BETWEEN CITIZEN AND CITY

STUDIES IN
GOVERNMENT AND PUBLIC POLICY

Charles H. Levine, Series Editor

BETWEEN CITIZEN AND CITY

NEIGHBORHOOD ORGANIZATIONS AND URBAN POLITICS IN CINCINNATI

JOHN CLAYTON THOMAS

UNIVERSITY PRESS OF KANSAS

To my mother
and in memory of my father

Published by the University Press of Kansas (Lawrence, Kansas 66045),
which was organized by the Kansas Board of Regents and is operated
and funded by Emporia State University, Fort Hays State University,
Kansas State University, Pittsburg State University,
the University of Kansas, and Wichita State University

Library of Congress Cataloging in Publication Data
Thomas, John Clayton.
Between citizen and city.
(Studies in government and public policy)
Bibliography: p.
Includes index.
1. Neighborhood government—Ohio—Cincinnati.
2. Citizens' associations—Ohio—Cincinnati.
3. Political participation—Ohio—Cincinnati.
4. Cincinnati (Ohio)—Politics and government.
I. Title. II. Series.
JS743.T48 1986   352'.007   86-7726
ISBN 0-7006-0303-4

Printed in the United States of America
10 9 8 7 6 5 4 3 2 1

Contents

List of Tables and Maps

MAPS

Preface

The idea for this book dates from a chance visit to a meeting of one of Cincinnati's community councils in the winter of 1976. As a student of urban politics, I was surprised and intrigued by the degree of neighborhood involvement in municipal governance evident at the meeting. A police officer was in attendance, apparently to hear—or talk—about law enforcement problems in the area. He was asked to check on a noisy bar and a possible house of prostitution. The group also showed a strong interest in zoning, with the council president asking for a good turnout to protest a proposed zoning change at a meeting of the City Planning Commission.

That initial fascination might have quickly faded had I not begun to see community councils at almost every turn. Municipal officials asked that questions on involvement with the councils be included in a large survey of city residents that I and others at the University of Cincinnati were planning. In a study of the city's mid-1970s budget crisis, the councils unexpectedly emerged as a factor in why some departments fared better than others (Thomas, 1981). These organizations of which I knew next to nothing suddenly seemed to be central figures in the city's politics.

Unfortunately, my interest in the councils peaked about the time that I was leaving Cincinnati. As a consequence, this research has been conducted mostly over a long distance. It has been possible to carry out the research only because many people in several cities have helped enormously.

Financial help has come from several sources. In Kansas City I have been supported most generously by the University of Kansas City Trustees through a UKC Faculty Fellowship. I have also received financial support from the Beistle Fund of the L. P. Cookingham Institute of Public Affairs and the Faculty Research Council at the University of Missouri–Kansas City (UMKC). My extensive research in Cincinnati in the summer of 1980 was made possible by the generous support of the Research Foundation at Texas Christian University. Finally, the survey that is the basis for Chapter 4 was funded by a special project grant through Title I of the federal Higher Education Act (Community Services and Education Program) and by the City of Cincinnati.

This research has also depended on the cooperation and assistance of many individuals. I am indebted to the many municipal officials and neighborhood leaders in Cincinnati who gave so generously of their time and records. I must give particular thanks in this regard to Ken Bordwell and Sister Ann Rene McConn, both of whom provided full access to valuable City Hall records that I did not know existed. I am also grateful to Peter Shocket, Don Heisel, and Tom Gau, all formerly of the Institute of Governmental Research at the University of Cincinnati, who helped in many ways to ensure that a transient scholar could pursue his research.

The data analysis and writing have been facilitated by colleagues at the Cookingham Institute and at the School of Business and Public Administration at UMKC. Dick Heimovics has been especially supportive over the past five years; Nick Peroff and Bill Eddy have helped by reading and commenting on various portions of the manuscript; and Steve DeLurgio advised me on the more complicated statistical techniques. I have also benefited from comments on the manuscript by colleagues at other schools—in particular Elaine Sharp and Mark Weinberg, as well as two anonymous reviewers. Various graduate students have helped along the way, including Bruce Rogers, Tony Schibler, and Mary West in Kansas City, Kim Webb at Texas Christian University, and Gayle Oosting in Cincinnati. In addition, the staff of the University Press of Kansas have helped to ensure that the manuscript would, in fact, become a book.

I am also indebted to all of the overburdened secretaries who have assisted in this endeavor. Paula Garrett had the unenviable task of putting the initial, lengthier, manuscript into presentable form, which she did with tenacity and good spirits despite having to do battle with rapidly changing word-processing technologies. Rosalie Long and Daphne Hunter then stepped in, with both patience and proficiency, to carry the final product to completion.

Finally, this book would not have been possible without my personal community in Cincinnati—Marilyn, Jason, and Bryan—who have supported me throughout this seemingly endless task. Jason and Bryan have helped to keep me going, if only by setting a model of boundless energy that I might try to emulate. Marilyn, for her part, has been a helpful reader as chapters were completed, an encouraging supporter when the book as a whole seemed unlikely ever to be completed, and my best friend at all times.

1

Introduction: "Seeds beneath the Snow"

At the grass roots of the neighborhood, there may be seeds beneath the snow. The rediscovery of the importance of a stake in society and the roots it provides appears in the householder of the neighborhood and in the warming sense of mutual support and significant action the building of homes and local community provide.

—Norton Long (1980: 32)

A steady rain turned to snow around midnight on a January evening in 1978 as a cold front swept across Cincinnati, leaving the city like a snow-covered ice rink. Strong winds created blizzard conditions for the next two days and brought the city to a virtual standstill. Grocery stores that managed to reopen despite the weather saw perishable goods vanish quickly as customers, fearing continued bad weather, stocked supplies for a potentially indefinite stay indoors.

Those fears were not ungrounded. That storm was the worst in a series of severe storms and cold snaps that produced the snowiest and coldest winter in Cincinnati's history. Nor was that winter itself an isolated experience. It came on the heels of an unusually harsh winter the previous year and was followed by yet a third severe winter the next year.

The weather forced many postponements. Schools closed for unprecedented periods, prompting speculation that "cabin fever" had become the city's primary health problem as parents and their children were confined together for long periods. Of less note to most city residents, the early 1978 snow and cold delayed the scheduled beginning of the Stimulating Neighborhood Action Program (SNAP), a program designed to accelerate the development of Cincinnati's neighborhood groups.

This coincidence of a harsh winter and the initiation of a new program for Cincinnati's neighborhoods gave nearly literal meaning to Norton Long's metaphorical description of the potential role for neighborhoods in older cities in the United States. Cincinnati, one of those older cities, was virtually buried beneath those snows, and the figurative "seeds" of the SNAP effort lay beneath the snow, able to grow only when weather might permit.

Metaphorically, Long's description had even more meaning for Cincinnati. The city had experienced the harsh, enduring, figurative winter to which Long alluded: the racial riots and other urban discontents of the late 1960s and early 1970s, succeeded by the fiscal crises of the late 1970s and 1980s. Yet beneath those oppressive problems, Cincinnati was seeing a revival of neighborhoods and neighborhood organizations. Many such groups were thriving by early 1978; SNAP was less a cause than a consequence of that revival. And this rebirth of interest in neighborhoods held for many Cincinnatians the promise that Long's phrase suggests for the neighborhood movement.

That optimism is widely shared in the 1980s by an impressive mix of urban observers covering most points on the political spectrum. For the left, neighborhood organizations represent part of a "backyard revolution," a continuation of the New Left's push for participatory democracy in the late 1960s. In terms similar to Long's, Harry Boyte (1980: 4) pictures this revolution occurring underneath an unhealthy, dominant culture: "Like the 1950s, the 1970s, too, had an underside. Beneath the surface of American political and intellectual discourse, little-understood kinds of ferment at the level of people's actual lives spread through the recesses of the society. Myriad forms of protest, self help, community building, and insurgency grew and flourished at the grassroots, sending ripples through the entire culture."

At the other end of the spectrum, conservatives praise the organizing of neighborhoods as part of a broader revival of "mediating institutions" (e.g., Berger and Neuhaus, 1977). These institutions are the groups and organizations—including the family, the church, and voluntary associations, such as neighborhood organizations—that mediate between the individual and large-scale institutions, government in particular. Their revival means for many conservatives a new surge of "private initiative" in which people " 'help themselves' rather than . . . rely on assistance from government" (Joyce, 1982: 201).

For the establishment center, neighborhood organizations offer potentially better ways of doing things at a time of dissatisfaction with the way government does them. The nonpartisan International City Management Association has even suggested that "government that is decentralized to the level of communities and neighborhoods may be the wave of the future" (Rutter, 1980: 26).

As these sentiments indicate, the neighborhood movement takes on the role of a savior in much contemporary writing. The movement is seen as capable of such diverse accomplishments as reversing the decay of older cities, reviving the flagging civic spirit of middle-class urban America, and performing more efficiently and more effectively services that have traditionally been performed by government. Very little seems beyond its reach.

These claims almost certainly exaggerate the potential of the neighborhood movement and its constituent neighborhood organizations. It is unclear, though, what degree of optimism is warranted. What improvements in the political and economic climate of cities can be expected from neighborhood organizations? Who benefits from these improvements? And would any careful analysis of the accomplishments of these organizations leave the left, the right, and the center still as effusive about the neighborhood movement? If those questions are to be answered, a number of other questions must be answered first. The effects of the neighborhood movement cannot really be defined until more is known about the movement's origins, its composition, the goals it seeks, and the role of the movement in contemporary urban government and politics.

Origins. On the question of origins, neighborhood groups are known to have developed during a tumultuous quarter-century of urban politics, a period extending from the "good government" years of the 1950s and early 1960s, through the turbulent later 1960s, when cities were shaken by riots and federal antipoverty efforts, and into the retrenchment years of the later 1970s and early 1980s. There is no agreement, however, on when and why the groups grew during these years.

The groups are most commonly characterized as indigenous, originating in the "grass roots" of city life. Cunningham (1981), for example, argues that the contemporary revival of neighborhood groups began as a "communal revolution" against a nearly exclusive traditional concern of city leaders with satisfying powerful economic forces. That "revolution" could have been helped along by the civil rights movement, given that urban blacks had more reason than most groups to be dissatisfied with any domination by economic elites. The civil rights movement could have seized upon that dissatisfaction as a basis for mobilizing neighborhood organizations in minority areas in the 1960s (e.g., Jackson, 1978).

Others also see a healthy, indigenous neighborhood movement but place its greatest growth later, primarily during the 1970s, and on the basis of very different causes. The 1970s brought escalating housing and energy costs as well as changes in life style, all of which may have rekindled interest in living in the city (e.g., Clay, 1979). That interest could, in turn, have increased commitment to the home neighborhood and its organizational life.

Alternatively, the origins of neighborhood organizations could be indigenous but not particularly healthy if, as Goering (1979: 510) argues, many of these groups are motivated by racism: "The resistance to racial change has been and continues to be a central ingredient in the purposes of many neighborhood associations. Local defense and control often mean, in the code words of insiders, keeping blacks out.''

Or, finally, these indigenous influences could be less important than the external encouragement neighborhood groups have received. In the eyes of some observers, the principal cause of revived neighborhood organizations is federal encouragement, beginning with the War on Poverty programs of the 1960s and their emphasis on participation by the poor, then continuing through the many federal ''citizen participation'' requirements and other neighborhood-directed programs of the later 1970s (see Bell and Held, 1969; Yates, 1977).

Composition. With so much confusion about the origins of the neighborhood movement, it is no wonder that the resulting composition of the movement is not well understood either. Here the issue focuses, in particular, on whether neighborhood organizations represent the disadvantaged or only perpetuate the traditional bias of urban political life. That bias favors the affluent, with most forms of organizational and political participation increasing with socioeconomic status. Some evidence suggests that this bias generalizes to participation in neighborhood groups (Cole, 1974; Steggart, 1975), but much of the rhetoric about the groups envisions a different pattern. War on Poverty legislation, for example, spoke optimistically of ''maximum feasible participation of the poor'' in programs that affected them, and some research suggests that low-income and minority populations have, in fact, become very active in the neighborhood movement (Lamb, 1975; Ambrecht, 1976). Yet a third possibility is that the movement means better representation for the working and middle classes, with the lower and upper classes changing little from their traditional patterns of participation. Rich (1980a) argues that these in-between classes are more involved because they have both the *need* (e.g., crime, threats of neighborhood housing decline), which the upper class lacks, and the *initiative,* which an apathetic lower class may lack.

Governmental involvement. The neighborhood movement has been touted from time to time as helping to open the governmental process to more citizen involvement. According to some experts, neighborhood organizations have been able to use federal citizen participation requirements to force open the doors of municipal government in such areas as community development planning, the municipal budgeting process, and the delivery of services (Kettl, 1979; Hallman, 1980; Ahlbrandt and Sumka, 1983). Neighborhoods and government may even have developed a cooperative relationship (e.g., Rutter, 1980; Cole, 1981).

Other observers are not so sanguine about this possible opening of the governmental process. Some question whether broader participation could mean *less* effective government. The entry of the newly legitimized neighborhood groups could overwhelm the governmental process in what Yates (1977) has described as ''street-fighting pluralism,'' a brand of chaotic politics in which a ''bewildering array'' of groups makes too many demands of government officials who have too few resources. The result could be an "ungovernable city."

A different kind of question is raised by those who suspect that the supposed opening of government is only a technique for seducing citizen groups (e.g., Hunter, 1979; Gittell, 1980). Accepting the invitation of the open doors could co-opt neighborhood groups, such that they surrender their ability to advocate without getting anything for their neighborhoods in exchange. These suspicions may be fed by knowledge of the "reformed" governmental structures prevalent in so many cities. Early twentieth-century reformers disdained the interests of the parts of the city, such as neighborhoods, in an effort to escape the corrupt ward politics of the urban political machine. To suppress those interests, they pushed a battery of reforms (e.g., election at large rather than from districts, civil service systems of employee selection) that have tended to slight geographic interests within cities (Lineberry and Fowler, 1967; Karnig, 1975). Elective officials chosen from the city at large were left with little incentive to consider the desires of particular neighborhoods. Administrators, insulated from the public by civil service protections, were encouraged to listen more closely to the norms of their professions than to the preferences of citizens. One could reasonably question why elective or appointive municipal officials should now be expected to be sympathetic to neighborhoods, particularly in any city with a reformed government.

Effects. The questions return, finally, to the possible effects of the neighborhood movement. To begin with, there is a question of whether neighborhood groups have had much, if any, effect on the way things are done in cities. Despite all the exuberant rhetoric, relatively little evidence can be found of actual neighborhood influence over urban policies (e.g., Kettl, 1979; Busson, 1983), and some evidence can be found to suggest that the groups for the most part are *not* influential (e.g., Jones, 1981; Bachelor and Jones, 1981). In addition, the evidence is inconclusive on the likely beneficiaries of any influence neighborhoods might be able to exert. The movement has been variously described as favoring the low income, the middle income, or the upper income. It hardly seems likely to favor all equally.

Nor is there agreement on how the neighborhood movement may affect the public interest citywide. The presence of too many neighborhood groups could distract municipal officials from cultivating that citywide interest, with the interests of the whole perhaps subordinated to the interests of the parts (see Kettl, 1979). It is also possible, however, that the citywide interest could gain a net benefit from the new life of neighborhood groups. Such is the implication of the current enthusiasm for "coproduction" (e.g., Whitaker, 1980; Ahlbrandt and Sumka, 1983), the joint production of public services by government and the citizenry, and of the Reagan administration's zeal for "voluntarism" and "private sector initiatives" (e.g., Hawkins, 1982). Neighborhood organizations may actually be able to help their financially burdened municipal governments by aiding in the delivery of services.

This book attempts to answer these and other questions about the place of neighborhood organizations in contemporary urban politics. The answers are sought from an examination of the history, composition, and current governmental involvement of these organizations in the city of Cincinnati, Ohio, a city known as "a leader in the neighborhood movement" (Woods, Andersen, and Grober, 1979). That leadership can be seen, for example, in the roughly fifty neighborhood organizations active in Cincinnati in the early 1980s.

Otherwise, Cincinnati is fairly typical of large northeastern and midwestern cities and so could hold lessons generalizable to those cities. The 1980 population of 384,000 people is close to the average for large cities, as is the black proportion of approximately one-third. Also typical of many of these cities, Cincinnati's income distribution overrepresents the lower and middle classes but includes sizable segments of the upper-middle and upper classes as well. Finally, Cincinnati knows firsthand the rigors of the harsh figurative winters from which so many of these cities have suffered.

Much of what has been written about the politics of cities in these regions counsels skepticism about any true significance for neighborhood organizations. The inducements are too few and the barriers too high, according to the conventional view, for groups like neighborhood organizations to achieve a real presence in urban politics (see Peterson, 1981; Jones, 1981). The Cincinnati story will suggest a different conclusion. Neighborhood organizations have become a significant force in Cincinnati, apparently as the consequence of a variety of changes in urban politics that are likely to have affected other cities in a similar manner.

The principal task of this book is to argue the case for how this has happened. Chapter 2 presents the argument in summary form, explaining how the incentives for urban groups have grown even as the barriers facing those groups were being lowered. The body of the book then elaborates the argument in light of the Cincinnati experience. The early chapters explore the roots of the community councils, as neighborhood organizations are known in Cincinnati. Chapter 3 profiles how the various councils began, Chapter 4 examines who is involved in the councils and why, and Chapter 5 describes how those factors merge to form the current pattern of organizational resources of the different councils.

The later chapters follow the neighborhood movement into the process of municipal governance. Chapter 6 examines the many mechanisms Cincinnati has developed to facilitate community involvement in municipal affairs and attempts to explain why those mechanisms developed at all. Chapter 7 moves from the formal mechanisms to the actual process of governance, explaining how that process has changed as the result of the neighborhood movement and these mechanisms. Chapter 8 turns to the substantive policy questions that bring neighborhood organizations to City Hall, describing both the nature of the issues and their varying salience for different types of neighborhoods. Finally, Chapters 9 and 10 consider whether the community councils exert any real influence in City Hall—either positively to advance the private interests of the different neighborhoods or negatively to hinder the pursuit of the citywide interest.

Considering all of these issues in the context of the Cincinnati experience should provide insights into the meaning of the neighborhood movement for the contemporary city. Chapter 11 attempts to make these insights explicit with a concluding discussion of the current and future significance of the neighborhood movement.

2

The Argument:
Neighborhood Organizations
and the New Urban Politics

"Local politics is groupless politics." So says Paul Peterson in *City Limits* (1981: 116), a much-acclaimed treatise on contemporary urban politics. The area between citizen and city, Peterson contends, is arid ground hostile to the survival of political life. Urban issues provide too little nourishment to sustain most forms of political groups. Peterson is not alone in this belief. Many other urban observers, political scientists especially, are skeptical that many political groups are—or can be—a significant force in urban politics. Bachelor and Jones (1981: 534–35) attribute this impotence to "the increasing ability of decision makers to limit the scope of citizens' decisions to matters that do not threaten their authority." Neighborhood organizations, because they "are institutionally weak," can hardly be expected to challenge this ability.

This skepticism obviously does not square with the enthusiasm neighborhood organizations have aroused in other quarters. The organizations of which Bachelor and Jones write could hardly be the same groups that journalist Neal Peirce (1980) says "fit, indeed symbolize the times": "They fill the void created by the decline of political machines, churches and civic groups. They respond to Americans' search for community after disillusionment with central government 'solutions' to social problems. They are decentralized, accountable to citizens, and as diverse as the neighborhoods they represent."

The more persuasive case to this point, however, has probably been made by Jones and Peterson and the other skeptics. Despite a variety of theories about particular aspects of neighborhood organizations (e.g., Orbell and Uno, 1972; O'Brien, 1975; Rich, 1980a; Gittell, 1980), no one has explained why the skeptics might be wrong in seeing no place for these organizations in contemporary urban politics. This chapter develops such an explanation, styled in conscious counterpoint to the dominant skeptical attitudes as drawn primarily from Peterson's work.

8

THE ROOTS
OF THE NEW NEIGHBORHOOD ORGANIZATIONS

The idea that influential political groups are lacking in the city has many supporters in addition to Peterson. Jeffrey Pressman (1975), for example, wrote of the "non-politics of Oakland" that included a "lack of organized politically interested groups." Peterson, however, provides the best explanation of why the groups should be lacking.

The limited incentives for urban groups. His explanation has two parts, the first concerning the formation of groups; the second, their influence. In the first part Peterson points to three problems that deter urban political groups from forming:

1. The limited stakes of local politics: The benefits available in the urban political competition, Peterson (1981: 120–21) contends, are insufficient to arouse much group interest. "The most important public policies are determined by the national government. . . . The stakes at the local level are by comparison of only secondary importance."[1]

2. The ability to "exit": On those few occasions when the stakes do reach substantial magnitude (e.g., when a neighborhood is threatened by highway construction), forming a group to fight the change is not the only option: "In local politics, as distinct from national politics, the individual always has the choice between 'fighting' and 'switching.' And it is no accident that a number of instances of community conflict end with the losers leaving town. Undoubtedly, the availability of 'exit' locally but not nationally contributes to differentials between patterns of citizen participation at national and local government levels" (p. 121).

3. The "free rider" problem: Even if those two problems can somehow be surmounted, a third problem would still deter individuals from forming or joining an organization. With voluntary groups, people may enjoy group successes—parks improvements won by a neighborhood organization, for example—without giving time to achieving those successes. These people can "ride free," as it were, in that they share in the benefits of group successes without incurring any of the costs. As a consequence of that possibility, however, few people may get involved and few groups form.

This characterization has some obvious validity. The lesser stakes of local politics and the greater ability to exit the local situation are readily evident. But the characterization also errs in important respects, most obviously by understating the stakes of local politics. Those stakes have increased in recent years as part of a changing urban politics. Moreover, in the context of the increased stakes, the other deterrents to group action carry less force than Peterson's arguments suggest.

The new salience of the homeownership stake. The first stake that Peterson overlooks is, curiously, an individual-level analogue to the citywide "developmental'' policy stakes that he sees as primary for cities. Developmental policies focus on a city's economic development through support for shopping centers, industrial parks, tax concessions to businesses, as well as any community improvements that increase the attractiveness of the city to taxpayers and businesses. Cities will emphasize these policies, Peterson (p. 41) contends, because they "strengthen the local economy, enhance the local tax base, and generate additional resources that can be used for the community's welfare." Individuals, analogously, should favor policies that promote their personal economic development; and although Peterson is right that many of these policies are national in origin, some involve local government as much as any level of government.

This is the case particularly with policies affecting the most important financial investment for millions of Americans: the home. National policies on interest rates and mortgage insurance affect whether people can buy a home of their own, but once a person has a home, local policies—on zoning, property taxation, highway construction, and the like—may be primary in determining the home's future value. As a consequence, people who own their homes have a significant latent stake in local politics. Renters lack a comparable stake because the value of their personal wealth is unlikely to be linked as directly to what happens locally.

Homeownership of itself, however, may provide only a modest impetus toward participation in local affairs (see Alford and Scoble, 1968). The impetus becomes strong only when local problems impinge on the homeowner by threatening, or being perceived to threaten, the value of the investment in the home. Threats can make manifest what has been only a latent stake in local affairs, in the process increasing the likelihood of action by the homeowner to protect the investment. Possible gains in home values do not provide a comparable impetus to participation because, as Hansen (1985) has argued, "people are more easily mobilized in response to threats than in response to prospects."

Homeownership can be overlooked as the basis for a stake in urban politics because a lack of threats usually keeps the stake latent and therefore unseen by most observers. Threats are minimized because home buyers, by selecting their homes with the care a primary investment deserves, try to choose locations removed from threats. In the 1950s and 1960s, however, these threats became more difficult to avoid in many northeastern and midwestern cities. Migration of rural blacks from the South was accelerating rapidly to these cities, creating pressures for turnover in the existing stock of residential homes. At the same time, cooperative federal-local urban renewal and highway construction programs were displacing large slum populations— again mostly blacks—to add to the pressures for residential turnover elsewhere in these cities (e.g., Greer, 1965; Snow and Leahy, 1980; Mollenkopf, 1981). That magnitude of residential change inevitably threatened the value of many homes, all the more so because of the perceived sensitivity of home values to racial change in residential composition (see Downs, 1981: 96-98). The homeowner's stake in local affairs had achieved a new salience.

So why not exit, as Peterson argues, instead of becoming active in a neighborhood organization? The truth is that many people did leave, as the massive suburbanization of these years attests. What Peterson fails to recognize, however, is that exit brings its own problems, especially for homeowners for whom exit means finding a new neighborhood and a new home, both as good as or better than the old, then selling the old home at a price at least sufficient to pay for the new, and, finally, accommodating to the new. Renters, by contrast, face only some of these problems when they contemplate moving.[2] These "transaction costs" of exiting (Cox, 1982) will lead many homeowners to opt instead for "voice" (Hirschman, 1970), where they stay and take action designed to neutralize the threats. During the 1950s and 1960s that frequently meant forming or joining a neighborhood organization.

The threats of rapid residential change declined in most northeastern and midwestern cities by the mid-1970s, but by that time threats from the gradual physical decay of neighborhoods had become more salient. This decay was probably no greater than in any earlier era, but exiting from the decay was becoming more difficult. The economic stagnation of the 1970s joined with the escalation of home costs, interest rates, and energy costs to make exiting unaffordable for many. Constrained from leaving, threatened homeowners became more inclined to exercise the option of voice through a neighborhood organization.

The free rider problem, the final deterrent to local activism in Peterson's formulation, may have deterred neighborhood activism only minimally through this entire period. For one thing, according to the scholar most responsible for popularizing the concept (Olson, 1971), the free rider problem deters participation in small groups, such as neighborhood organizations, less than it deters participation in large groups, such as national interest groups. In addition, the rewards possible from the public goods to which the free rider problem applies are not the only reasons people join voluntary groups. Many people join to enjoy the social life of the group or to pursue philosophically important goals (Clark and Wilson, 1961; on neighborhood organizations specifically, see Rich, 1980b), thus explaining some group involvement in disregard of the inequitable distribution of public goods. The people most interested in these less tangible rewards tend to be the more affluent, such as homeowners, if only because they have more of the resources necessary to pursue the rewards. The free rider problem consequently deters the neighborhood activism of homeowners only minimally—or less, in any event, than it deters activism at other levels of American government.

The stakes of new inducements. Activism can be spurred by inducements as well as by threats. Peterson's formulation underestimates the significance, in particular, of the new inducements to be found in many urban programs of the 1960s and 1970s. These nurtured many new neighborhood groups as part of a larger process wherein the growth of government was encouraging all manner of interest groups (Walker, 1983).

The new inducements first appeared with the Great Society in the 1960s, especially its Community Action and Model Cities components for low-income urban neighborhoods. Although later Republican administrations viewed urban programs less favorably, total federal funding to cities continued to increase until the late 1970s, often in ways directly relevant to neighborhoods. The landmark Community Development Block Grant (CDBG) legislation of 1974, for example, had a strong neighborhood emphasis. Many private foundations eventually joined in the effort with programs to revitalize neighborhoods and neighborhood organizations (see Hallman, 1984: 282–83).

The various programs have offered several kinds of funding for neighborhood organizations. Some funds were available to pay participants in the organizations, as with Model Cities stipends to residents attending neighborhood meetings and Community Action funding for neighborhood staff salaries. Staff compensation also has been possible through more recent programs, including the Mott Foundation's Stimulating Neighborhood Action Program (SNAP) of grants for the development of neighborhood organizations. Some programs funded new social services or assistance in obtaining existing services through neighborhood organizations. Community Action agencies in particular were designed as service-oriented neighborhood organizations for low-income areas (see Judd, 1979: 306–8). Since the beginning of CDBG, many programs have permitted contracts for neighborhood organizations to perform redevelopment projects (e.g., housing rehabilitation).

These funds increased the stakes of urban politics at the neighborhood level, thereby making group activity at that level more likely than Peterson's formulation suggests. In addition, the other factors Peterson says deter local activism become largely irrelevant in the context of the new stakes. The ability to exit is relevant only in situations involving reasons to leave, not inducements to stay; and the free rider problem diminishes because the inducements can sometimes serve as "selective incentives," rewards that go only to those who participate in the organization (Olson, 1971).

These inducements are also significant for their targeting principally to neighborhoods and residents less affected by the incentives for homeowner activism. At the outset the programs were targeted almost exclusively to low-income neighborhoods, but political pressures from other neighborhoods and from national Republican administrations (see Mollenkopf, 1983: 126–27) eventually resulted in local governments being given more latitude concerning where federal funding could be spent. The CDBG legislation, for example, initially included very few restrictions on where cities could spend funds (see Dommel et al., 1982:'41–44), prompting many cities to spread funds across more neighborhoods than had benefited from earlier funding (Kettl, 1981a). Benefits were also spread through new federal tax policies, such as the deductions available after 1976 for the costs of restoring urban historical structures. These deductions were more attractive to the higher-income developers and "new gentry," people with the funds necessary to undertake rehabilitation projects, than to the low-income clienteles of the Great Society programs (Schill and Nathan, 1983: 24–25).

By the late 1970s, in short, many urban neighborhoods were sharing in the new stakes of urban politics. The stakes were well enough entrenched that they could even withstand the Reagan administration's push for cutbacks. Funding levels for these programs have declined in the 1980s, but only fractionally from the levels of earlier years (e.g., Nathan and Doolittle, 1984). The new stakes have combined with the new salience of the traditional stake of homeownership to alter the incentive structure of urban politics. The incentives for neighborhood activism in particular are much greater than they were as recently as twenty years ago, as well as much greater than Peterson estimates. The increases make understandable and perhaps inevitable the renaissance of neighborhood organizations.

THE INFLUENCE OF NEIGHBORHOOD ORGANIZATIONS

The harder part of the argument lies ahead. Despite the strong case Peterson makes for the absence of groups, the evidence indicates that at least some groups are present, and neighborhood groups may occasionally be so numerous as to be "bewildering" (e.g., Schumaker and Getter, 1983; Yates, 1977). With the issue of influence, by contrast, both the theory and the evidence point toward a lack of influence by urban political groups. The theory, for its part, argues that several characteristics of municipal decision making work against influence by political groups:

1. "Closed decision-making processes": Municipal decisions are not made openly, Peterson argues. Instead, local boards and commissions commonly meet in secret or at times unannounced to the general public. In addition, these bodies often call for closed executive sessions when discussing particularly significant topics, such as personnel or land use (pp. 122–23).

2. Limited geographic representation: Neighborhood groups may not face a particularly sympathetic audience even if they do somehow penetrate this closed system. Officials elected citywide, as in reformed cities like Cincinnati, may feel little need to attend to the unique demands of particular neighborhoods. In any event, groups representing the city's geographic parts do tend to suffer under reformed systems of municipal government (e.g., Lineberry and Fowler, 1967; Karnig, 1975).

3. Lack of formal accountability: Actually, the power of elected officials in many cities may have been eclipsed by the power of appointive administrators (see Lowi, 1968). Most of these administrators lack formal accountability because merit system principles or collective bargaining concessions assure job tenure, regardless of changes in public opinion or political leadership. With elected officials, neighborhood dissatisfaction can at least be translated into votes in the electoral process. With administrators, even that occasional recourse may not be available.

4. An imbalance of resources: Administrators could be aided in this local domination by their greater resources of expertise, time, salaries, and staff. Pressman (1972: 514–15) has documented how these resources helped the city manager dominate the mayor in Oakland, and others have documented how school superintendents have used a similar resource imbalance to dominate school boards (see Kerr, 1964). If these elective officials can be so easily dominated, groups such as neighborhood organizations seem to stand little chance when pitted against municipal administrators. As Jones (1981: 699) puts it, neighborhood organizations, ''with their small paid staffs and volunteer labor, cannot provide the day-to-day incentives that are necessary to keep government agencies constantly in touch with citizens.''

5. The dominance of professional values: Making matters worse, these administrators may feel their primary allegiance should be to professional norms rather than to community values. Many urban functions, ranging from planning to police to general management, have become increasingly professionalized over the course of this century, resulting in potentially less sympathy toward citizen and community interests. As Kirlin (1973: 321) explains, ''the thrust to 'professionalization' strengthened the influence of organizational members over their own activities, while reducing the influence of the citizens they serve.''

Taken together, these five characteristics of municipal decision making could reflect the success of the urban reform movement's effort to minimize the influence of political groups, especially geographic groups such as neighborhood organizations. Implicitly or explicitly, the reform movement favored at least four of the five characteristics. Their supposed pervasiveness could mean that the reforms were more successful than they could have hoped.

The reform of reform. But all is not right in this picture, for the evolution of urban political forms did not end with the ideas of the early twentieth-century reform movement. In the 1960s and 1970s, most large American cities were pressured to reform the reforms, to restore some of the local responsiveness to the differentiated needs within the population. From below, the stirrings in black communities, as expressed dramatically in urban riots, told municipal governments that the fastest-growing segment of their population was unhappy with governmental responsiveness. From above, the federal government funded new programs for blacks and the poor and encouraged municipal government to involve those groups more in local decision making. These and other pressures changed municipal decision making and the decision makers themselves in several ways conducive to a new power for neighborhood organizations:

1. Formal opening of the decision-making process: The federal requirement for "maximum feasible participation" of the poor in War on Poverty programs set a precedent for a generation of federal-urban programs. Citizen participation became almost a uniform requirement in these programs, with local governments often having to document the participation as a condition for further funding (Advisory Commission on Intergovernmental Relations, 1979). "Sunshine laws," requiring that meetings of public bodies be open to the public, were becoming popular at much the same time, making a closed decision-making process all the more difficult to maintain. Many cities did not even try to maintain closed decision making, opting instead for extensive reforms to bring citizens and citizen groups into municipal decision making (e.g., Hallman, 1980).

Skeptics sometimes view these responsiveness reforms as simply ineffective or as only cynical symbolic posturing never intended to be effective. That view might be credible were it not for the other changes that accompanied this formal opening of the decision-making process.

2. A better balance of power: Power arrangements were changing, for one thing, as circumstances helped to redress the balance of power between neighborhood groups and municipal officials. The mere presence of more groups was one factor. A neighborhood group, however limited its resources, may be able to muster veto power, particularly on changes proposed for the neighborhood itself. That is hardly insignificant if government wants, for example, to run a highway through a neighborhood; and more groups mean more widespread veto power. The power of the groups was enhanced, in addition, by the new funding increasingly available from the federal government and private foundations.

3. A new generation of political leadership: As long as cities ran smoothly, political leaders may have been willing to defer to the judgments of professional administrators and, consistent with those judgments, to slight geographic interests within the city. With cities no longer running smoothly by the later 1960s, these leaders had to change that stance or risk an end to their tenure in office. The result was a new generation of political leaders—many new leaders along with some old leaders with new ideas—more sympathetic to the interests of neighborhoods and minorities (see especially Clark and Ferguson, 1983: 104-10). These leaders changed municipal policies in ways helpful to those groups and also urged recalcitrant administrators to change their attitudes.

4. "Guerrillas in the bureaucracy": Despite being increasingly stereotyped as insulated and unresponsive (e.g., Lipsky, 1971), the municipal bureaucracy probably was becoming more responsive in these years, and not

solely as a result of coercion by political leaders. The expansion of urban government in the 1960s brought an infusion of new employees to municipal bureaucracies, employees whose thinking was shaped more by the liberal social philosophy of the 1960s than by the traditional public interest orientation of the professions (e.g., Howe and Kaufman, 1979). These new bureaucrats often favored responsiveness to disadvantaged groups, in contrast to the stonewalling characteristic of the traditional municipal bureaucrat (Lipsky, 1968). Guerrillas had infiltrated the municipal bureaucracy (see, for example, Needleman and Needleman, 1974).

5. The changing professions: As time went by, these guerrillas found their personal preferences for responsiveness less inconsistent with the values of their professions, as professional values changed to reflect societal change. This is no better illustrated than with the planning profession. Long a bastion of reform public interest ideals, planning in the 1960s increasingly meant "community planning" and "advocacy planning," where the needs of the neighborhood took precedence over the needs of the city as a whole. The "new public administration" signaled that most other municipal professions were similarly updating their norms to fit the times (e.g., Marini, 1971; Murphy, 1976).

6. Municipal advantages to neighborhood involvement: If personal and professional values initially impelled municipal administrators toward more responsiveness, selfish concerns may have sustained the momentum. Contemporary theories of decision making recognize that involving more people in decisions often can be advantageous for those in authority (Vroom and Yetton, 1973). Consistent with this principle, municipal officials began to see how they could benefit from increasing neighborhood involvement in municipal decision making. There is an obvious advantage, for example, in avoiding the veto power—or, in a milder form, the harassment power—neighborhood groups can exercise to frustrate municipal plans. In addition, gaining neighborhood assistance in the delivery of services could mean more services at lower cost. Finally, given the frequent preoccupation of neighborhood groups with "private urban renewal" (Zeitz, 1979), the groups could help in promoting the developmental preferences of these officials. Any or all of these advantages could result from more neighborhood involvement in decision making.

Individually, any of these six changes might not greatly affect neighborhood involvement in municipal governance. In combination, however, their effect may be profound, particularly on the administrative side of local government. It is there, after all, that many important municipal decisions are made, especially in reformed cities (see Harrigan, 1981: 164–70), a fact neighborhood organizations would inevitably recognize. The administrative side of government is also susceptible because it has been the locus for many of the changes conducive to increased neighborhood involvement.

Could this involvement be co-optation, in which government gains neighborhood support but permits no real neighborhood influence over municipal decisions? Despite what some observers think (Hunter, 1979; Gittell, 1980; Mollenkopf, 1981), that seems unlikely to be the dominant pattern, mainly because municipal bureaucrats seem unlikely agents of co-optation. Assuming they are sincere in their commitment to responsiveness, the new bureaucrats are unlikely to want to co-opt. The earlier generation of bureaucrats for their part may lack the capability given that the task of deftly manipulating neighborhood groups calls for skills considerably different from those necessary for the traditional task of avoiding the groups.

Second, the argument for co-optation seriously underestimates the power of the neighborhood organizations. Despite what Gittell (1980) contends, the dependence of these groups on governmental funding does not necessarily leave the groups powerless relative to government. True, the groups need the funding, but government needs the groups in order to maintain legitimacy by spending what has been budgeted. As an ample literature on intergovernmental relations documents, this mutuality of need usually results in a bargaining process in which grant recipients share power with grantor agencies, rather than being dominated by those agencies (e.g., Pressman, 1975; Ingram, 1977). Neighborhood groups seem unlikely to be exceptions to this rule.

Finding neighborhood influence. But a logical case cannot substitute for evidence. Even if this argument for neighborhood influence seems persuasive, the preponderance of evidence seems to support the view that neighborhood groups and most other political groups, except those representing economic elites, have failed to affect municipal decisions significantly. The allocation of urban services in particular has been found, in city after city throughout the country, to be seldom affected by political factors such as neighborhood groups (e.g., Levy, Meltsner, and Wildavsky, 1974; Lineberry, 1977; Jones, Greenberg, Kaufman, and Drew, 1978). Instead, as Mladenka (1980: 996) said of Chicago, "distributional outcomes are largely a function of past decisions, population shifts, technological changes, and reliance upon technical-rational criteria and professional values."

A closer look, however, reveals that this research has not adequately tested the influence of contemporary neighborhood organizations. For the most part, in fact, the research never gave these organizations the opportunity to be influential. Neighborhood organizations and other organized urban groups are omitted from the research in favor of unorganized social groupings and social classes—blacks, whites, the rich, the poor (for an exception, see Jones, 1981). Findings on how services are distributed by these groupings are important for questions of race and class discrimination, but those findings say nothing about the influence of *organized* groups.

Perhaps more important, the decisions examined in the service distribution research are not the sort that neighborhood organizations could be expected to influence. For one thing, as Mladenka's description indicates, many parts of the decisions were made decades ago. Considering that most of the new neighborhood organizations did not exist then, they could hardly have been expected to influence the decisions. Nor could neighborhood groups realistically be expected to reverse these decisions in more recent times. The decisions too often involve the "location of expensive facilities," such as parks, fire stations, and police stations, which are not easily moved and so not readily subject to change by current political forces (Boyle and Jacobs, 1982: 377).

Even the contemporary discretionary component of this spending, the money remaining once the influence of the historical decisions is removed, might not constitute a good target for neighborhood influence. First, the discretionary money may not be sufficient to arouse group interest, particularly if the money has to be divided to satisfy both group and municipal preferences. Second, the money may not be available for purposes of interest to neighborhood organizations. Neighborhoods are only infrequently interested, for example, in funding for fire services. The potential gains from competing for these funds consequently might seem not worth the effort required, leaving neighborhood groups mostly indifferent to how the funds are allocated.

Neighborhood interest in spending decisions will be assured only when significant discretionary funds are available for neighborhood purposes. That means newer urban programs, rather than traditional municipal services, because only newer programs have large components of discretionary funding. That, in turn, means for the most part programs financed by federal grants, those grants being the primary source of significant new municipal funding in recent decades. The programs that will interest neighborhoods will be, in short, the programs characterized earlier as constituting the new stakes of urban politics. This locus of interest could also be anticipated from the fact that neighborhood organizations exist in part because these programs took an interest in their existence. Once nurtured by the programs, neighborhood organizations may understandably devote their primary political energies to shaping the future course of the programs. Not to do so would be foolhardy, especially when the prospects for seizing any traditional municipal service spending are so bleak.

Seen in this light, federal CDBG spending becomes the obvious candidate for contemporary neighborhood influence. The magnitude of CDBG spending in many cities is annually in the millions or tens of millions, certainly enough to arouse group interest. Originating in 1974, the funds are new enough to be minimally constrained by history, and loose federal guidelines have imposed relatively few other constraints (see Dommel et al., 1982). Finally, CDBG funds are available for uses likely to interest neighborhood groups: housing, parks improvement, neighborhood economic development, and so on. The surprise might consequently be if neighborhoods were *not* interested in how CDBG funds are spent (see also Kettl, 1979).

CDBG is unlikely to be the only program of interest to neighborhoods, however. Any new program—federal or other—targeted *to* neighborhoods is likely, in turn, to be targeted *by* the neighborhoods. As the history of many federal programs teaches (Walker, 1983: 400), once a program finds a clientele, that clientele is seldom absent or quiet when the program's future is debated. Nor is neighborhood influence likely to be exerted only to win larger shares of particular spending programs. To the contrary, this influence may occasionally be greatest when a neighborhood wants to keep money out of the neighborhood, rather than to bring more in. Many neighborhood organizations began as efforts to block changes proposed for their neighborhoods, and they have often succeeded in vetoing those changes. For wealthier neighborhoods wanting to maintain the residential status quo and not needing large infusions of outside funds, this veto power may represent the most important form of neighborhood power.

The nature of neighborhood influence. In applying veto power, neighborhood organizations may occasionally dominate a decision area, overriding the preferences of other actors. The bias toward inertia in American politics is strong enough that a group wanting to veto a policy change can sometimes dominate. For the most part, however, neighborhood organizations can expect to affect decisions only as one of several influences, rather than as the controlling influence. By the nature of an intergovernmental decision-making process, the role of grant recipient gives neighborhoods some power, but other power remains with the grantor municipal government and with the federal government, where it is the original source of funding.

That divided power is important because the three actors are likely to have different spending preferences. Municipal governments, although now more sympathetic to neighborhood needs, should still be impelled by the interests of the city as a whole to prefer developmental policies, policies that supposedly build the economy and tax base of the city by favoring the interests of economically well-off city residents and businesses (Peterson, 1981: 41). This may mean that municipal governments will try to direct more money into prosperous or potentially prosperous areas of the city.

By contrast, the federal preference in urban programs has traditionally been redistributive, favoring the transfer of benefits "from the better off to the less well off segments of the community" (p. 43). That preference reflects both an effort to compensate for the local bias toward the well off and the greater freedom of the federal government to engage in such efforts. Where local governments are deterred from redistribution by the need to compete with neighboring jurisdictions for businesses and affluent residents, the federal government has more latitude because people and businesses, if dissatisfied with redistributive policies, are less able to move to another country. This is not to say that the federal government always favors redistribution. On the average, however, and including the current conservative Reagan years, efforts at redistribution seem more likely to be undertaken by the federal government than by local governments.

This contrast of federal and municipal policy preferences helps to explain the controversial "triage" strategy sometimes employed with urban programs (see Downs, 1981: 156–58; Marcuse, Medoff, and Pereira, 1982). Torn between federal preferences for redistributing to low-income areas and local preferences for spending in more prosperous areas, municipal governments may compromise by sending funds only to those low-income areas that are perceived to have a good potential for improvement. Low-income areas perceived as lacking that potential may receive little or no assistance, being designated for triage as areas too deteriorated to be salvageable with the limited public funding available.

Neighborhood organizations for their part usually favor something along the lines of an "allocational" approach (pp. 44–46); that is, each organization wants at least its proportionate share. Summed across all the organizations, that preference produces "heavy pressures to distribute benefits widely," as Kettl (1981a: 17) has said of local CDBG decision making. Alternatively, as a slightly different allocational approach, the organizations may favor competition among themselves for funds. Any such competition is likely to result in stronger organizations' getting more funds, either because of superior expertise or greater political clout. The result may still be allocational rather than developmental because the stronger organizations are not necessarily found only in more prosperous neighborhoods.

When each of the three actors holds some power, the eventual decisions should reflect a compromise of the several preferences, much as federal-local intergovernmental spending decisions have usually reflected a compromise of federal redistributive and municipal developmental preferences (pp. 82–83). Involving the neighborhoods should mean only that the decisions now embody allocational criteria as well.

Any new power for neighborhoods is not without risks for cities. The citywide public interest an earlier generation of urban reformers sought so zealously to protect could be compromised anew if the many individual neighborhoods pursue their own interests to the neglect of the interests of the city as a whole. CDBG spending, for example, could be widely dispersed, rather than being concentrated in the manner necessary to induce significant development (see Kettl, 1979: 451). That danger need not become a reality, however. The earlier reforms have not entirely lost their hold on city halls, and so may continue to promote citywide interests. In addition, neighborhood organizations are probably not comparable to the corrupt ward organizations of the machine politics era. Finally, the cooperative city-neighborhood relationship encouraged by recent changes in municipal politics could even incline neighborhoods to be sympathetic with the citywide interest.

A final question remains of whether the entire neighborhood movement is worth its costs. The direct costs of the various government programs in particular can be questioned. Where some observers believe those costs are more than offset by the resulting benefits, others see mostly costs and few benefits (contrast Lamb, 1975, to Bell and Held, 1969). The argument of this chapter does not, unfortunately, suggest a clear answer to this question. Cincinnati itself may.

3

Beginnings: The Rise of the Community Council in Cincinnati

Scarcely a generation ago, in the late 1950s and early 1960s, the American urban neighborhood was being given up for dead, an apparent victim of a transition to mass society that was eroding all sorts of personal relationships, including those based on residential proximity (see Wellman and Leighton, 1979: 368–71). In its place, supposedly, was the depressing impersonal sameness of the assembly-line suburb, as satirized in folksinger Pete Seeger's lyric, "little boxes on the hillside, all made out of ticky-tacky, and they all look just the same."

At about the same time, but without comparable fanfare, Cincinnati's neighborhood resurgence began with the creation of the city's first community council. Ironically, the first of these councils formed in reaction against threats to the supposed depressing sameness of the neighborhoods. In a relatively short time, however, many other factors sparked the formation of other councils. How that happened is the subject of this chapter.

A CITY OF COMMUNITIES

The story begins millions of years ago when nature shaped the topography of the Cincinnati area. A combination of volcanic action and glacial runoff left an area of rolling hills alternating with narrow valleys and rivers, the most prominent being the Ohio River, along with one so-called basin area (see Map 3.1), a large plateau unique for being well above the Ohio River yet below the hills that border the river for hundreds of miles. The basin had strategic value in the days when transportation moved most easily by river, the more so because two other rivers—the Little Miami to the northeast and the Licking

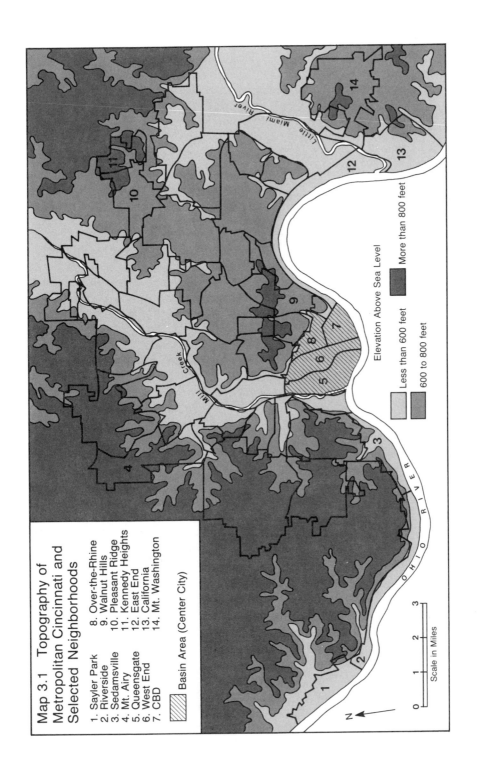

Map 3.1 Topography of
Metropolitan Cincinnati and
Selected Neighborhoods

1. Sayler Park   8. Over-the-Rhine
2. Riverside   9. Walnut Hills
3. Sedamsville   10. Mt. Airy
4. Mt. Airy   11. Kennedy Heights
5. Queensgate   12. East End
6. West End   13. California
7. CBD   14. Mt. Washington

▨ Basin Area (Center City)

Elevation Above Sea Level

☐ Less than 600 feet   ■ More than 800 feet

■ 600 to 800 feet

Scale in Miles
0   1   2   3

N

OHIO RIVER

Little Miami River

Mill Creek

River from the hills of Kentucky—drained into the Ohio near the basin. This value attracted settlers in the eighteenth and nineteenth centuries, and the basin area was eventually christened Cincinnati early in the nineteenth century.

As the city grew, its hills, valleys, and rivers provided natural demarcations for many neighborhoods, facilitating the development of more clearly defined neighborhoods than are found in most cities (e.g., Needleman and Needleman, 1974: 65–66). That development began in the mid-1800s with the building of five inclines, trolleylike systems used to transport people between the basin area and the surrounding hills. Residents working in the increasingly crowded basin were now free to live in new suburbs in the surrounding hills. The subsequent arrival of railroads and streetcars permitted even longer commutes, and a second ring of suburbs formed. Most began as independent villages that became neighborhoods only when annexed to Cincinnati around the turn of the century.

This topographical legacy can be seen in the names of the city's contemporary communities (see Map 3.1). More than a third contain a reference to hills, ranging from Walnut Hills to Mount Airy to Kennedy Heights to Pleasant Ridge. Although no names refer to valleys, many of the other communities trace their origin to that status. The most visible are the riverside communities below the hills: Sedamsville, Riverside, and Sayler Park to the west and the East End and California to the east.

Man, of course, can alter topography in ways that affect neighborhood boundaries. Transportation links such as railroads and highways are well known for affecting these boundaries (e.g., Needleman and Needleman, 1974: 65). Early in Cincinnati's history, for example, a canal dug through the basin area to facilitate river traffic became the boundary between the Over-the-Rhine community and the Central Business District (City of Cincinnati, 1972). In more recent years, highway construction has figured even more prominently in defining and mobilizing many of the city's neighborhoods.

As important as topography can be to a sense of community, ultimately that sense depends on people's perceiving neighborhoods and acting as though they exist. As Downs (1981: 14–16) says, a neighborhood is only "what the inhabitants think it is." The likelihood that inhabitants will think in terms of neighborhoods at all probably depends first on population.[1] In relatively large cities, such as Cincinnati with its 1980 population of 384,000 people, neighborhoods can provide the smaller residential areas with which many people want to identify. Even more important, however, may be the ethnic diversity of the people. As population diversity increases, the similarities within particular areas of a city should become more obvious, such that thinking in terms of neighborhoods becomes more likely. Race has been the most prominent dimension of population diversity for the current revival of neighborhoods (see Cole, 1974: 47; Taub, Taylor, and Dunham, 1984). Race is an obvious basis for thinking in terms of similarities and differences, and it often overlaps other differences, such as those of social class. The extensive racial changes in many cities during the 1950s and 1960s made such contrasts especially salient in recent decades.

Race clearly differentiates many neighborhoods in Cincinnati. The city's population was slightly more than one-third black in 1980 (33.8 percent), but, as in most racially mixed cities, the percentage of blacks in the large majority of the communities was well above or well below that figure, as either predominantly white or predominantly black. City Hall's own listing of statistical communities reported only nine of forty-eight communities in the broad range from one-fifth to two-thirds black (City of Cincinnati, Planning Commission, 1981).

Most of the city's predominantly black communities are distinctive in terms of social class; high concentrations of their populations have low incomes, are renters rather than homeowners, are female-headed households with children, and are service workers—all characteristics of late twentieth-century American poverty, in other words. These communities are somewhat more diverse geographically with locations in the core of the city, along a path of northeastern migration from the core, and in several public housing communities in the near northwest area of the city.

The city does contain some racially mixed neighborhoods, which, though small in number, are distinctive because they are relatively integrated, prosperous, and stable. In addition, as will become clear, they figure prominently in the rise of community councils in Cincinnati. These "pluralistic neighborhoods," as they are often termed, vary from one-third to three-fourths black in population yet have median incomes above or close to the citywide median. All are located some distance from the city's center at the outer edge of the black migration.

The predominantly white communities, constituting a majority of the city's communities, fall into several types on the basis of social class and life-style differences. For natives of the city the clearest distinction is between the cosmopolitan East Side and the more parochial West Side. Along with the university community of Clifton to the north of downtown, several upper-middle-class East Side communities are known for providing a disproportionate share of the political and social leadership of the city. The relatively prosperous communities on the city's West Side, where baseball star Pete Rose grew up, are more middle or working class in composition and much less involved in citywide affairs.

That West Side stereotype is sometimes extended to the city's lower-income white communities, but they really constitute a separate type. These smaller communities, all with populations of about 4,000 or less, are found principally on the near West Side but also to some extent to the north and the east. All are predominantly white, with median incomes below that for the city as a whole, and, as is characteristic of white urban poverty nationally, with disproportionate numbers of elderly. In addition, characteristic of Cincinnati white poverty particularly, these communities include large numbers of white Appalachians who migrated from the South after World War II.

Finally, the city also contains several of the newest type of urban neighborhood; that is, the predominantly white community favoring a nontraditional life style less oriented to child-rearing. Mt. Adams, high above and immediately to the east of the basin, is the most obvious example; the first of Cincinnati's old communities to be restored in the 1960s, it is the home of many single adults and artists (see Schill and Nathan, 1983: 32–38). Several other communities have begun similar evolutions in more recent years.

THE ERA OF THE CIVIC ASSOCIATION, PRE–1956

Although neighborhood organizations in Cincinnati date at least from the turn-of-the-century era of machine politics, the dominant neighborhood groups through most of this century were civic associations, described in other cities (Bell and Held, 1969: 144) as "the old, established, predominantly upper middle class, business, and 'good government' organizations." In Cincinnati, this often meant that, according to one veteran of the Cincinnati neighborhood movement (Crum, 1974), "the main philosophy of the group was that what was good for the neighborhood businesses was good for the neighborhood." Alternatively, some of the groups acted more like fraternal than like civic organizations. Some limited membership to white male adults—at least one did so until the late 1970s—and many emphasized social over communitywide activities. A few gave evidence of a pattern that would soon dominate the city's neighborhood groups, one in which a group forms to deal with a perceived threat to the community. The East Price Hill Improvement Association, for example, formed in the early 1940s in an effort to save the Price Hill incline.[2]

The number of civic associations, although probably considerable at earlier points in Cincinnati's history, had been reduced to eleven by the early 1980s largely because of the rise after 1956 of other neighborhood groups that rejected the dominant business or fraternal orientation. The survival of the eleven probably can be explained by two factors. First, some of the groups adapted to become more like residentially oriented community councils than like traditional civic associations. One, the Clifton Heights–University Heights–Fairview (CHUHF) group, had even abandoned the civic association label in favor of the community council label. Second, and probably more important, the stable nature of these communities has minimized challenges to the authority of their neighborhood organizations. As shown in Map 3.2, these communities—with the understandable CHUHF exception—are outlying areas largely insulated from the residential change that has been so extensive in other parts of Cincinnati in recent decades. In particular, the communities have

Map 3.2 The Civic Association Survivors
from Before 1956

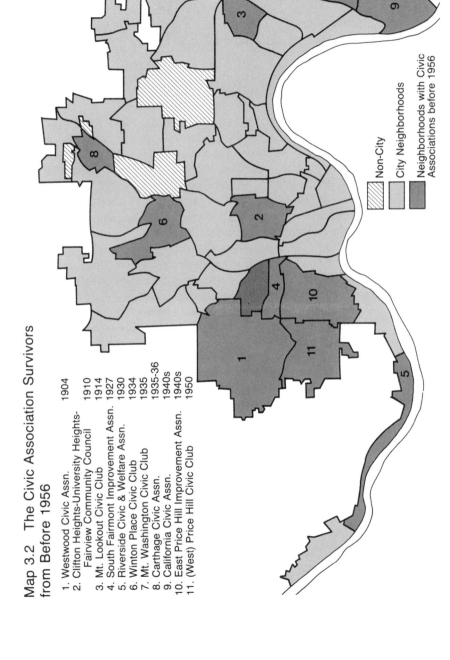

1. Westwood Civic Assn.   1904
2. Clifton Heights-University Heights-
      Fairview Community Council   1910
3. Mt. Lookout Civic Club   1914
4. South Fairmont Improvement Assn.   1927
5. Riverside Civic & Welfare Assn.   1930
6. Winton Place Civic Club   1934
7. Mt. Washington Civic Club   1935
8. Carthage Civic Assn.   1935-36
9. California Civic Assn.   1940s
10. East Price Hill Improvement Assn.   1940s
11. (West) Price Hill Civic Club   1950

Non-City

City Neighborhoods

Neighborhoods with Civic
Associations before 1956

been almost untouched by the recent growth in Cincinnati's black population. None of the eleven had a black proportion by 1980 as large even as the median for all the city's communities, and most had black proportions of less than 5 percent.

Adding to the impression of stability, ten of the eleven communities had homeowner proportions greater than the citywide median, with six having an absolute majority of homeowner households. This stability presumably has permitted these organizations to persist in many of their traditions—at least, in any event, in the tradition of the civic association name.

THE BIRTH OF THE COMMUNITY COUNCIL, 1956–65

In 1956 the decline of the civic association began in Cincinnati—and the city's modern neighborhood movement was born—with the formation of the first community council in the Avondale neighborhood. This council formed at the instigation of a visionary city planning director named Herb Stevens, who thought that planning ought to be done cooperatively with city residents. Anticipating correctly that many blacks would migrate to Avondale when urban renewal forced them to leave the basin area's West End, Stevens worked to organize Avondale residents to prepare for the influx.

Stevens's efforts could not stop the decline of Avondale—it became predominantly poor and black and was the eventual site for the city's riots a decade later—but they did provide a model that other communities followed in forming their own community councils in subsequent years. Although they received no City Hall assistance, these other councils followed the Stevens model in at least two crucial respects. First, they formed to deal more with residential concerns than with the commercial and fraternal concerns of the earlier civic associations. Second, they usually formed in response to perceived threats to the residential nature of neighborhoods, threats linked to the city's rapid development and associated racial change.

The racial transformation of Cincinnati. The importance of racial change might be surmised from the fact that the black proportion of the city's population more than doubled, from 15.5 to 33.8 percent, between 1950 and 1980. Even those figures understate the magnitude of racial change in Cincinnati between 1950 and 1970, the relevant years for the first community councils. For one thing, most of Cincinnati's black population growth came in those two decades, when, according to census data, the number of blacks increased from 78,196 in 1950 to 108,757 in 1960 to 125,031 in 1970. The growth since then, with the end of the black migration from the South, has been only negligible—up to 130,467 in 1980.

In addition, those figures suggest only how many blacks were new to the city, ignoring entirely the additional numbers who moved *within* the city during those years. Those numbers were sizable because City Hall in Cincinnati, beginning in 1956 and continuing into the 1960s (Hessler, 1961: 106), displaced many blacks from the West End to make way for expressway construction and urban renewal (e.g., a new municipal convention hall, a new industrial area). The magnitude of the displacement is suggested by the population decline in West End census tracts from 67,520 in 1950 to 17,068 in 1970, with the number of blacks declining from 54,090 to 16,051. That translates to a loss of 50,452 people, of whom 37,589 were black. Other accounts (Shapiro and Miller, 1976: 42–43) suggest that most of those people were displaced, although some may have chosen to move.

Adding those figures to the figures on the city's black population growth produces a conservative estimate of the number of blacks who moved into Cincinnati neighborhoods, other than the West End, between 1950 and 1970. (It is conservative because it ignores entirely any interneighborhood black movement that did *not* begin in the West End.) That estimate totals 84,424, or the equivalent of more than *two-thirds* (67.5 percent) of Cincinnati's total black population in 1970. Given the racial sensitivities common in American cities (Downs, 1981: 91–93), this represents a radical change.

The impact of that change on the development of community councils becomes clear when the path of the black migration is compared to the location of the new councils. The path initially headed into the basin community of Over-the-Rhine and northeast to Walnut Hills, both of which showed large numbers of blacks as early as 1950. Blacks continued to move into those areas after 1950, but they also moved in a variety of other directions, as indicated in Map 3.3.[3] The racial migration transformed a number of communities, as these census data on racial change from 1950 to 1960 reveal:

1. Walnut Hills, from 39.8 to 55.5 percent black
2. East Walnut Hills, from 0.8 to 44.6 percent black
3. Evanston, from 8.0 to 72.5 percent black
4. Corryville, from 0.5 to 27.7 percent black
5. Avondale, from 13.9 to 68.9 percent black
6. North Fairmount, from 0.5 to 22.7 percent black
7. South Cumminsville, from 9.5 to 48.6 percent black

The percentages continued to grow in most of these neighborhoods after 1960, but blacks also began to move into more distant neighborhoods, producing these changes between 1960 and 1970:

1. Mt. Auburn, from 9.8 to 73.9 percent black
2. North Avondale–Paddock Hills, from 1.6 to 37.6 percent black
3. Bond Hill, from 0.1 to 26.2 percent black
4. Winton Hills, from 2.4 to 52.7 percent black
5. Kennedy Heights, from 17.5 to 58.1 percent black

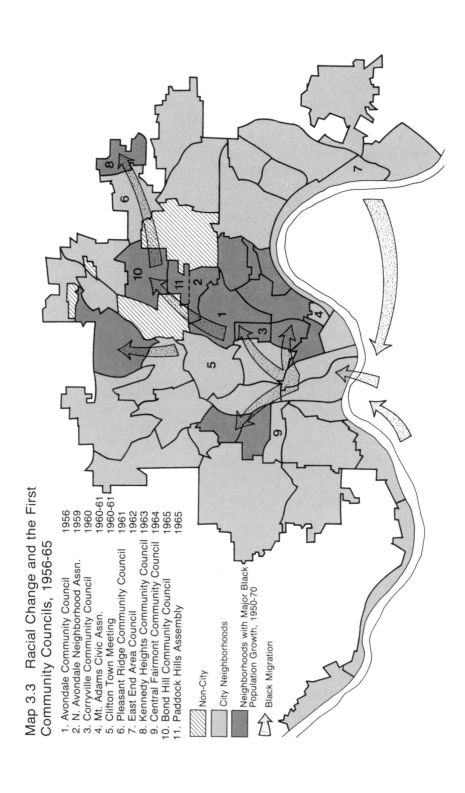

Map 3.3 Racial Change and the First
Community Councils, 1956-65

1. Avondale Community Council   1956
2. N. Avondale Neighborhood Assn.   1959
3. Corryville Community Council   1960
4. Mt. Adams Civic Assn.   1960-61
5. Clifton Town Meeting   1960-61
6. Pleasant Ridge Community Council   1961
7. East End Area Council   1962
8. Kennedy Heights Community Council   1963
9. Central Fairmont Community Council   1964
10. Bond Hill Community Council   1965
11. Paddock Hills Assembly   1965

Non-City

City Neighborhoods

Neighborhoods with Major Black
Population Growth, 1950-70

Black Migration

The black proportion also increased in the West End but primarily because displacement had left few whites behind.

The effects on community council development. As this migration proceeded, community councils frequently developed along its actual or anticipated path. Six of the new groups formed in recently integrated neighborhoods (see Map 3.3), and race appears to have been a factor in the formation of all six. In addition to the Avondale group, the North Avondale, Kennedy Heights, and Paddock Hills groups all are on record as forming to promote stable neighborhood integration. As well, the Bond Hill and Corryville groups formed in part because "white-only" membership clauses left the existing civic associations poorly equipped to cope with racial change.

Race may also have figured in the rise of the other neighborhood groups that began in this period. None of these neighborhoods experienced extensive racial change in these years, but all five could see that change occurring just across their borders. A 1970 comment (Charter Research Institute of Cincinnati, 1970: 60) on the Mt. Adams group, for example, hints at the relevance of that nearby racial change: "Mt. Adams has maintained an identity as a middle class residential area throughout these years, while the neighborhoods surrounding it have been increasingly populated by lower income blacks."

Many of these groups took surprisingly liberal stands on the race issue, seeking to stabilize racial change rather than to prevent it. The Kennedy Heights Community Council formed in 1963 as an interracial group to fight a zoning change that would have allowed increased housing density and probably a rapid racial transformation (Kennedy Heights Community Council, 1978: 10). It was subsequently involved in fighting "block busting" attempts. The success of this and some of the other groups is reflected in the continuing pluralistic character of some of these neighborhoods.

Race was not the only factor in the birth of these councils, however. At least five were also influenced by threats from the city's widespread highway construction and urban renewal in this era of extensive federal support for those activities. The groups in Clifton, Central Fairmount, and the East End, for example, all originated to fight highway or road plans of some kind (Charter Research Institute of Cincinnati, 1970). There may have been others, too. Jim Krusling, then city engineer, contended in a 1980 interview, with some chagrin, that "the highway program probably was responsible for the development of community organizations" in Cincinnati.

Other kinds of urban development helped to bring groups into existence in Corryville and Bond Hill. For Corryville the problem was the City Hall–supported expansion of the adjacent University of Cincinnati and hospital complexes, an expansion that increasingly encroached on the neighborhood's residential area. For Bond Hill the problem was a City Hall proposal to build a new stadium for the Cincinnati Reds in the neighborhood. The Bond Hill group was already in existence, but, according to one of its early leaders, when the city proposal was announced, "we had a thousand members in ten seconds flat." Those numbers apparently were effective; the Reds now play in Riverfront Stadium well south of Bond Hill.

These five cases reflect the *direct* influence of highways and renewal on the early community councils, but they say nothing about the *indirect* role those developments played by helping to accelerate racial change within the city. The combined importance of the direct and indirect influences can perhaps be guessed from the fact that no council formed until the city's urban renewal began in 1956.

These findings tend to confirm the widespread perception that federally assisted programs were largely responsible, although in an unintended manner, for the first phase of the new neighborhood movement. The only surprise is that the indirect role, where organizations formed to combat spillover effects from construction in other neighborhoods, could exceed the direct role, where organizations formed to oppose construction in their own neighborhoods.

Where councils did not form. Where these first community councils did *not* form is equally revealing. To begin with, as Map 3.3 shows, they did not form in most of the areas that experienced the greatest racial change: Walnut Hills, East Walnut Hills, Evanston, Mt. Auburn, South Cumminsville, and North Fairmount. The reason may be the lower socioeconomic status of these areas as compared to the areas where councils did form.[4] All of the racially changing areas without new councils were relatively poor, with 1960 median incomes below the citywide median. By contrast, with the exception of Avondale and Corryville, all of the integrated areas that developed councils were relatively affluent, with median family incomes well above the citywide median. That affluence is important for two reasons. First, it means more residential investment in the community through homeownership. Most of the communities with new councils did, in fact, have above-average homeowner proportions in 1960, giving residents more reason to fight threatened changes in the neighborhood. Second, affluence brings more of the resources—time, money, attitudes—that facilitate making the fight, as by forming a community council.

Yet affluence and its investment in the neighborhood alone could not spur the formation of the new councils. Otherwise there might have been new groups in such prosperous areas as Mt. Lookout, Sayler Park, Westwood, and California, where no group formed or traditional civic associations persisted unchallenged. What these latter areas lacked were threats: None apparently had reason to fear disruption of its residential area because all were well removed geographically from the racial change and construction boom that were transforming other parts of the city.

Most of the early community councils developed, in other words, on the basis of the coincidence of *(a)* above-average home investments by residents and *(b)* threats that could erode the value of those investments. When those conditions hold, community organizations become more likely, and as Taub,

Taylor, and Dunham (1984) have documented, racial tipping may become less likely.

Three of the eleven new councils—those in Avondale, Corryville, and the East End—cannot be explained in these terms. All three appear to have had only below-average community economic resources yet still managed to form community councils when confronted by serious threats to their neighborhoods. In Avondale the limited resources within the community were supplemented by outside resources—those provided by Herb Stevens—to enable a group to form. The other two exceptions are not as easily explained but may illustrate the simple unpredictability of neighborhood leadership: Despite limited economic resources, a community may develop an organization if, by chance, the one or a few necessary leaders are available to get the group going.

THE COMMUNITY ACTION REVOLUTION, 1965–66

Although the poor were largely left behind in those first years of community council activity, momentum was building nationally that would make them primary in the next phase of the neighborhood movement. That momentum grew, first, from the increasing recognition of how urban renewal and highway construction were disrupting the lives of the urban poor. In addition, leaders of the Democratic party may have foreseen partisan gains if they formulated new federal programs for the growing poor population, the urban black poor in particular (Piven and Cloward, 1971).

In any event, whether for humanitarian or Machiavellian reasons, the War on Poverty was formulated early in Lyndon Johnson's administration and became law as the Equal Opportunity Act late in 1964. By early 1965 a variety of programs were operating through the new Office of Economic Opportunity (OEO). Of those programs, the most important for neighborhoods was the Community Action Program (CAP), which provided funds to establish service centers in many urban neighborhoods and rural areas. The Cincinnati-area Community Action Commission (CAC), for example, received $3,745,000 during the initial 1965–66 period, with approximately half of the city's share of those funds going to neighborhood service centers (Yankelovich, 1967: 13–14). The ostensible purpose of these centers, according to the legislation, was to coordinate and improve services for the poor. But the legislation had also included a little-noted requirement for "maximum feasible participation" of area residents. OEO administrators, perhaps hoping to empower the previously politically impotent poor, seized upon that requirement to insist that the centers involve the poor in their operation.

The impact on neighborhood organizations was immediate and profound (e.g., Lamb, 1975). In Cincinnati, twenty new neighborhood groups formed in the first two CAP years, almost twice as many as had formed during the previous decade.[5] The CAC assistance is usually credited with starting fourteen of the groups, and four others were in CAC areas and so probably benefited from the assistance. (Assistance also went to Avondale and the East End, where groups had already formed, and would later fund the formation of two groups after 1966.) The only major exceptions to this pattern were the College Hill and Madisonville groups, both of which formed to combat perceived residential threats.[6] The effects of the new stakes of urban politics were being felt.

The minority concentrations in these communities—most of the CAC-assisted areas had black majorities by 1970—could suggest that the civil rights movement also figured in the rise of the new groups. If so, its role was no more than secondary, for what really distinguishes these communities is the Community Action assistance, not their minority concentrations or the level of civil rights activity. For the most part, in fact, that activity was focusing then on national policy changes rather than on local organizing in northern cities.

A different kind of neighborhood group. As the minority concentrations suggest, these new groups radically altered the face of the neighborhood movement in Cincinnati. As shown in Map 3.4, the CAC groups were located primarily in the areas that had been experiencing the most extensive racial change, without new neighborhood groups forming, over the previous decade or so. The CAC areas were also marked by poverty, as the OEO charge required; all had incomes below the citywide median family income of $8,894, according to the 1970 census, and most were more than $4,000 below that figure. The predominantly white and affluent movement of the early 1960s suddenly, as the result of federal intervention, included many predominantly black and low-income communities.

These new groups differed in structure and function from most of the city's earlier neighborhood groups, even from the community councils whose label the new groups usually adopted. As creatures of the OEO, the new groups were required to draw at least one-third of their elected governing board members "from the poverty segment of the community" (Charter Research Institute of Cincinnati, 1970: 9) to satisfy the maximum feasible participation requirement. In addition, the CAC-assisted groups were more likely than the city's other neighborhood groups to draw their leaders from the service and welfare professions, the professions that provided employees for the neighborhood service centers. In a 1980 interview Herb Stevens recalled, for example, that the staff for these centers "became sort of a staff to some community organizations."

As his comment suggests, many of the CAC groups chose to function in part as advocates for their communities in government, a functional interest they shared with most of the community groups born in the previous decade (see also Yankelovich, 1967: 25). For the most part, however, the new groups

Map 3.4 The Community Action Revolution, 1965–66

1. Camp Washington Community Council
2. College Hill Forum
3. Columbia Neighborhood Association
4. Evanston Community Council
5. Madisonville Coordinating Committee
6. Mt. Auburn Community Council
7. North Fairmont* * *
8. Over-the-Rhine* * * * * *
9. South Cumminsville-Millvale* * * *
10. Walnut Hills Area Council
11. West End Community Council
12. Winton Hills Citizen Action Council

* Number of groups where
more than 1 formed

Black Proportion of
Neighborhood Population, 1970

10-30%

31-50%

Over 50%

Non-City

City Neighborhoods

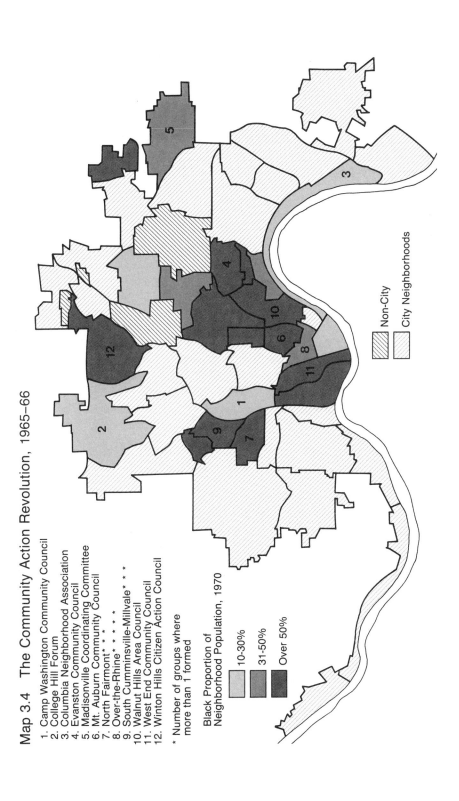

tended to be service organizations, unlike the earlier councils, in a pattern
critics have often lamented (e.g., Gittell, 1980). Even in those early years one
Cincinnati critic complained that for the local CAC, "community organization
has been secondary to the extension of individual services to the poor"
(Yankelovich, 1967: 3). Some of that primary concern for services may be
unavoidable, however, given the nature of the residents of these areas: more
low income, more one-parent families, more elderly, and generally the more
dependent populations likely to be most interested in services.

SPREAD AND CONSOLIDATION, 1967–80

By the end of 1966, as the result of three distinctive phases, neighborhood
groups could be found in most of Cincinnati's communities. The growth of new
groups was far from over, however; another twenty groups would form before
1980 as the community idea spread to almost every part of the city (see Map
3.5). Many factors are thought to have figured in the rise of these groups,
ranging from residential threats to CAC assistance to church concerns over
racial conflicts (Charter Research Institute of Cincinati, 1970). As much as
anything, the new groups may have developed because they perceived the
neighborhood organization idea as successful. Many of the first community
councils could have been perceived as succeeding in stabilizing their neighborhoods, and the Community Action groups had succeeded in drawing federal
funds. In addition, as this era progressed, the potential value of the neighborhood idea grew as more and more neighborhood groups became eligible for
various kinds of outside funding. Federal Community Development Block
Grant funding, for example, was made widely available to the neighborhoods
upon its arrival in Cincinnati in 1975 (Woods, Andersen, and Grober, 1979).
Not long thereafter, in 1978, the Mott Foundation's Stimulating Neighborhood
Action Program made funding available to every one of the city's forty-seven
neighborhoods. In an era when federal funds were being "spread" (Nathan,
1978: 78–82) to larger numbers of local governments, funds within Cincinnati—
and within some other cities (Kettl, 1981a)—were being spread in analogous
fashion to larger numbers of neighborhoods.

   Probably in part as a consequence of that spread, the community council
idea spread in this period principally to areas that had not been involved in the
earlier phases. Thus thirteen of the new groups formed in areas that previously
did not have their own group. Of the thirteen, nine represented small
communities, areas with populations below the median for all Cincinnati
communities, suggesting that smaller communities, because of fewer resources, may have taken longer to organize. The small communities were not
the only ones to organize in these years, however; such larger communities as
Hyde Park, Northside, and Oakley also developed their first modern neighborhood organizations.

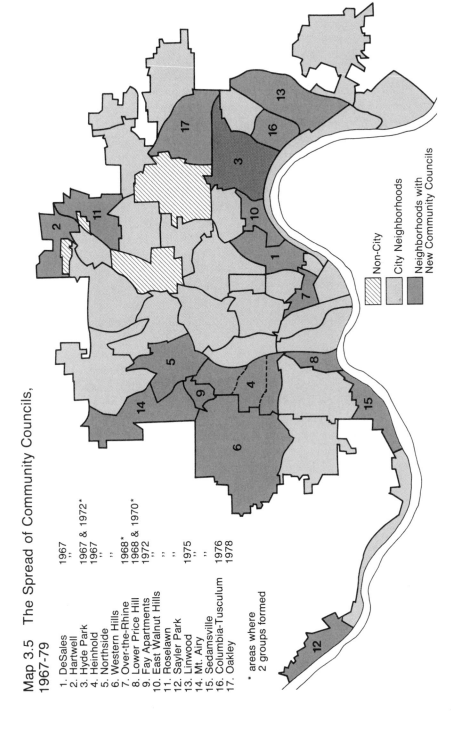

Map 3.5 The Spread of Community Councils, 1967-79

1. DeSales   1967
2. Hartwell   ,,
3. Hyde Park   1967 & 1972*
4. Heinhold   1967
5. Northside   ,,
6. Western Hills   1968*
7. Over-the-Rhine   1968 & 1970*
8. Lower Price Hill   1972
9. Fay Apartments   ,,
10. East Walnut Hills   ,,
11. Roselawn   ,,
12. Sayler Park   1975
13. Linwood   ,,
14. Mt. Airy   ,,
15. Sedamsville   1976
16. Columbia-Tusculum   1976
17. Oakley   1978

* areas where
  2 groups formed

Non-City

City Neighborhoods

Neighborhoods with
New Community Councils

Nor were unrepresented areas the only ones to develop new groups. Some of the new groups formed as apparent competitors of existing organizations: the Lower Price Hill Action Group of 1970 competing with the Lower Price Hill Community Council of 1968, the Hyde Park Residents Association of 1972 with the Greater Hyde Park Community Council of 1967, and the Mt. Airy Town Council of 1975 with a civic association survivor of an earlier era. Finally, two of the new groups developed as umbrella coordinating organizations for other neighborhood groups: the Heinold Area Council for several groups in the near northwest part of the city; the Over-the-Rhine Community Council for the several groups already in that community.

The one thing missing in these findings is evidence of groups forming because escalating housing and energy costs made exit to the suburbs more difficult. Only a group in Columbia-Tusculum clearly fits that pattern, having formed to promote the rehabilitation of an older community by a new gentry. The lack of any broader pattern could be traced to the fact that many Cincinnati residents had already chosen voice over exit by forming new community councils in the 1950s and 1960s, such that new organizations were not needed to exercise voice in the 1970s. The problems of the 1970s might instead have prompted increased participation in these groups, perhaps helping to explain membership increases in the two-thirds of the councils that continued through the 1970s (see Table 3.1).

"A bewildering array"? By the early 1970s the spread may have produced something akin to the "bewildering array of street-level community organizations that seek to give voice to one neighborhood demand or another," which Douglas Yates (1977: 23) said characterized urban politics in the 1970s. Yates, with Bell and Held (1969), viewed this proliferation of groups with dismay, seeing it as a federally induced outcome that made governing cities more difficult.

The Cincinnati evolution provides some support for that criticism. Some public officials could have been bewildered and confused by the rapid growth of neighborhood groups and the many resulting cases of multiple groups claiming to represent the same area, as in Over-the-Rhine and Columbia–East End. Ultimately, however, the criticism fails on a number of counts with the Cincinnati case. First and most important, the criticism exaggerates the influence of federal incentives. Most of Cincinnati's neighborhood groups—the civic associations, the early community councils, and most of the groups formed in the 1967–80 period—were begun without significant federal support. Only the Community Action groups appear to owe their existence to that support. If the movement would be easier for local officials to manage without these latter groups, it also would not be as representative for having left out most low-income areas. Federal aid, in other words, has done more for the representativeness of neighborhood groups than for their sheer numbers.

Second, the criticism also exaggerates the confusion over what areas groups represent. For the most part, rather than voicing only "one neighborhood demand or another," each of the Cincinnati groups represented an identifiable geographic area and was usually the only group representing that area. That would be confusing only if one did not understand the geographic divisions of the city. Even where groups did compete to represent an area, the competition often was neither confusing nor longstanding. The usual competition between traditional business-oriented civic associations and newer residential community councils would be confusing only if officials did not understand the opposition of business and residential interests, perhaps the most common opposition in both cities and suburbs. Any confusion could not long persist, in any event, because one of the groups, probably the community council, usually soon won out over the other.

Consolidation. Over the decade of the 1970s, in fact, the number of neighborhood groups in Cincinnati was gradually reduced through mergers and attrition, further undermining the possibility that local officials would be overwhelmed by the sheer number of groups. The changes came principally where multiple groups had been active, with mergers in such areas as Millvale and Hyde Park and attrition in such other areas as Lower Price Hill, North Fairmount, Over-the-Rhine, South Fairmount, and Westwood. The effect was to reduce the number of groups to one in most of the city's communities, with only the business-dominated CBD left without a "neighborhood" group as such at the end of this period. This consolidation probably was inevitable. Given the limited resources available, most neighborhoods have difficulty maintaining one organization, let alone several (e.g., O'Brien, 1975). Even when indigenous resources are supplemented by external support from federal or local governments, the support is unlikely to be so generous that several groups can be sustained in the same area.

It also may have been inevitable that the losers in the consolidation would be the low-income Community Action areas of the 1960s. Each of these areas still had a neighborhood organization at the outset of the 1980s, but, as revealed in Table 3.1, they had lost more than their share of the groups that had disappeared, even as their surviving groups did not experience as much membership growth as did the city's other community councils. This is hardly surprising in a decade when both federal and local funds were being distributed more widely.

COMMENT: THE MANY CAUSES
OF THE NEIGHBORHOOD MOVEMENT

This chronology describes a movement with many causes. They begin with the roots neighborhood organizations have in the traditions of cities, in people's

TABLE 3.1
WINNERS AND LOSERS IN THE CONSOLIDATION

| Neighborhood | Councils | | Membership Trend | |
Type	Disappeared	Continuing	Decreasing	Increasing
Community				
Action areas	62% (8)	31% (15)	55% (6)	32% (7)
Other areas	38 (5)	69 (33)	45 (5)	68 (15)
Totals	100 (13)	100 (48)	100 (11)	100 (22)

Source: Membership trends reflect a comparison of 1970 reported memberships (Charter Research Institute of Cincinnati, 1970) to 1978 memberships, as reported to the city. Council disappearances and continuations were assessed as explained in note 2 of this chapter.

Parenthetical numbers in this and all subsequent tables reflect the sample size on which the percentage is based.

historical sense of belonging to particular neighborhoods. That sense derives in part from topography, as evident in how the natural flow of land and water demarcates many Cincinnati neighborhoods. These traditional roots live on, for example, through the many civic associations that have survived in Cincinnati neighborhoods for periods ranging from one-third to three-quarters of a century. These groups could survive, if changing along the way, because their home communities have themselves changed very little—remaining predominantly white enclaves—during a turbulent quarter-century for the city as a whole. They may represent an anachronism in the neighborhood movement, but nonetheless they constitute a large component of the movement.

If similarity and stability of residents explain the persistence of many civic associations, diversity and change in the population were clearly the catalysts for the rise of the modern community council and the new neighborhood movement as a whole. Moreover, of all the possible elements of population diversity and change, race as overlapped by class was unquestionably the most important. Race best differentiates the city's neighborhoods, with most either predominantly white or predominantly black. As well, the few neighborhoods that are racially mixed are well known for their pluralistic nature and for the influence of that nature on the formation of the first community councils. Race also figures prominently in the expansion of neighborhood groups during the Community Action years, though in a very different fashion. Most of the areas where Community Action groups formed had predominantly black populations and may have received funding primarily for that reason (see Donovan, 1973: 107).

The multiple roles of government. The racial change that triggered so many new community councils in the years after 1955 was not entirely the product of migration from agricultural areas in the rural South. It was also based on the cooperative efforts of business and government, both federal and local, in urban renewal and highway construction. Those efforts created much of the movement of blacks within Cincinnati during the critical early years of the neighborhood revival. Therein lies the irony of urban renewal and highway construction. Programs intended to revive the inner city may, quite unintentionally, have done as much or more to revive neighborhood organizations in outlying areas of the city. The threats these programs posed, both directly from construction and indirectly through the spillover from population displacement, figured in the formation of most or all of the city's first community councils.

The role of these programs does not fit either of two common images of these years. One image pictures an era when city governments responded to the first federal citizen participation requirements by creating elite "blue ribbon" committees that only rubber-stamped City Hall plans. Not so, it appears, in Cincinnati. The first community councils, far from being elite committees imposed on the communities, were mostly indigenous in origin, reflecting reactions to perceived threats to the communities. And if their members were relatively prosperous, they were still not citywide elites speaking for communities where they did not live.

Nor were these first community councils composed of the urban poor angrily mobilized against urban renewal displacement, the other common but contrasting image of these years (Mollenkopf, 1981; Henig, 1982b). Very few of the new groups formed in the low-income areas that experienced urban renewal directly or were transformed by the accompanying displacement. Instead, the groups formed mostly in more prosperous areas to cope with the secondary effects of urban renewal. Only these areas had the resources, as well as the threats, necessary to form and sustain neighborhood organizations (for similar findings, see Wilson, 1963; Kovak, 1972). The poor are not easily mobilized, even in the face of threats, because they lack the resources necessary for that mobilization.

The poor were mobilized in Cincinnati only when the federal government intervened through the War on Poverty in the middle 1960s, causing a proliferation of new neighborhood groups in low-income, predominantly black areas. The new stakes of the poverty program, stakes targeted specifically to low-income neighborhoods, created neighborhood organizations where the earlier devastation of urban renewal could not.

The wisdom of this federal effort is still debated in Cincinnati and elsewhere. Gittell (1980: 64–65), for one, argues that long-term dependency on support from outside the community weakens the ability of community groups in low-income areas to advocate to the powers that be. Along slightly different lines, some Cincinnati observers argue that the service orientation of the Community Action groups depressed community initiative to the extent that, as one critic said, "the communities sit and wait for the services to come." Although those criticisms may have merit, the fact remains that the War on Poverty produced groups in many low-income, high-minority areas where previously there had been no groups or only dormant groups. Most of those groups survive today, no small accomplishment in the turbulent world of neighborhood groups. Without the War on Poverty, these groups might be less dependent, but they might also be fewer in number and even less outspoken in advocacy.

Maturation. Causes are not as easily specified for the latest phase of the evolution, the years since 1966. To be sure, ostensible reasons can be found for the rise of most of the groups that began in these years, but those reasons are not entirely persuasive. The evolution in these years may reflect as much as anything a maturation process in which, first, many new groups began as the viability of the community council idea continued to grow and, second, many groups disappeared as the movement discovered its upper limits.

The growing popularity does not appear to have been, as sometimes argued, an unhealthy product of federal policies. It was only partially produced by those policies, and the effect may have been to make the movement healthier by improving its representativeness. In addition, much of the putatively unhealthy profusion of groups was only temporary, as many of the new groups vanished within a decade. Moreover, even at its zenith, that profusion may have been good for cities. A healthy economic environment is now viewed (e.g., Birch, 1981) as one in which, in addition to more new businesses beginning and succeeding, more businesses *fail*. The health appears to lie in the willingness to try and the pressures to compete, not in the rate of success. Similarly with neighborhoods, the rise of so many new groups between the mid-1950s and the mid-1970s may have reflected a healthy interest in neighborhoods, with competition among groups serving to determine which groups could best represent particular neighborhoods. From that perspective, there may be more risks in the consolidation of the 1970s than in the proliferation of earlier years, but risks of too little rather than too much vitality.

4

People:
The Several Faces
of Neighborhood Activism

The origins of Cincinnati's community councils are now history, far enough in the past to be forgotten by all but a few veterans of the city's neighborhood movement. The movement survives in the 1980s on the basis of a new pool of neighborhood activists who reflect the interests of another generation. The makeup and motivations of that pool can seem difficult to predict, given the many ways in which neighborhood activism has been described. Although sometimes advertised as reflecting a "people's" movement, an uprising of a cross-section of the population (Boyte, 1980), this activism has frequently been found to have unrepresentative biases akin to those that characterize most traditional organizational and political participation (see Cole, 1974: 90-92; Steggart, 1975: 13). Yet any temptation to treat neighborhood activism as simply another form of traditional participation dissolves in the face of ample evidence of significant differences (Cox and McCarthy, 1980; Sharp, 1980). Blacks, for example, are much more likely to be active in neighborhood groups than in other modes of participation (e.g., Shingles, 1981).

This confusion about neighborhood activism leaves at least two issues unresolved. The first concerns representativeness. Although most observers may agree that neighborhood activism is not entirely representative, they do not agree on the manner or degree of unrepresentativeness. Nor do they agree on the reasons for this activism. Although some students of neighborhood activism seem willing to settle for simple explanations, choosing to ignore many exceptions to their rules, other observers are elaborating complicated explanations that seem to do too little summarizing. A recent survey by Wandersman (1981), for example, listed at least nine major explanations of participation in neighborhood groups and included additional constituent elements within each of the nine.

This chapter seeks to clarify both issues by examining neighborhood activism in Cincinnati. The principal data for the examination come from a citywide survey of 2,334 Cincinnati residents conducted in early 1978, a survey that included questions about the city's community councils.[1] Supplementary information comes from in-depth interviews with forty-four community council leaders by telephone in the summer of 1979 and, in person and at greater length, with a smaller group of fourteen council leaders in the summer of 1980.

REPRESENTATIVENESS AND BIAS

Questions about the representativeness of neighborhood organizations are best answered by examining responses to two questions in the 1978 survey. First, "Is there a neighborhood association or community council (or its equivalent) in your neighborhood?" The broad phrasing was used because of the many names taken by the city's neighborhood groups (e.g., Paddock Hills Assembly, College Hill Forum, Clifton Town Meeting). Just over half of the sample, or 50.8 percent, answered yes. That also means, of course, that almost half of the sample—and thus probably half of the Cincinnati population— were unaware of a local neighborhood group, despite the fact that almost all of the neighborhoods had such a group by that time.

The level of membership. An initial indication of the representativeness of Cincinnati's neighborhood movement comes from answers to the second question, asked only of those who reported a group in their neighborhood: "Do you belong in some way to your community council?" (The phrase "in some way" was included because the councils vary in how they define membership.) The greater the numbers answering yes to this question, the more the councils as a group can claim to have mobilized the Cincinnati population in a manner reflective of one kind of representativeness. That mobilization is an important concern of the councils. Several council leaders spoke of their interest in building group memberships or of their pride in having already done so. As one leader said when asked about his group's recent accomplishments, "The typical answer to that would be physical improvements, but I would like to think that the accomplishments go more with level of people activities. . . . One of our tremendous accomplishments is the fact that people now feel that they participate more in community activity."

The survey data raise some doubts, however, about the extent of the mobilization achieved by the councils. Across the entire sample, only 12.6 percent, or 293 respondents, reported belonging to a neighborhood organization. Stated in different terms, only approximately one of every eight Cincinnati adults belongs to a neighborhood group, judging from this sample. Even that probably overstates the formal registered membership in the city's community councils. Survey respondents are known for often exaggerating what seems socially desirable behavior, such as community activism. That tendency could be especially strong here because the phrase "in some way" invited respondents to use a liberal definition of "belonging."

In fact, the rates of membership reported by the community councils themselves are considerably lower than the survey estimates. How much lower is difficult to say because the councils vary so much in how they count members: Some count individuals, others count family units, and a few even count other units (e.g., members of a steering committee selected from the community). To cope with this confusion, council-reported membership figures were compared separately to total population *and* to total households, thereby producing minimum and maximum estimates of formal membership as a proportion of potential membership. Comparing 1980 council-reported memberships to 1980 census data produced membership estimates of 3.3 percent of the *total population* and 8.0 percent of *all households,* both significantly below the survey percentage.[2]

What these several figures suggest is that somewhere between 3.3 and 12.6 percent of the eligible Cincinnati population are involved in community councils. Regardless of which figure is preferred, that hardly suggests the mobilization of a representative "people's movement." Even the maximum 12.6 percent figure falls well below the usual 25 to 30 percent figure for voter turnout in Cincinnati local elections, a good standard of comparison for other local political involvement. On the other hand, any of the membership estimates is large enough to argue that the neighborhood movement constitutes a significant interest group movement in the city, especially given the often underdeveloped group politics in cities such as Cincinnati (see Pressman, 1975: 28–30).

The bias of council membership. The other question about representativeness asks whether neighborhood activists are drawn more from some groups than from others. The survey data, although perhaps exaggerating overall membership levels, probably can be trusted for answering this question because they do accurately reflect where membership levels are higher or lower. Membership proportions developed for each of twenty-four neighborhoods with survey samples of twenty or more correspond closely (r = .638) to proportions based on council-reported figures, despite the vagaries of those council-reported memberships.[3] Data that so accurately describe differences between communities are also likely to capture the actual differences between groups.

The data reveal definite biases in neighborhood activism, including most prominently the usual socioeconomic bias of other forms of participation. Council membership increases (gamma = .264) with a measure of socioeconomic status that combines the income and education of the respondent, although most of the increase comes at the highest socioeconomic levels.[4] A similar bias can be seen by homeownership, with one in five of those who own their homes (20.1 percent) reporting this neighborhood organization membership as compared to only one in fifteen (6.6 percent) of those who rent. Membership does not appear to be much affected, however, by such other factors as having dependent children or having resided longer in the city.

Council membership also rises with use of each of three neighborhood-level services (neighborhood health centers, recreation programs and facilities, and parks programs and facilities) and even more so with a combined measure of use of all three services (gamma = .306). This bias, too, is not necessarily inconsistent with the usual bias of participation given that service use increases slightly with socioeconomic status.

In one pattern that does run counter to the customary bias, Cincinnati's blacks, despite having on the average much lower socioeconomic status than the city's whites, are more inclined to report council membership, with a rate of 15.2 percent compared to 11.5 percent for whites. Curiously, this does not seem to produce any distortions in the racial representativeness of the individual councils. The racial mix of each council, as perceived by neighborhood experts in City Hall, almost mirrors the census-reported racial mix of the community as a whole (gamma = .965), as indicated in Table 4.1.[5] The lack of racial bias in council membership rates could be partially attributable to the earlier War on Poverty efforts that were concentrated in predominantly black neighborhoods. Membership rates are slightly higher in any event in the former Community Action neighborhoods, despite their persistent severe poverty, than in other Cincinnati neighborhoods (13.8 percent members versus 12 percent).

Taken together, these various patterns indicate that community council membership is not broadly representative of the full Cincinnati population. Some people, such as homeowners and those of higher socioeconomic status, are more involved than others. Still, the degree of bias, by socioeconomic status in particular, is less than that commonly found with political and organizational participation (e.g., Verba and Nie, 1972). The neighborhood movement may not be representative, but it is perhaps not as *un*representative as most other participation.

Explaining activism. That also means, however, that council membership cannot be readily explained by any one or two demographic factors. Rather than having one or two characteristics (e.g., socioeconomic status) that clearly set them apart from the rest of the Cincinnati population, these activists appear to be only a little more of this and a little less of that. They can appear that way because the patterns of activism in the city are actually several, rather than only one. Moreover, the patterns contrast so sharply that treating council members as a single group inevitably obscures any sense of pattern. The patterns, or different orientations to neighborhood activism, can become evident only if each of four demographic groupings is examined separately: white homeowners, black homeowners, black renters, and white renters.

TABLE 4.1
RACIAL REPRESENTATIVENESS OF THE COMMUNITY COUNCILS

Percentage Black in the Community	Community Council Racial Composition				
	All or Almost All White	Majority White	50-50	Majority Black	All or Almost All Black
0–7%a	70% (16)	13% (1)	0%	0%	0%
10–35%	30 (7)	50 (4)	0	0	0
50–57%	0	38 (3)	33 (1)	25 (1)	0
58–87%	0	0	67 (2)	50 (2)	33 (3)
90% +	0	0	0	25 (1)	67 (6)

gamma = .965

Sources: Community percentages are taken from a report by the Cincinnati Planning Commission, Planning and Management Support Services Division (1981). Council racial composition was reported by CAT quadrant leaders in terms of these five categories in the summer of 1980.

a Categories for percentage black in the community are intentionally not exhaustive (e.g., there is no place for communities with 36–49 percent black) to reflect the actual proportions in Cincinnati's communities.

These groupings were chosen for two reasons. First, the groupings differ substantially in their rates of neighborhood activism (see Table 4.2), suggesting that they are distinct groups in reality. Council membership rates are highest for black homeowners, somewhat lower for white homeowners, much lower for black renters, and almost minuscule for white renters. Second, each of the groups exhibits its own distinctive pattern of activism that can be explained in terms of factors already known to be operative in urban politics.[6]

THE INVESTMENT ORIENTATION:
WHITE HOMEOWNERS

Most community council members, a majority of 52.4 percent, are white homeowners. Black homeowners have a slightly higher rate of council membership (22 percent as opposed to 19.6 percent), but there are so many more white homeowners that their lower rate of participation still produces a majority of all community council members in the city. White homeowners are motivated in this activism principally by the considerable financial stake in local affairs that investment in a home implies. The impact of that stake on

TABLE 4.2
NEIGHBORHOOD ACTIVISM BY RACE AND HOMEOWNERSHIP

Group	Full Group		Council Membership		
	Number	Sample %[a]	Number	Sample %[a]	Member %[a]
White homeowners	774	33.7	152	52.4	19.6
Black homeowners	246	10.7	54	18.6	22.0
White renters	846	36.9	35	12.1	4.1
Black renters	429	18.7	49	16.9	11.4
Citywide	2295	100.0	290	100.0	12.6

[a] "Sample %" is the group number as a proportion of the entire sample, in the first case of all respondents and in the second case of all respondents who said they were council members. "Member %" is the proportion of the group (e.g., white homeowners) who said they were council members.

neighborhood activism is evident, to begin with, in the sharp contrast between the almost 20 percent membership rate for white homeowners and the low 4.1 percent rate for white renters.

The role of socioeconomic status. More evidence of the importance of this investment comes from the influence of socioeconomic status on council membership. That status is the best single predictor of council membership among white homeowners (gamma = .460), with their membership rates ranging from around 10 percent at the lowest socioeconomic levels to 36.6 percent at the highest level. This relationship can be explained in part independent of investment in a home. Socioeconomic status could be stimulating neighborhood activism, first, by providing the greater personal resources that facilitate any kind of group participation, and second, by nurturing the stronger civic values that impel people toward various forms of participation in public affairs. That cannot be the entire story, however, because socioeconomic status does not also impel renters to neighborhood activism. Membership rates do not change appreciably with socioeconomic status for either white or black renters. The influence of socioeconomic status is contingent on homeownership, underscoring the centrality of that investment for neighborhood activism.

The racial threat. Race also plays a role in linking the home investment to membership in community councils. White homeowners in American cities have long viewed racial change as one of the most serious threats to the value of their homes. As a consequence, when racial change is imminent, the typical white homeowner may seek to protect the home investment either by moving to a neighborhood not experiencing racial change or, while staying put, by exercising voice through action designed to combat the perceived threat (Hirschman, 1970; Sharp, 1984). The latter option may mean joining a neighborhood organization, as many Cincinnati residents apparently did in response to the racial threat of the late 1950s and 1960s. What held then may still hold, such that contemporary white homeowners will be more likely to join community councils when faced with the threat of racial change.

Although no direct measure of this threat is available, the threat can be measured indirectly by the black proportion of the population in the respondent's neighborhood, a figure available from the 1980 census. That proportion usually reflects for whites the proximity of racial change, a likely basis for their perceptions of racial threats to the neighborhood (see Taub, Taylor, and Dunham, 1984: 160–62). It will not necessarily reflect accomplished integration because racially mixed neighborhoods in the segregated American city are most often composed of black areas adjacent to white areas, rather than one large integrated area. As a leader of one of Cincinnati's most racially balanced neighborhoods said of her area, "It's not true integration in that you have one black house, one white house" (*Cincinnati Enquirer,* 1981b).

That proximity of blacks strongly influences the neighborhood activism of white homeowners, as suggested by the data in Table 4.3. Council membership rates for this group climb from 14.7 percent in predominantly white neighborhoods to 31 percent in majority black neighborhoods. With white renters, by contrast, the inclination to join community councils is unaffected by the community's racial mix.[7] The salience of the threat, in other words, depends on the investment in the home.

Individual socioeconomic status adds to that effect, as higher status leads white homeowners to respond even more strongly to the presence of blacks in the community. When both the black proportion of the community and the individual's socioeconomic status are high, community council membership rates are very high, peaking at 59.1 percent for higher-status white homeowners in majority black communities. Those individuals are the most involved, presumably because they have the most to lose if the neighborhood experiences complete racial turnover. They are not necessarily acting out of racist motives. Such motives might be inferred from this sensitivity to racial change, but unfairly so in many cases. For one thing, these owners have chosen to stay and cope with racial change, rather than fleeing to a suburb far removed from the change. For another, as noted in Chapter 3, the community councils they have joined have frequently taken progressive stands on racial issues, seeking stable integration rather than racial separation.

The magnitude of the investment. White homeowners are also influenced in their neighborhood activism by the value of their homes. Greater market value for a home means a greater investment for the homeowner, which in turn

TABLE 4.3
THE INVESTMENT ORIENTATION I:
COUNCIL MEMBERSHIP RATES OF WHITE HOMEOWNERS
BY COMMUNITY RACIAL MIX AND INDIVIDUAL SOCIOECONOMIC STATUS

Community	Individual Socioeconomic Status[a]				
Racial Mix	Low/Mid	Middle	Up/Mid	Upper	Totals
Under 10% black	8.2%[b]	8.4%	12.3%	27.9%	14.7%
	(73)	(131)	(138)	(122)	(464)
10–35% black	17.9	8.3	19.6	43.4	25.7
	(39)	(48)	(56)	(83)	(226)
50% + black[b]	18.8	15.4	30.0	59.1	31.0
	(16)	(26)	(20)	(22)	(84)
Totals	12.5	9.3	15.9	36.6	
	(128)	(205)	(214)	(227)	

[a] For the relationship of socioeconomic status to membership, gamma = .460. For the relationship of community racial mix to membership, controlling for socioeconomic status, gamma = .335. Groupings of socioeconomic status favor the middle- to upper-status categories because white homeowners fall more into those categories.
[b] No community in the city is between 35 and 50 percent black.

means a higher likelihood of joining a community council to protect that investment. In theory, this tendency should affect all neighborhoods. It would be difficult to discern in the racially mixed neighborhoods, however, because the racial threat and socioeconomic status so dominate the activism of white homeowners there. The tendency can be better isolated in predominantly white neighborhoods, where 60 percent (464 of 774) of the white homeowners in the sample live.

One measure of home values is the average sale value of one- to three-family homes, a figure reported regularly by the Ohio Transfer Service Property Data and compiled by the Cincinnati City Planning Commission (1981) for each of the city's neighborhoods for the year 1980. For this analysis those averages were grouped into four categories, chosen to respect natural breaks in the distribution of home values across neighborhoods. These categories obviously cannot give a precise reading on the value of any particular respondent's home, but they should provide a good estimate given the tendency toward homogeneity of home values within particular neighborhoods.

The influence of these home values can be seen in Table 4.4. Council membership rates of white homeowners increase steadily as these values increase. Of those who live in areas with the lowest home values, only 6.3 percent belong to community councils, compared to 27 percent of those who live where home values are highest. The table also shows that the influence of home values is felt in conjunction with individual socioeconomic status, with membership levels peaking when the two predictors both peak.

TABLE 4.4
THE INVESTMENT ORIENTATION II:
COUNCIL MEMBERSHIP RATES OF WHITE HOMEOWNERS
BY HOME SALE VALUE AND SOCIOECONOMIC STATUS[a]

Neighborhood Home	Individual Socioeconomic Status				
Sale Value (1980)[b]	Low	Low/Mid	Up/Mid	Upper	Totals
Low	7.5%	5.3%	0%	0%	6.3%
(Up to $33,000)	(67)	(19)	(6)	(3)	(95)
Average	4.5	13.7	15.8	22.2	10.3
($35–47,000)	(67)	(51)	(19)	(9)	(146)
High	9.1	12.8	20.0	43.8	16.7
($50–58,000)	(44)	(47)	(25)	(16)	(132)
Very high	20.0	14.3	30.8	40.0	27.0
($62–93,000)	(25)	(21)	(13)	(30)	(89)
Totals	8.4	12.3	19.0	36.2	
	(203)	(138)	(63)	(58)	

[a] Only for those neighborhoods with less than 10 percent black, neighborhoods that contain 59.9 percent of all white homeowners.
[b] For the relationship of home sale value to membership, controlling for socioeconomic status, gamma = .282.

Perspectives from community council leaders. The survey data give no evidence on one of the more important distinctions among white homeowners, the now well-known distinction between the traditional homeowner, trying to preserve the quality of a relatively affluent neighborhood, and the "new gentry," the homeowner trying to return a once prosperous neighborhood to its earlier glory. The survey was simply not designed to discriminate between these two groups.

That distinction did emerge as important, however, when fourteen leaders of the community councils were interviewed in depth. Several of the fourteen resembled new gentry activists, whereas others resembled the traditional homeowner activist. The former included two council leaders who are developers of deteriorated properties and one who is the primary paid staff of a neighborhood development corporation; all three are white homeowners. One of the developers even described himself, in terms appropriate for the new gentry, as a "hustler" who had chosen his neighborhood of residence as "a wholesome place for us to live and to make money."

By contrast, the more traditional white homeowners among these leaders explained their neighborhood involvement primarily in terms of a general concern for community problems, seldom making any mention of selfish concerns for the value of their properties. Several, for example, traced their initial involvement to racial problems, as with one leader who was recruited through his church at a time of racial tensions in the late 1960s. These findings are not atypical either; neighborhood leaders in other cities (Rich, 1980b) have also explained their decisions to lead more in terms of civic concerns than in terms of selfish concerns for home investments. These findings do not cast doubt on the importance of the investment orientation. The earlier evidence for the primacy of that orientation is simply too strong to view the orientation as subordinate to some civic concern, no matter how much neighborhood leaders might protest that a sense of civic duty really underlies their activism. The suspicion arises, instead, that a professed civic orientation could sometimes disguise a selfish concern for one's investment in a home.

But a civic orientation may be important, too. The investment orientation may be the prerequisite for neighborhood activism by white homeowners; without the home investment, even council membership is unlikely, as the survey evidence clearly demonstrated. What may be needed beyond the prerequisite, however, is something to overcome the free rider problem, the inclination to let others do the hard work. A sense of civic duty could overcome the problem by making activism desirable as a means to satisfy one's conscience. In other words, the neighborhood activism of white homeowners is probably a function of both the investment orientation and a sense of civic duty. That sense may not have emerged as more important in the survey data only because respondents were not asked about civic orientations. As it is, a role for civic concerns is suggested by the influence of socioeconomic status on activism, as that status usually nurtures concerns for the broader community.

THE SERVICE ORIENTATION:
BLACK RENTERS

There may be no sharper contrast in the American city than that between the white homeowner and the black renter. The considerable economic advantage that whites enjoy over blacks combines with the substantial economic and social differences between owners and renters to produce a stark contrast on almost any demographic comparison of the two groups. The contrast is not so stark, however, when it comes to joining neighborhood organizations. Despite lacking both socioeconomic status and ownership of their homes, black renters still report council membership rates of 11.4 percent, almost three-fifths the rate for white homeowners. Their membership rates can be that high because they do not join community councils for the same reasons as white home-owners. Where the membership rate of white homeowners derives in part from socioeconomic status, any activist tendency among black renters is unaffected by socioeconomic status (gamma = .05). And neighborhood home values bear no relationship to their inclination to join.

The meaning of the service orientation. What does affect the neighborhood activism of black renters is the use of neighborhood-level services provided by the city: Membership rates rise from 6.4 percent at the lowest level of use to 25 percent at the highest level (gamma = .410). No other factor exerts a comparable influence on their membership rates.

There are probably several reasons service use has this effect on black renters. First, that use gives them a stake in the community analogous to what investment in a home gives the white homeowner, a stake that could provide an initial impetus toward neighborhood activism. That cannot entirely explain this activism, however, because the same linkage is not evident among white renters. Council membership rates for white renters vary only minimally with use of neighborhood services. Something specific to blacks must link service use to neighborhood activism.

One factor is the greater need blacks feel for having an intermediary in communicating to public agencies on questions or problems concerning public services (e.g., Sharp, 1980). Given persisting distrust of public institutions once reputed to be very antiblack, blacks prefer to channel their service concerns through groups such as neighborhood organizations, groups more likely to have the symbolically important black leadership (see Shingles, 1981). That preference probably increases the neighborhood activism of those blacks most interested in municipal services.[8] The other factor is the legacy in black neighborhoods of the much-aligned War on Poverty. The community councils in most of Cincinnati's black neighborhoods grew out of the "neighborhood service centers" established under Community Action, as explained in the last chapter. Most have retained at least some of the service emphasis of their early years, thereby encouraging public service users in minority areas of the city to channel their concerns to neighborhood organizations—and, apparently, to join those organizations (see also White, 1981).

As these arguments imply, black renters are more inclined to join neighborhood organizations in areas that *(a)* experienced Community Action and/or *(b)* have predominantly black populations. As shown in Table 4.5, membership rates for black renters rise with both factors even when use of neighborhood services is controlled. This pattern was personified by one of the community council leaders. A black renting in a public housing area, he initially

TABLE 4.5
THE SERVICE ORIENTATION:
MEMBERSHIP RATES OF BLACK RENTERS
BY USE OF NEIGHBORHOOD SERVICES AND TYPE OF NEIGHBORHOOD

Type of Neighborhood[a]	Number of Services Used[a]				Totals
	0–1	2–5	6–8	9+	
Neither majority black nor CAP[b]	0% (27)		5.0% (20)		2.1% (47)
Majority black *or* CAP	3.0 (33)		10.5 (19)		3.8 (52)
Majority black *and* CAP	7.1 (126)	12.2 (74)	12.7 (63)	28.4 (67)	13.6 (330)
Totals	6.4 (156)	8.7 (104)	11.8 (93)	25.0 (76)	

[a] For the relationship of service use to membership, gamma = .411. For the relationship of type of neighborhood to membership, controlling for service use, gamma = .516.
[b] CAP = Community Action Program of the War on Poverty.

joined a neighborhood organization through the War on Poverty. After moving, he became more involved with a different council when back problems forced him to abandon his job as a construction worker and to become more reliant on public services. His listing of the concerns of his community included an unusually high number of service problems, indicative, again, of a strong service orientation.

His example and the broader pattern could reflect a redistributive federal program's having its intended compensatory effect. As noted earlier, the neighborhood activism of black renters is unrelated to their socioeconomic status. Yet their use of neighborhood services is strongly related to socioeconomic status (gamma = .437). This means that in the process of being translated to neighborhood activism, service use by black renters *loses* its socioeconomic bias. These neighborhood organizations thus appear to have attracted members more from among the economically disadvantaged, consistent with the initial redistributive War on Poverty mandate.

To be sure, the magnitude of the effect is modest. It takes a high level of service use and the right kind of neighborhood for any effects to be felt. Membership rates for black renters exceed 15 percent only at the highest service use in majority black neighborhoods with a Community Action history. By contrast, the effects of socioeconomic status and the investment orientation on white homeowners were felt much more rapidly and eventually produced much higher levels of community council membership. The investment orientation obviously carries more weight than the service orientation in explaining neighborhood activism.

The service orientation may also give a different quality to neighborhood activism than that imparted by the investment orientation. The political impotence that Gittell (1980) laments in many contemporary neighborhood organizations could conceivably derive from the dependent service orientations that motivate these black renters. Lacking a similar dependency, investment-oriented white homeowners may provide a better power base for neighborhood organizations.

The linkage of services to council membership does not necessarily mean, however, that black renters are more dependent on the city's services. The issue is not who uses *more* services (white homeowners actually use more of the parks and recreation services, though less of the neighborhood health center services) but how that service use is linked to neighborhood activism. The use does not figure in whether white homeowners join community councils, but it is central to whether black renters join.

THE TWO ORIENTATIONS COMBINED:
BLACK HOMEOWNERS

Black homeowners may be the most intriguing of the several groupings because, as both blacks and homeowners, they have reasons to be affected by both the investment and the service orientation. In fact, both orientations influence the neighborhood activism of black homeowners, resulting in the highest council membership rate for any of the four groups: 22 percent of the sample of 246.

The strongest role is played by the service orientation, with council membership among black homeowners influenced more by service use (gamma = .441) than by any other factor. Membership rates for this group rise from 11.1 percent at the lowest level of use to 39.6 percent at the highest level. Neighborhood service concerns draw both black homeowners and black renters to community councils presumably because, first, blacks often prefer to approach municipal service issues indirectly through community councils and, second, the OEO-induced service orientation of councils in black neighborhoods encourages that preference.

Black homeowners are similar to black renters in another respect, also consistent with the notion of a residual War on Poverty impact. The relationship between socioeconomic status and council membership among black homeowners (gamma = .299) is less than the relationship between that status and the use of neighborhood services (gamma = .411); and this relationship of socioeconomic status to membership essentially disappears when the effect of that service use is controlled. In other words, with black homeowners as with black renters, socioeconomic status does not influence council membership, despite being strongly linked to the service use that is central to that membership. One legacy of the War on Poverty, it would appear, is a reduced socioeconomic bias to the neighborhood activism of blacks.

The service orientation is not, however, the only basis for the neighborhood activism of black homeowners. While the type of neighborhood influenced the membership rates of black renters in a manner consistent with the service orientation, it has no effect on the membership of black homeowners, even when their service use is controlled. Instead, these homeowners are partially influenced by their investment in homes.

A different kind of investment orientation. A role for the investment orientation is evident in the contrasting membership rates of black homeowners and black renters at similar levels of service use; those rates range from 5 to 15 percent higher for black homeowners at each level of use. But the investment orientation does not otherwise affect black homeowners quite as it affects white homeowners. Council membership rates of black homeowners are unaffected, for example, by either the market value of neighborhood homes or the black proportion of the neighborhood population, two factors primary to the neighborhood activism of white homeowners. These factors should not be expected to influence black homeowners as they did white homeowners, however. Most black homeowners are confined, by personal economics and by continuing residential segregation, to areas with relatively low home values. Fully 94 percent of Cincinnati's black homeowners live in neighborhoods where housing values are average to below average (i.e., a 1980 maximum value of $47,000). Yet most of the influence of those values on white homeowners appeared in the two above-average categories in which 35 percent of all white homeowners fall. A similar pattern among black homeowners could affect only 6 percent of their number and so could not explain much of the variation in their council membership rates.

In addition, black homeowners live mostly in predominantly black areas— 81 percent in Cincinnati live in neighborhoods with majority black populations— where they could not be much affected by the varying black proportions so important to the council membership rates of white homeowners. Black homeowners may also be less likely to be frightened by the prospect of having other blacks as neighbors (but see Taub, Taylor, and Dunham, 1984: 135–36). Black homeowners might be influenced, however, by something analogous to the changing black proportion of the neighborhood; that is, by some other perceived threat to the value of their homes. Black homeowners certainly face such threats because they often live in the unstable "transition zones" (Downs, 1981: 87–89) most vulnerable to takeover by lower economic classes, which can reduce property values. The signs of these threats for black homeowners might come in the form, not of racial change, but of deteriorating physical conditions in neighboring homes, along the lines of these problems asked about in the survey:

1. Are there other buildings or residences in your neighborhood which you feel are dangerous?
2. Are there buildings or lots in your neighborhood which detract from its appearance to the extent that some of the residents might move out or other people might refuse to move into the neighborhood?

Perceiving these threats does, in fact, motivate more neighborhood activism by black homeowners. Concerned presumably for their investments in the neighborhood, black homeowners who reported either or both of these problems were more likely to belong to community councils (gamma = .393). Significantly, other types of neighborhood problems do not have the same effect on this activism. Problems with traffic signals, street repair, waste collection, and the like were not individually related to the membership rates of black homeowners, and a combined measure of all these other problems is only weakly related (gamma = .097). Only nearby housing problems affect activism, probably because only those problems are perceived to threaten seriously the value of the home investment. The same effect is not evident among white homeowners, most likely because they will exit a neighborhood when faced with such serious threats to housing values. Black homeowners cannot exit as easily, given the discriminatory residential housing market, and so must consider more seriously exercising voice by joining a community council.

The influence of these perceived housing problems adds to the influence of service use (see Table 4.6). Membership rates for black homeowners climb steadily with the two factors, reflecting the joint influence of the service and investment orientations.

NEITHER ORIENTATION: WHITE RENTERS

With a few exceptions, rates of community council membership never reach high levels with any segment of the Cincinnati population. Within this limited involvement, however, one group still stands out as virtually uninvolved. White renters have a membership rate of only 4.1 percent, no better than a third the rate of any of the other three groups. White renters are uninvolved because they share neither of the orientations that attract other city residents to the movement. They lack the investment in a home that attracts homeowners and the orientation blacks have to link service use to neighborhood activism. When both orientations are missing, socioeconomic status, which white renters have to a greater degree than do either black renters or black homeowners, cannot by itself produce significant neighborhood involvement.

TABLE 4.6
THE TWO ORIENTATIONS COMBINED:
MEMBERSHIP RATES OF BLACK HOMEOWNERS
BY SERVICE USE AND NEIGHBORHOOD HOUSING PROBLEMS

Number of Perceived	Number of Services Used[a]				
Housing Problems[a]	0–1	2–5	6–8	9+	Totals
0	12.0%	11.8%	16.1%	30.0%	15.6%
	(50)	(34)	(31)	(20)	(135)
1–2	9.7	22.6	47.6	46.4	29.7
	(31)	(31)	(21)	(28)	(111)
Totals	11.1	16.9	28.8	39.6	
	(81)	(65)	(52)	(48)	

[a] For the relationship of service use to membership, gamma = .441. For the relationship of housing problems to membership, controlling for service use, gamma = .314.

Actually, socioeconomic status and such other possible predictors as service use, housing values, and community racial mix are essentially unrelated to the membership rates of white renters. The only factor that even modestly affects those rates is the number of problems white renters perceive in the neighborhood (gamma = .271). When those problems reach their highest level, membership among white renters reaches 11.4 percent (13 of 114). Short of that maximum problem level, however, membership rates remain unaffected.

This lack of involvement could be read as an indictment of the representativeness of the neighborhood movement because it means that the largest of the four groups—the 36.9 percent white renter proportion of the survey sample—is essentially absent from neighborhood organizations. That may not be a fair criticism, however. The evidence does not suggest, after all, that white renters have been prevented or discouraged from joining community councils. They appear, instead, to lack the concerns that draw others to neighborhood groups. When white renters develop those concerns, as when the stakes of renting increase (e.g., Navarro, 1985), they may become involved.

COMMENT:
A CURIOUS CLASS STRUGGLE

Science has always valued parsimony in its explanations, preferring the explanation that requires the minimum number of elements, other things being equal. That parsimony has been lost, unfortunately, in much of the recent theorizing about neighborhood activism, as scholars have often resorted to an unwieldy number of explanations (e.g., Wandersman, 1981). The current research restores that parsimony through a three-part explanation involving the neighborhood-specific investment and service orientations and the more general socioeconomic spur to participation. Those three factors do a relatively good job of accounting for the varying neighborhood activism both within and between different segments of the Cincinnati population. Coupling the concern for investment in a home with the general stimulant of socioeconomic status largely explains the varying activism of white homeowners; the interest in neighborhood services provided by the city explains much of the more limited neighborhood involvement of black renters; and the investment and service orientations together account for much of the activism of black homeowners as well as the almost complete lack of activism among white renters.

These several patterns reveal a kind of curious class struggle contained within the neighborhood movement. It is curious in that the dominant class of activists—the white homeowners—apparently acts primarily from personal economic concerns for homes but disguises that self-interest in altruistic talk of civic concern for the community as a whole. This is not entirely a disguise because civic concerns probably are a factor, useful especially in overcoming the free rider problem. The disguise in part may also be unwitting in that these homeowners may believe they are acting solely from altruistic motives. The fact of the disguise remains, however; the evidence points unequivocally to a personal economic interest in a home as essential to the activism of white homeowners. This class struggle is also curious in that the "downtrodden" within it are not attempting to seize the investment that the white home-owners—and, to a lesser extent, the black homeowners—are protecting. Those with the investments need fear, at most, only the unintended threats that those without create by migrating within the city. Those without are principally concerned for public services, to the extent that they are mobilized at all at the neighborhood level. This neighborhood class struggle is curious, finally, because it includes a significant transition group: the black homeowners who share interests with both white homeowners and black renters. Black homeowners are a transitional group in more than one sense, considering that they frequently live in unstable transitional areas of the city.

Actually, this class struggle is not as curious as it at first appears. Seen in the broader context of Western society, much contemporary activism is based on those who have trying to protect or improve upon what they have, while those who do not have may be motivated by the services that have supposedly been used to mollify the economically disadvantaged (see Brown and Erie, 1981; Isaac and Kelly, 1981). Those caught in the middle—the black home-owners—may understandably be interested in the services *and* in their home investments.

All of this implies that the neighborhood movement in Cincinnati may be moderately unrepresentative. The movement involves no more than one of every eight adults in the city, and those who are involved favor, to use one Cincinnati administrator's description, "the pushers and movers" in the neighborhoods. The majority of the community council members are white homeowners, and their participation increases with their resources (i.e., socioeconomic status, home value). The movement might be extremely unrepresentative, however, were it not for the War on Poverty and its legacy in Cincinnati's black neighborhoods. Without that legacy neighborhood involvement in those communities might be negligible today, perhaps approximating the minuscule involvement of the city's white renters. Whatever the disadvantages of the dependent service orientation fostered by the War on Poverty, that orientation has at least given the neighborhood movement in Cincinnati a quality of representativeness probably otherwise unattainable.

5

Organizations:
The Unequal Resources
of Community Councils

The legacy of history and the interests of the current generation of activists shape the resources of contemporary community councils. This chapter examines those resources: what they are, where they are, and why, as a consequence, councils are stronger in some neighborhoods than in others.

MEMBERSHIP: THE SINE QUA NON?

The core resource for a neighborhood organization, as argued in Chapter 4, is membership. Without membership, an organization's claim to represent a community can sound hollow, perhaps undermining credibility with public officials. Other organizational resources may be of minimal value at that point because they do not really address representativeness. The most telling evidence of the importance of membership in Cincinnati came from three municipal officials—two department heads and a member of City Council—who, after a promise of anonymity, were willing to say which councils they perceived to be the strongest in the summer of 1980. These perceptions, combined into a single measure, were more closely linked to council membership levels (r = .582) than to any other community or organizational resource, suggesting that council reputations in City Hall depend primarily on membership.

Where are the numbers? The last chapter largely explained who the members are but spoke only indirectly to where they are; that is, which neighborhoods have larger or smaller community council memberships. That issue will be explored here by examining how membership levels vary with a number of neighborhood characteristics, including principally the neighborhood demographics (taken from 1980 census and 1978 R. L. Polk reports) and the

61

War on Poverty involvement thought to be primary in the building of neighborhood organizations:

1. Homeownership investment: percentage of homeowners, number of homeowners, median home sale value.
2. Threats to the residential neighborhood: percentage of residential units vacant, percentage of residential units turning over in the previous year, total black population, percentage black.[1]
3. Socioeconomic status: median income, percentage in professional occupations, percentage below the poverty line.
4. War on Poverty involvement: involvement with Community Action and/or Model Cities programs; involvement with those programs and with current Community Services Administration programs.

Membership levels could also vary with neighborhood differences in life style (e.g., degree of child-rearing orientation, degree of commercial development) or population. For that reason, these other demographics are also included:

5. Life style orientation: percentage of families with dependent children, percentage of retired heads of household, persons per household, percentage of commercial units as a proportion to residential units.
6. Population: total population, number of households.

Membership variations. Actual membership levels, as reported by the councils, varied greatly in Cincinnati in 1980.[2] Most councils, a majority of almost 60 percent, had relatively small memberships numbering 200 or less, but the remaining 40 percent ranged upward to over 1,000 members, with Westwood the leader at 1,430. Two councils reported higher figures, but those reports were discounted because both councils defined residency as conferring membership.

Even with that discounting, the membership figures still contain too much variation in how membership is defined for any meaningful analysis to be possible. That problem can be solved only by limiting the analysis to those councils that require dues; that is, the councils that use a similar definition of membership. These councils number thirty, or almost two-thirds of the total of forty-seven. With a median membership of 195, the thirty are somewhat larger than the fourteen councils without dues requirements, where the median is only 100 members.[3] Membership may be a more important resource to understand with these thirty than for the other fourteen, however, because it can produce revenue as well as build legitimacy. As one indication of that importance, perceived strength is more strongly linked to membership for the dues-based councils ($r = .657$) than for the others ($r = .544$).

The membership figures must also be adjusted to control for the positive skewness created by a few cases of extremely high membership figures. This can be done by using as the dependent variable the square root of membership, rather than membership itself. That conversion moderates the influence of extreme values without sacrificing their essence and produces the approximately normal distribution necessary if membership levels are to be compared statistically to other neighborhood characteristics.

In Table 5.1 the number of households in the neighborhood is shown to be the strongest factor ($r = .487$) underlying variations among the dues-based councils. More households presumably mean a larger potential membership— more people who can be subject to the various threats and inducements that draw people to community councils. For example, the number of households is closely related to the number of homeowners, probably also explaining why a homeownership factor is not otherwise prominent in this analysis.

TABLE 5.1
MEMBERSHIP LEVELS AND COMMUNITY RESOURCES
FOR DUES-BASED COUNCILS

Neighborhood Demographic	Relationship to Membership Level[a]	
	Zero-Order Correlation	Regression Coefficient
Number of households	.487[b]	.487[b]
Percentage black	− .104	
Percentage families with children	− .449[b]	
Percentage residential units vacant	.082	.335[c]
Percentage commercial units	− .039	
Median income	.202	
Home sale value	.435[b]	
Number of homeowners	.415[b]	
Percentage professional	.385[c]	.349[c]
War on Poverty history	− .102	
R^2		.453
Adjusted R^2		.390
N of cases	30	30

[a] The square root of membership is used in the analysis in order to moderate the influence of the few councils that report extremely high membership levels. All significance tests in this and the subsequent tables are one-tailed because all significant relationships are in the predicted direction.

[b] Significant at .01 level.

[c] Significant at .05 level.

The socioeconomic influence on membership is nearly as strong, with membership levels significantly related to several indicators of socioeconomic status. As suggested in Chapter 4, however, the important consideration is not the *average* level of socioeconomic status as much as the proportions at the *highest* levels of socioeconomic status. Percentage professional in the neighborhood thus proves to be the most important of these indicators, once the influence of the number of households is controlled, while median income is not even significantly related to membership.[4]

Threats to neighborhoods also appear to affect membership levels, but only as a tertiary factor. Once population and percentage professional in a neighborhood are controlled, council memberships rise as the proportion of vacant residential units increases, probably because residents—such as the black homeowners described in the last chapter—join councils to combat the threat posed by vacant structures.

No role is evident, surprisingly, for the service orientation thought to be primary for community council membership among blacks. Membership appears to be unrelated to either percentage black or OEO programs in the neighborhood, the two likely indicators of that orientation.[5] The lack of a relationship in the initial correlations is perhaps not surprising given that the socioeconomic bias to membership could obscure the service orientation's probably lesser effect on a predominantly low-income population. It is surprising, however, that a relationship does not emerge in the regression analysis once the socioeconomic bias is reduced by controlling for population and percentage professional. Indeed, neither indicator of the service orientation emerges as a factor even when the socioeconomic bias is further reduced by restricting the analysis to the city's low-income communities (data not shown). Membership levels for OEO-supported groups prove to be no higher than those for groups in other low-income communities.

The sense of "belonging" to neighborhood groups reported by blacks in Cincinnati in Chapter 4 thus appears often not to include formal registered membership in a community council. Instead, it may frequently reflect a much less active involvement, as through the occasional turning to councils—or to the OEO-initiated neighborhood services centers that might be confused with councils—on issues related to municipal services.

ORGANIZATIONAL COMPLEXITY:
ORGANIZING FOR INFLUENCE?

Membership may be critical for establishing the legitimacy of a neighborhood organization, but other resources could figure more directly in whether organizational goals are achieved. The ability of leadership, for example, could be much more important than membership when a council is lobbying City Hall. These other resources could also be growing in importance if, as some suspect, neighborhood organizations are becoming increasingly bureaucratic (see Cooper, 1980).

For organizations in general, the most important of these other resources are leadership, subordinate units, and financial resources (e.g., Walker, 1983). To capture those dimensions with the community councils, this analysis examines (1) paid staff, (2) number of active committees, (3) number of block clubs, and (4) budget size. Data are taken from a 1978 survey (Robinson, 1978) for the city manager and from 1980 interviews with City Community Assistance Team officials familiar with the councils. Those data, as reported in Table 5.2, reveal considerable variation in the extent to which the councils can claim the different resources.

TABLE 5.2
OTHER RESOURCES OF COMMUNITY COUNCILS

Budget Size (1978)			Paid Staff (1980)		
No budget, no dues	27%	(12)	No	23%	(11)
Dues, no budget	36	(16)	Part-time	32	(15)
Under $1,000	11	(5)	Full-time	45	(21)
$1,000–3,000	14	(6)	Totals	100	(47)
$5,000–11,000	11	(5)			
Totals	99	(44)			

Active Committees (1980)			Block Clubs (1978)		
None	17%	(8)	None	52%	(23)
1–2	43	(20)	1–9	32	(14)
3+	40	(19)	10+	16	(7)
Totals	100	(47)	Totals	100	(44)

Sources: Robinson (1978) and interviews with Community Assistance Team staff in 1980.

For the most part, councils do not appear to substitute one resource for another. Instead, having one resource increases the likelihood of having others, as these associations demonstrate:[6]

	Budget	*Committees*	*Block Clubs*	*Paid Staff*
Membership	.485 (44)	.839 (47)	.360 (44)	.216 (47)
Budget		.471 (44)	.139 (44)	.302 (44)
Active Committees			.732 (44)	.407 (47)
Block Clubs				.381 (44)

In light of this overlap, the several resources, excluding membership, were combined into a single "organizational complexity" measure, equaling the sum of the scores across the four dimensions for each council. Adding the scores gives each of the three-category variables approximately equal weighting in the summary measure. Budget as a five-category variable receives somewhat heavier weighting, as may be appropriate for the only indicator of a council's material resources. (No measure was developed for three councils when data were lacking on two resource dimensions.) The importance of this organizational complexity is suggested by its strong relationship to perceived council strength: correlations of .454 for all councils and .767 for councils that do not require dues.

Building organizational complexity. Organizational complexity in Cincinnati is built from several sources, judging from the data in Table 5.3. Membership is the most important factor; as membership rolls grow, so apparently do other organizational resources.[7] Once the influence of membership is controlled, percentage professional and percentage black in a community emerge as additional significant sources of organizational complexity. The role of percentage professional again reflects the influence of neighborhood socioeconomic status. Here that influence indicates that organizations in more affluent neighborhoods are able to build more organizational complexity than their membership figures alone would suggest, probably because members in those neighborhoods can contribute more resources—time, money, and leadership skills—than can members in lower-income areas. The surprise may be that this socioeconomic bias is not more pronounced.

The role of percentage black is more complex. It is not simply a matter of blacks being more interested in community councils (e.g., Sharp, 1980). Any greater interest of a generally lower-income black population can hardly be expected to bring more time, money, and organizational skills to these councils when it could not earlier produce larger memberships for the councils. What this racial factor may reflect instead is, first, how larger black proportions in neighborhoods prompt white homeowners to contribute more to neighborhood organizations. Such a tendency makes intuitive sense given what earlier chapters have said about the salience of the racial threat for Cincinnati's white homeowners. It is also consistent with the way council organizational complexity varies by era of origin. As Table 5.4 shows, the highest levels of complexity are found among the first community councils, those which formed primarily to confront racial threats in the 1956–65 period.

The role of the War on Poverty. The racial factor also reflects in part a residual influence of the War on Poverty. The poverty programs were targeted principally to predominantly black areas; Table 5.4 shows that the councils most influenced by those programs, the Community Action groups of the period 1965–66, have more organizational complexity than any other set of council cohorts except those of the 1956–65 era. Other community resources could hardly account for that complexity, as the Community Action groups have by far the lowest indigenous resources of any of the four neighborhood cohort groups.

TABLE 5.3
EXPLAINING ORGANIZATIONAL COMPLEXITY

Neighborhood Characteristic	Relationship to Complexity	
	Zero-Order Correlation	Regression Coefficient
Council membership (1978)	.612[a]	.612[a]
Number of households	.486[a]	
Percentage black	.220	.275[b]
Percentage families with children	−.363[b]	
Percentage residential units turning over	−.133	
Percentage commercial units	−.206	
Median family income	.223	
Home sale value	.405[a]	
Number of homeowners	.443[a]	
Percentage professional	.411[a]	.322[b]
War on Poverty history	.065	
R^2		.530
Adjusted R^2		.495
N of cases	44	44

[a] Significant at .01 level.
[b] Significant at .05 level.

TABLE 5.4
ORGANIZATIONAL COMPLEXITY BY
ERA OF COUNCIL ORIGIN

Era of Origin	Levels of Complexity (%)			Totals	N
	Low 0–.50	.75–1.25	High 1.50–2.25		
Pre–1956: Traditional civic associations	40	30	30	100	10
1956–65: First community councils	11	33	56	100	9
1965–66: Community Action revolution	23	46	31	100	13
1967–79: Spread of councils	42	25	33	100	12
All councils	30	34	36	100	44

The clearest OEO/CSA impact comes through paid staff, with eight community councils receiving part-time paid staff directly from the local Neighborhood Services arms of the Community Services Administration. The impact of that assistance is predictably redistributive, reducing the socioeconomic bias to organizational complexity, as can be seen when complexity *with* paid staff is compared to an alternative measure *excluding* paid staff (even those not supported by the CSA). That exclusion strengthens the correlations between organizational complexity and most socioeconomic variables, with the understandable exception of percentage black:

	Complexity (staff included)	*Complexity (staff excluded)*
Number of households	.486	.565
Percentage professional	.411	.489
Home sale value	.405	.446
Percentage black	.220	.153

The poverty program assistance also affects other aspects of organizational complexity, though only indirectly. This becomes evident when the measure of organizational complexity *excluding* paid staff is analyzed as a possible function of a variety of neighborhood characteristics, including the OEO/CSA experience (operationalized in terms of two trichotomies, one for experience with early Community Action and Model Cities programs, the other for experience with those programs and with continuing CSA support). The analysis is restricted to the city's low-income communities, those with 1980 median family incomes below $16,000, to reduce the confounding effect of community socioeconomic status.[8]

Those other components of organizational complexity appear to have benefited from the OEO/CSA assistance (see Table 5.5). The primary determinant of those components in the low-income communities may be population—larger populations lead to more complex organizations—but the neighborhood's OEO/CSA experience is an important secondary influence. The extent of that influence might even be understated in that it partially overlaps the influence of population.

It might seem paradoxical that poverty program assistance could help to build more complex neighborhood organizations but be of little value in building active memberships in the organizations. The paradox can be explained, however, by the OEO tendency to, as one Cincinnati critic put it, "organize around the agency, not around the neighborhood." That strategy could easily produce more complex organizations—"horribly cumbersome administrative structures" in the words of another critic—but no larger memberships. Some neighborhood OEO leaders may have pursued this strategy for fear that their leadership roles would be threatened by larger memberships. That could explain why, as another observer contended, some who used the War on

TABLE 5.5
SOURCES OF ORGANIZATIONAL COMPLEXITY
IN LOW-INCOME COMMUNITIES[a]

Neighborhood Characteristic	Relationship to Complexity	
	Zero-Order Correlation	Regression Coefficient
Council membership in 1978	.609[b]	.245[c]
Number of households	.810[b]	.810[b]
Percentage black	.412[c]	
Percentage residential units turning over	.070	
Median family income	− .313	
Percentage professional	.167	
OEO history	.448[c]	
OEO/CSA history	.491[b]	.355[b]
R^2		.824
Adjusted R^2		.791
N of cases		20

[a] With paid staff excluded from organizational complexity.
[b] Significant at .01 level.
[c] Significant at .05 level.

Poverty to climb to power in Cincinnati "immediately began to get rid of the ladder so no other citizens could climb up." Whatever the reasons, the War on Poverty has effected some redistribution of power among Cincinnati's community councils by building organizations in low-income, predominantly black communities, but it has failed to make these councils the broad-based membership organizations envisioned in the early talk of maximum feasible participation.

COMMENT: THE SOURCES OF ORGANIZATIONAL CAPACITY IN COMMUNITY COUNCILS

The revived interest in neighborhood organizations has prompted growing discussion of where the strongest of them are located, with various experts saying low-income areas (Boyte, 1980), middle-income areas (Rich, 1980a), or, disregarding class, areas experiencing residential change (Henig, 1982b). This profile of the resources of Cincinnati's community councils suggests that each view contains some truth, but the complete truth has escaped all of them. The reality of the resources of neighborhood organizations is too complex to be described by any one pattern.

The strongest pattern is that common to all types of organizations. Community councils are stronger in members and other resources where neighborhoods have more indigenous resources, particularly larger populations and larger professional populations. The population factor, linked as it is to the number of homeowners, also hints at a possible role for the home investment orientation.

The importance of residential threats for community council resources points in the same direction. Neighborhood organizations are able to mobilize more resources when the neighborhoods themselves can most easily be perceived as threatened, as by higher proportions of vacant structures, higher residential turnover, or higher proportions of black residents. Those threats probably have their primary effect on homeowners, who have the most to lose if the quality of the residential neighborhood declines.

The resources of these organizations also grow from some indigenous community characteristics that could not be captured in these analyses. Observers in Cincinnati argue, in particular, that "precipitating incidents," such as proposed development projects, frequently mobilize neighborhoods almost overnight. These organizations sometimes benefit, in addition, from "accidents of leadership" in which, by chance or "accident," a neighborhood contains the one or a few individuals with the skills, time, and interest necessary for energizing a neighborhood organization. The inability to capture these idosyncratic community resources probably accounts for much of the variance that remains unexplained in the regressions.

But strong community councils are not built only from below, from ample community resources catalyzed by residential threats. These organizations also have depended increasingly in recent years on outside assistance, much of which has come so recently that its influence could not yet be assessed. A hint of the possible extent of that influence comes, however, from the long-term positive impact of the War on Poverty on council organizational complexity. Whatever the shortcomings of the OEO effort in terms of mobilizing people, it is clear that had the effort not been made, the neighborhood movement in Cincinnati would have an even more pronounced socioeconomic bias than is already the case. The War on Poverty did at least modestly broaden a movement whose inherent tendency appears to be elitist.

Taken together, the diversity of factors that underlie the resources of community councils could seem to mark the organizations as a particularly unique urban entity. In reality, however, this explanation transforms neighborhood organizations from what previously appeared to be a peculiarly urban phenomenon into something that now looks akin to most contemporary interest groups. Like those interest groups (Walker, 1983; Hansen, 1985), neighborhood organizations build their resources from a combination of *(a)* the extent of shared interests (e.g., neighborhood population), *(b)* threats to those interests, *(c)* socioeconomic status, and *(d)* government support. Perhaps all that remains to be seen is whether neighborhood organizations are able, like other interest groups, to wield their resources effectively in the halls of government.

6

Channels:
The Development of Mechanisms
for Community Involvement

For as long as they have existed in Cincinnati, community councils have been involved with municipal government. That involvement has changed dramatically, however, since its beginnings in the City Hall intervention to form the first council in Avondale in 1956. Along the way, municipal government itself has been transformed as the neighborhood movement has affected how decisions are made, what policies the city adopts, and who benefits from those policies.

The story of this transformation begins in this chapter with a description of the mechanisms Cincinnati has developed for involving communities in municipal decision making. An effort is also made to explain why the mechanisms have developed, for Cincinnati at first glance appears an unlikely candidate for a revolution in community involvement. This account is drawn from a variety of City Hall records, newspaper accounts, and interviews with key historical figures.[1]

THE SURPRISING SETTING: CINCINNATI'S
REFORMED "PUBLIC INTEREST" GOVERNMENT

American cities have been dominated through most of this century by a "reform" or "good government" philosophy, which holds that municipal government should be concerned primarily with the citywide "public interest," rather than with the separate "private" interests of the parts of the city (e.g., political parties, electoral districts). Toward that end the reform philosophy recommends, first, that city councils consist of a small number of members who are elected on a nonpartisan ballot and at large, rather than from districts of the city. The mayor, according to this philosophy, should have only minimal formal powers (e.g., no veto power, no appointment power) and be selected by the council members from among their number, rather than being separately elected. The strongest figure in the government can then be the city manager, a council-appointed administrator whose commitment to professional standards will aid in the pursuit of the public interest. To assure the dominance of those standards, this manager should have the power of appointment for most higher-level administrators, and most other municipal employees should be assured of job security, short of job malfeasance.

These principles were followed closely in the shaping of municipal government in Cincinnati. The City Council numbers only nine, and all are elected at large on a nonpartisan ballot. Council members do identify with political parties, but the parties are not listed on the ballot, and one is the reform Charter party. The mayor is selected by the council members from among their number, a technique that has usually had the intended result of producing relatively weak mayors (see, for example, Pressman, 1972; Kotter and Lawrence, 1974: 107). Most of the power in City Hall consequently lies with the city manager, one of the stronger managerial positions in the country, and with the other municipal administrators, most of whom have job security. The strength of these administrators was suggested by a City Council member who, when asked to name the city's most powerful interest groups, replied with a smile, "Other than the City Administration?"

This is a surprising setting for a revolution in community involvement. To begin with, any organization of long standing is likely to resist change in the way it operates (Lipsky, 1968), especially when change means sharing decision-making power, as with community involvement. Reformed governmental structures should reinforce that inclination. The at-large system of elections, for example, gives City Council little incentive to listen to neighborhood demands because a council member's tenure will be decided citywide, not by a particular area of the city. And the reform emphasis on professional standards encourages municipal administrators to be more concerned with what their professions recommend than with what any local interest groups might want.

In operation, these reformed structures have proved very effective in slighting the interests of geographical parts of cities (see Lineberry and Fowler, 1967; Karnig, 1975). Reform-dominated Cincinnati has chosen, nonetheless, to open its governmental process to these interests. Part of the task of this chapter is to explain how that could happen.

AWAKENING, 1965–70: CITY HALL
RECOGNITION OF NEIGHBORHOOD DISCONTENTS

Prior to 1965 citizen participation in most cities referred only to the advisory role of elite committees in federally assisted programs. The Federal Housing

Act of 1954 had mandated citizen participation in housing and urban renewal programs, but local governments usually responded by appointing blue ribbon committees of well-known city figures, rather than groups representative of target areas (Zimmerman, 1972: 4–5). Often the committees were used only to rubber-stamp municipal preferences. The force of events gradually changed that pattern, beginning in Cincinnati with a period of awakening that extended from about 1965 to 1970.

The impetus for change came from both above and below. From below, the growth of community groups in the 1956–66 years caught City Hall attention as, according to municipal officials of that era, the groups came to fight the disruption and displacement threatened by highway construction and urban renewal. Race riots in Avondale in 1967 and 1968, part of the national phenomenon, added to the sense of pressure from below, shocking many city leaders into a new awareness of the city's black communities. From above, the impetus was the federal War on Poverty. It asked cities to become more concerned with low-income neighborhoods and gave those neighborhoods staff assistance to make their own demands of cities. In Cincinnati, for example, according to former Planning Director Herb Stevens, Community Action staff frequently came to City Hall as advocates for neighborhoods. The poverty program also gave some communities a new experience with control over public resources, as former Model Cities staffer Bud Haupt recalled: "Model Cities really only related to four neighborhoods, but it set a new mark for community control. There was no experiment before or since that put so many dollars into the hands of citizens to decide what to do with it, with little or no control or restraint." That experience may well have increased community interest in other governmental programs.

The OEO effort helped, finally, to create a leadership group sympathetic to the concerns of low-income communities, both in Cincinnati and elsewhere (e.g., Moynihan, 1969). Many of the leaders recruited for the OEO programs in Cincinnati, for example, have continued in influential roles in their communities or elsewhere in the city.

Isolated experiments. Within City Hall itself, however, the new awareness of the communities produced only isolated experiments with community involvement in these years, experiments mostly with no long-term significance. In one case, in 1970, the city manager made an abortive effort to involve the city's communities in decisions on allocating capital improvement funds. The effort died quickly in the face of community objections to the manager's arbitrary division of the city into seven "sectors" and City Council objections to the personnel costs required for the effort (Johnson, 1975: 9).

One innovation that did have long-term significance was the West End Task Force, a joint city–community planning effort. By 1965, urban renewal, highway construction, and natural urban decay had reduced the once thriving

West End to only 8,000 residents and 150 industrial firms. Despite the population decline, the community was suffering from fierce competition for available land, "residents seeking to solve housing and recreation problems and industry seeking to solve expansion, parking, and loading problems" (Geiser, 1968). Facing those problems, and aided perhaps by Community Action funds, the West End Community Council came to the City Planning Commission in 1965 to ask for discussions on the community's future. Planning Director Stevens backed the West End proposal and suggested to the city manager the formation of a task force of community leaders and City Hall officials. The manager rejected the idea, but Stevens reported the rejection and his frustration to the head of the city's Human Relations Commission, who suggested a joint meeting of the City Council and West End community leaders. The meeting was scheduled, and the City Council majority of "enlightened Republicans," as Stevens describes them, approved the task force idea.

The task force proved to be a hybrid of the elite blue ribbon committees of the 1950s and the more representative citizen participation committees of recent years. It was more representative in that a number of West End residents were involved, but the 1950s legacy was evident in the remaining membership of municipal officials and in the task force head, an investment banker named Edgar "Buddy" Mack. Mack, despite living in the affluent suburb of Indian Hill, was chosen because, in his own words, "you need someone with clout as head of a neighborhood group."

The success of the task force is arguable. By most accounts, Mack's leadership was effective in bringing some municipal assistance to the West End, but that assistance may have had little impact on the community's fate. The task force's greatest significance may consequently lie in the joint city–community planning that marked the beginning of city efforts to plan *with* communities what the city government would do in the communities. It was a slow start, however, as the effort expanded into only two more communities— Mt. Auburn and Over-the-Rhine—over the next four years; any further expansion was stymied by two city managers who vetoed Stevens's annual requests for funding of an additional community planning team.

Those vetoes come as no surprise given how city managers have traditionally championed the reform philosophy that is so unsympathetic to neighborhoods. The surprise is that a few other municipal officials, despite their own traditional allegiance to reform principles, did not join the managers in this opposition. City Council members, though products of reformed electoral machinery, seemingly departed from reform principles in approving the West End Task Force. And they did so at the encouragement of a planning professional who even more obviously departed from his field's traditional reform orientation. Some of the traditional support of reform principles was wavering in the face of neighborhood discontents.

INNOVATION, 1971–74:
THE COMMUNITY IDEA IN ASCENDANCE

The growing awareness of neighborhoods did not translate to extensive innovation, however, until the community idea ascended to power as the result of City Council elections in 1971. Those elections replaced a previous Republican majority with a new Democratic-Charterite coalition that had campaigned on a proneighborhood platform. Where Republicans had emphasized downtown development over the previous fourteen years, "Cincinnati's Charter-Democratic coalition majority in City Council intends to put a new emphasis on revitalizing neighborhoods" (*Cincinnati Enquirer*, 1971a). Once in office, according to one of its members, the coalition "started to make a real move in terms of neighborhood health clinics and recreation centers. That was something visible which people could rally around."

Actually, the new council's most important impact on community involvement may have come through its choice of city managers. Stevens, for one, argues that the council turnover "didn't affect the funding of my community planning teams" but did affect "the selection of managers, who became more modern, more receptive to citizen participation." The new council did not wait long either, hiring E. Robert Turner as manager in early 1972 to head the new neighborhood initiatives.

The expansion of community planning. The era of innovation really began before the election when Stevens bypassed a resistant city manager to get council approval of $50,000 for a new community planning team in mid–1971. Despite the timing, the approval was influenced by the election as favorable votes came from a mix of Charter-Democratic council members campaigning on the neighborhood issue and Republicans making a "last-ditch attempt," according to one observer, to come down on the popular side of the neighborhood issue. Planning in Cincinnati, as Stevens had long hoped, would finally include a significant effort to prepare neighborhood land-use plans in cooperation with neighborhood residents.

The philosophy underlying the push for community planning in Cincinnati and other cities had at least three elements. First, the massive dislocations caused by urban renewal and highway construction, as in Cincinnati's West End, were interpreted by many as reflecting the failure of citywide planning (see Needleman and Needleman, 1974: 29–30). Second, proponents of community planning argued that contrary to the reform philosophy, community ideas should be more important than technical considerations in the formulation of plans. In the words of Ken Bordwell, one of Cincinnati's first community planners, "With a given lot, what should be there is a matter of opinion 80 percent of the time. Given that, community ideas should come first." Third, many planners also believed that community involvement could produce more popular plans. As Bordwell said of his boss, "My impression of Stevens's motivation was that you simply could get better plans and have less brouhaha later if you included the communities right from the beginning."

The roots of community planning in the failures of urban renewal and highway construction were evident in how Cincinnati decided which communities should receive the initial planning assistance (Stevens, 1971). In an effort to compensate for "public and institutional actions," the new planning assistance was directed first to Evanston and the East End, two communities recently disrupted by the threat or reality of highway construction. The new program proved so popular that other communities were soon reportedly "clamoring for planning." That led to funding of two more community planning teams in the 1972–74 period. Each team gradually took on larger numbers of communities, such that by June 1974, eighteen of the city's communities had completed or were developing plans (Hartsock, 1974). The plans had by then been upgraded by the Planning Commission from an "opinion" status to the same official status accorded the city's 1948 Master Plan.

With the growth came a drift away from the original criteria for involvement in community planning. Any mention of a compensatory criterion had disappeared from departmental correspondence by 1973 (Stevens, 1972), as the department accommodated the increasing demands from middle-income neighborhoods. As the Needlemans have noted (1974: 68), "Some of the areas that get planners will be relatively affluent and problem free, but well organized." The pressures to "spread" the assistance (e.g., Nathan, 1978) were so effective, in fact, that ten of the eighteen Cincinnati communities involved in planning in 1974 had median incomes *above* the citywide median.

Citizen participation in municipal goal-setting. City Hall next began to experiment with citizen participation in the development of municipal goals and programs. A first experiment traced to the area's League of Women Voters, which, spurred by the national citizen participation movement, obtained a Carnegie Foundation grant to help Cincinnati and greater Hamilton County develop better citizen participation procedures (Johnson, 1975). The resulting Metropolitan Project sought to establish "a geographical approach to budgeting and service improvements" by, first, aiding the neighborhoods in translating their needs into budget requests and, second, persuading the municipal departments to listen to those requests. The effort began in April 1973 with a workshop on the budget process, which was intended for community leaders but was also attended by City Hall officials. Subsequently, the league's project staff worked with the communities to define their budget priorities, which were then submitted for consideration in municipal departmental budget processes.

The communities were initially skeptical of the project's merits, with only twenty-one communities submitting budget priorities. That skepticism diminished when the final city budget showed "more dollars for neighborhood programs," including the city's first Neighborhood Improvement Program (Woods, Andersen, and Grober, 1979: 48). By the next year, thirty-two communities were willing to participate (Johnson, 1975: 17).

Around the same time, City Manager Turner began his own citizen participation effort, the COPE (Community Organization Program Evaluation) project (League of Women Voters of the Cincinnati Area, 1975). This project sought to use citizens in setting *functional* goals for the city, as distinct from the geographic goals of the Metropolitan Project. Goals were developed by eight task forces, one for each functional area. Each task force was composed of representatives from the relevant municipal agencies, the University of Cincinnati, and the community councils.

Other experiments. The Metropolitan and COPE projects are only the most notable of many community involvement experiments City Hall undertook in these years. According to an internal memo in early 1975, experiments were also under way in the departments of Urban Development, Management Services, Police, Recreation, and Public Works, and in the Citizens Committee on Youth and the Cincinnati Human Relations Commission. The most interesting of these efforts found municipal government, unbeknown to its leadership, doing community organizing. The effort began in 1973 when Chuck Hirt was assigned, without any precise job description, to the Field Services Division (later renamed Research and Neighborhood Affairs) of the Cincinnati Human Relations Commission. Having trained as a community organizer, Hirt decided to define "his nebulous job description . . . in terms of a community organizing commitment." He worked principally with the neighborhoods of Sedamsville and Camp Washington and with the Inner-City Neighborhood Coalition, an alliance of several groups from low-income neighborhoods. His efforts are cited by observers as aiding all three groups in becoming viable.

Hirt and some of Cincinnati's early community planners are the city's best examples of "guerrillas in the bureaucracy" (e.g., Needleman and Needleman, 1974), people who are paid by the public bureaucracy but feel their primary allegiance is to low-income groups outside the bureaucracy. These guerrillas have been an important component of the neighborhood movement in Cincinnati and elsewhere.

The guerrillas were less important in Cincinnati in this period, however, than the reform establishment itself, which led the push for increased neighborhood involvement. The Charter Committee, the original voice of the reform movement in Cincinnati, helped to launch the period of innovation by campaigning successfully on the neighborhood issue in 1971. The innovations were then directed by a new city manager whose profession tied him historically to the reform movement. The reform-oriented League of Women Voters also joined the push for neighborhood involvement. "Reform" was losing some of its traditional meaning in Cincinnati.

CONSOLIDATION, 1975–77: RATIONALIZING
THE COMMUNITY INVOLVEMENT MECHANISMS

Such rapid innovation inevitably brought problems. First, the many fragmented experiments often created confusion and inefficiency. Community leaders were said to be "confused about the dovetailing of COPE and Metro" (Johnson, 1975), for one thing, as the conceptual distinction between the two experiments became blurred in actual operation. Second, the theories underlying particular experiments were sometimes found wanting when the experiments were actually implemented. The restricted physical assignments of community planners, for example, often proved inadequate in the face of the broad service interests of communities (see also Needleman and Needleman, 1974: 89–92).

The Total Neighborhood Assistance plan. These problems were not lost on City Hall leadership. Formal recognition came as early as June 1974, when consultant Paul Hartsock argued that the city needed to rationalize its various community involvement mechanisms. Hartsock (1974) proposed a Total Neighborhood Assistance (TNA) plan, the principles of which became the foundation for a consolidation eventually achieved two years later.

TNA was "an attempt to bring together . . . many of the concepts and systems the City has been using for neighborhood planning, implementation of the plans, and entry into the budget process." It recommended, first, an expansion of the community plans to cover all municipal services, rather than simply physical planning. Second, it suggested that the plans be formulated to "mesh with the budget cycle" by timing community plan requests to arrive as the departments began their budget planning. To facilitate this process, community planning would be reorganized and expanded into "community assistance teams," each composed of a team manager, a physical planner, an urban developer, a management analyst, a human services planner, and one other person for public works services. These teams would work with the communities in developing or updating community plans, which would be reviewed annually by the Planning Commission and then distributed to the appropriate departments.

The TNA proposal began a debate over how to revise the community involvement process. Its resolution was delayed when City Manager Turner left in early 1975 for a job in private industry. The new manager, Bill Donaldson, decided to do his own review, asking a team of city administrators to answer the question, "What can be done to reduce the confusion and duplication in the City's community involvement processes and mechanisms?" The team produced recommendations similar to those in the TNA proposal, but a financial crisis in late 1975 brought a hiring freeze, again delaying any changes that required new personnel.

The Community Development Block Grant process. The financial crisis did not prevent the city from instituting a new system for community involvement in decisions on federal Community Development Block Grant (CDBG) funds. The city's first CDBG plan had been formulated hastily in early 1975 because of late funding authorization, and the resulting community involvement was limited to a few public hearings. With more time to prepare the second-year plan, in late 1975 City Hall began a CDBG community involvement process largely consistent with TNA principles.

City Hall chose to make the basic CDBG spending decisions through a Community Development Advisory Council (CDAC), composed of twelve neighborhood representatives, twelve at-large representatives, and a chairperson (who has sometimes also been a neighborhood representative). The CDAC was asked to formulate an annual CDBG plan, after first soliciting proposals from the neighborhoods in a manner similar to what the TNA proposals envisioned for the general budget process. The plan would then be reviewed and approved by City Council. In operation, the extensive neighborhood representation on the CDAC has assured a substantial neighborhood component in the plans, and the plans themselves have seldom been much altered by City Council (Woods, Andersen, and Grober, 1979: 57).

Might this process have been the result of federal pressures rather than a reflection of local preferences? The federal government certainly did provide the opportunity that made the process possible. Otherwise, however, the process appears to have been locally developed. Both neighborhood and city officials argue that this was the case. In addition, evidence on national CDBG implementation in these years suggests minimal federal pressure for citizen participation (Dommel et al., 1982: 44).

The Community Assistance Teams. The next step came in mid-1976 when the obstacles to the new community assistance process were finally overcome and City Hall established the Community Assistance Teams (CATs) by converting the three existing community planning teams and hiring one new team, thus to have a team for each of the four city quadrants. The teams were somewhat smaller than initially envisioned; each consisted of a team captain, a physical planner, a human services planner, a technician (for graphs, demographic data, etc.), and a part-time secretary.

The CATs were assigned—and have performed—three principal responsibilities. They were asked, first, to provide "liaison service between each community and all City departments and agencies" (Hartsock, 1975). As Hartsock explained, "This will lead to a reduction in the confusion and duplication in the City's community involvement process, will provide communities with a single prime contact in the City (a community assistance team), and will provide departments with an ongoing structured means of contacting representative community groups." This new charge might at the same time resolve one of the central role conflicts in community planning. No longer restricted to physical planning, the CATs would be able to serve as the general-purpose representatives of City Hall that neighborhoods had frequently expected community planners would be (Needleman and Needleman, 1974: 89–92).

To deal with another role conflict, the CATs were asked to "provide follow-through to see that plans get implemented and that implementation follows the intent of the goals and objectives" (Martin, 1975). Planners had traditionally thought that they should plan and let others implement, but community planners who followed that advice risked seeing their efforts come to nothing and their standing in the community deteriorate (Needleman and Needleman, 1974: 91–92). With the conversion to CATs, however, that conflict might no longer exist. Actually, according to Planning Director Stevens, the pre-CATs planners were already moving in this direction by "doing more implementation of community proposals all the time."

As their third responsibility, the CATs retained the original community planning function, but even that was changing from what it had once been. With increasing numbers of communities having completed plans, and with many communities becoming more concerned with specific short-term improvements than with long-term general plans, the CATs would decide by 1977 to de-emphasize community plans in favor of Community Work Programs (CWPs), annual statements of municipal projects desired within a community.

There was one responsibility, finally, that the CATs were instructed *not* to assume. Community planners can be tempted to become advocates for the neighborhoods they serve, but they do so at the risk of getting caught between competing allegiances—those they feel to the communities versus those they have to the city that pays them. The official City Hall thinking recognized this problem as a "conflict of interest," and told the CATs to avoid advocacy and "let the communities be responsible for their own lobbying efforts" (Martin, 1975).

Opening of the budget process. The last major element in the consolidation of the community involvement mechanisms was the opening of the budget process in 1977 (see Hartsock, 1977). Movement in this direction had begun with the Metropolitan and COPE projects and gained momentum from the successful involvement of the communities in the CDBG planning process. That success, Ken Bordwell argues, got neighborhood leaders thinking: "A lot of neighborhood people, including one who had been head of the CDAC, started realizing that there's a hell of a budget out there, and we've been shuffled into this little $18 million budget [the CDBG funds], of which 20 percent goes for administration and so forth." By 1977 City Hall was ready to accommodate this thinking by making community submission of proposals the first step in the budget process.

What made this change possible was the move to Community Work Programs, which could serve as annual neighborhood budget requests. Preparation or revision of the CWPs, perhaps with CATs assistance, now begins the budget process each year. The CWP requests are distributed to the appropriate departments to arrive concurrently with the department's tentative budget allocation, thus facilitating consideration of the requests in departmental budget deliberations. The communities are able to lobby because they are told where their proposals have been sent. (For comparisons to similar budget processes in other cities, see Hallman, 1980.)

This process has continued to evolve to further facilitate community involvement. Since 1980 the process has begun each year with a day-long "Town Meeting" at which community leaders are able to talk with departmental officials, stationed in booths, about possible budget requests prior to their submission. Even more recently, training sessions have been added to teach new community leaders about the budget process.

The opening of the budget process probably was not as productive for the neighborhoods, initially at least, as was the opening of the CDBG process. For one thing, with the city government in retrenchment during the late 1970s, the discretionary component was much smaller in the general operating budget than in the CDBG budget, meaning a smaller potential "pot" available for neighborhoods to influence. In addition, officials in most departments were unlikely to be as sympathetic to neighborhood requests as the CDAC, with its strong neighborhood representation, might be. Still, the opening of the budget process is cited by both neighborhood and municipal officials as an important step in the evolution of community involvement in Cincinnati, a step that may also have grown in importance as the two sides have become more familiar with each other over the years.

ENTITLEMENT, 1978–?: NEIGHBORHOOD ENTRENCHMENT IN MUNICIPAL GOVERNMENT

By the late 1970s, the community councils were interested in more than simply the access to municipal government promised by the new community involvement mechanisms. They were also becoming increasingly interested in the possibility of financial assistance, particularly if it could be channeled directly into building and maintaining their organizations.

Neighborhood organizations face two special resource problems that help to explain this interest. First, the incentives for potential members to join are limited by the so-called public goods dilemma, the fact that the public goods that the groups seek will, if obtained, be equally available to all residents regardless of their contributions to the group (Olson, 1971; O'Brien, 1975). As earlier chapters have shown, that problem can occasionally be overcome by a threat that galvanizes many residents into action, but the resulting involvement may be mostly temporary, giving these organizations—as their second resource problem—a cyclical equality that can also undermine effectiveness (e.g., Jones, 1981).

These problems can be ameliorated if the organizations can obtain a steady diet of "selective incentives," rewards that go only to individuals who are involved in the organization. The question, of course, is where to find these incentives, as they may be unavailable in sufficient supply in the communities themselves. With appetites whetted by OEO and CDBG assistance, by the late 1970s the councils were wondering if government might be a good source.

The Stimulating Neighborhood Action Program. City Hall was not yet ready to finance direct support of the community councils, but it was willing to help the councils in seeking that support from other sources. The willingness became relevant when Chuck Hirt learned in 1977 of a new program designed to increase neighborhood involvement: the Stimulating Neighborhood Action Program (SNAP) sponsored by the Charles Stewart Mott Foundation of Flint, Michigan (City of Cincinnati, Office of the Manager, 1979). With the assistance of Hirt and with the approval of City Manager Donaldson, City Hall formally applied for program funding in August 1977 and was approved in December for an initial three-year $600,000 grant (later extended for two additional years with supplementary funding).

Although the grant went to City Hall, most of the funding was targeted to the community councils as "seed money" to help in building self-sustaining organizations. To move the groups toward that independence, the money was provided in smaller amounts each year, decreasing by $1,000 each year from an initial $5,000 for each council in 1978 to only $1,000 per council in the last year, 1982. The funds were initially available to forty-four community councils that, on advice of the CATs, had been designated in the SNAP proposal. (Provisions were also made to divide funds where more than one group existed in a neighborhood and to support three councils formed since the time of the proposal's submission.) The funds required applications for specific projects, with approval supposedly hinging on the project's relevance to the goal of building community organizations. In practice, however, most applications were approved as SNAP became a virtual entitlements program for all interested councils.

SNAP began in Cincinnati, on the heels of that harsh winter, in March of 1978, and councils spent their allotments on such modest items as community newsletters and organizational stationery and on such major tasks as building a recreation center, starting a community library, and rehabilitating abandoned housing for resale. Although SNAP money could not go directly to individuals as selective incentives, it could be used indirectly in that manner, as with special community celebrations in which organizational leaders were honored. Or, by aiding in increasing a council's paid membership, SNAP could generate revenue to pay staff, a salary being an obvious selective incentive.

The new roots of council membership. With the coming of SNAP, and with OEO/CSA and CDBG assistance continuing, the roots of the community councils were changing. The new roots can be seen by examining the determinants of membership change between 1975 and 1980, the most recent period for which membership data are available. The five-year span is also sufficiently long to capture substantial membership change. The average change for the period is minimal—a mean gain of 22.5 members and a median gain of 11.7 members—but substantial membership change is evident in the standard deviation of 130.2 members.[2]

The strongest single pattern in these changes, shown in Table 6.1, is an inverse relationship between membership at the outset of the five-year period and membership change during the period, indicating that the larger councils were mostly losing members while the smaller councils were growing. This probably reflects in part the different maturational stages of the councils. Most of the larger councils were also the older councils by this time, such that many were experiencing a natural membership decline or stagnation, while the smaller councils tended to be younger and more likely to be enjoying the natural growth of newer organizations. This pattern may also have been encouraged by the tendency in these years to spread outside assistance, such as SNAP and CDBG, across many neighborhoods.

TABLE 6.1
SOURCES OF MEMBERSHIP CHANGE, 1975–80

| Neighborhood Characteristic[a] | Relationship to Membership Change | |
	Zero-Order Correlation	Regression Coefficient
Membership in 1975	− .420[b]	− .420[b]
Number of households	.367[c]	
Percentage black	.041	
Percentage residential units turning over	.171	.284[c]
Percentage commercial units	.033	
Median family income	.025	
Home sale value	.033	
Number of homeowners	− .315[c]	
Percentage professional	.139	.317[c]
Mott Foundation assistance	.298[c]	.406[b]
CDBG spending per capita	.212	.251[c]
R[2]		.550
Adjusted R[2]		.478
N of cases		37

[a] Demographic data were taken from 1978 when possible (households, residential turnover) and from 1980 otherwise. Mott Foundation assistance is for the 1978–80 period, CDBG spending for the 1975–78 period.
[b] Significant at .01 level.
[c] Significant at .05 level.

Whatever the role of the spread, the assistance itself figures prominently in the membership changes. The level of Mott funding to a council is the second most important predictor and the CDBG funding per capita the fifth most important predictor of these changes. The Mott money is more important, despite fewer actual dollars per neighborhood than from CDBG, presumably because it was more available for general organizational maintenance (i.e., selective incentives).

Probably as a consequence of this assistance, these membership changes contain much less of the socioeconomic bias evident in overall council memberships in Chapter 5. None of the measures of socioeconomic status or of investment in a home is highly correlated with membership trends. To be sure, community resources remain important for building membership. Once the influence of the equalizing tendency and the two forms of outside assistance have been controlled, percentage professional in a community emerges as an important influence, indicating that higher socioeconomic status continues to influence council membership levels. Threats may also continue to be important, judging from the emergence of residential turnover as a factor in the regression. Some residents appear to have joined community councils in these years to fight the change high turnover rates could bring. But residential turnover and percentage professional together explain only 16 percent of the variation in membership changes, less than the 22 percent explained by the two forms of outside financial assistance. Council membership in recent years seems to have become more a function of outside assistance than of indigenous neighborhood resources.

The community councils have become part of what Samuel Beer (1976) has termed "public sector politics." This phenomenon is said to have reached significant proportions during the 1960s when the federal government designated other public sector actors (i.e., local governments and some quasi-public institutions, such as neighborhood groups) as potential recipients for federal grants. Foundations have also sometimes joined in offering such grants (e.g., Walker, 1983). The grants were often designed, as with SNAP, as seed money, but the recipients are likely nonetheless to lobby for continuation of the grants. The lobbying can be very effective, because the recipients are usually well organized and the organized opposition is usually minimal.

Consistent with that model, as the end of SNAP in Cincinnati approached, the community councils began to look for how the flow of outside funding could be maintained. Perhaps recognizing the difficulty of lobbying an out-of-town private foundation, the councils turned their attention instead to City Hall in Cincinnati.

The decline of the CATs. Their request was framed partially in terms of dissatisfaction with the CATs. Where the CATs had once been useful as intermediaries in dealing with City Hall, most of the council leaders interviewed in 1980 said they preferred by then to work directly with the various city departments. What the councils wanted now in City Hall, many of their leaders claimed, was the advocacy role the CATs had been told *not* to assume. As long-time community leader Pat Crum argued in a 1980 interview, "The main thing neighborhoods have to learn now is how to effectively advocate, how to fight City Hall and win, and it really isn't an appropriate role for someone at City Hall to do that."

This was not good news for the CATs. Without a strong base of support in the communities, the CATs became easy prey when budget problems once again beset the city in the early 1980s. A policy of attrition was imposed on the CATs, with positions left unfilled whenever employees left. By June 1982 the CATs, after having been launched with so much fanfare only a few years earlier, had declined in average team size from the original four people to slightly fewer than two. In that context the communities asked in mid–1980 that City Hall fund "community support workers," staff and advocates *for* the councils (*Cincinnati Enquirer*, 1980c). From the perspective of public sector politics, however, what they may really have been seeking was continued outside financial support once the SNAP funding ended.

The Neighborhood Support Program. Despite the risks political leaders can invite if they oppose this kind of united front, City Hall did not give in easily or totally to the wishes of the neighborhoods. The Neighborhood Support Program (NSP) approved by City Hall in late 1980 offered each community council up to $8,000 per year, but with some strings attached to the offer (City of Cincinnati, Department of Neighborhood Housing and Conservation, 1981). Following the SNAP model, the City Council insisted that the neighborhoods would have to apply for the funds, and only activities designed to develop the councils would be eligible for funding, thereby ruling out the possibility of using the funds to pay salaries directly. (The "development" criterion also permitted City Hall to use CDBG funds to pay for the program, rather than having to tap the already tight general operating budget.) Finally, the council refused to commit to a continuing entitlement, specifying instead a three-year experiment.

That limitation may have left the neighborhoods feeling anything but entrenched in the municipal system. By late 1981, as a consequence, with the termination of SNAP now imminent and the eventual termination of NSP also possible, the councils were searching for new funding sources. This time, recognizing the reality of a shrinking public sector, the councils turned to the larger Cincinnati community in an effort to build a $1 million "Neighborhood Fund," an endowment that could provide interest income to support the councils. The hope was to build the fund partially from contributions from the councils themselves, which in the process would buy into the eventual income from the fund, and partially from other community sources (e.g., business contributions, community enterprises, carnivals).

The million-dollar goal may have been too ambitious, but the idea of the endowment proved viable. By mid–1985 Invest in Neighborhoods, as the fund had been renamed, had raised approximately $500,000, half of that coming from $5,440 contributions from each of forty-five community councils (*Eastern Hills Journal*, 1985). The goal of a stable, if modest, base of interest income was in sight, and the place of the councils in Cincinnati was becoming more secure.

As it turned out, the councils had probably underestimated how solidly they were entrenched in City Hall. The debate in 1983 on whether to continue NSP was "a real battle," according to one observer, but the neighborhoods did not come out the losers. Despite the fact that the city's CDBG allotment was down by more than a third from its early 1980s peak, NSP was continued for three more years with *more*, not less, funding. Each council's share would increase from $9,000 to $9,500 to $10,000 per year over the three years. Having obtained increased funding at a time of decreased municipal resources, the community councils appeared to have a secure hold on a continuing program of municipal entitlements.

COMMENT: COMMUNITY INVOLVEMENT AND THE REFORM OF REFORM

From an initial stance of skepticism and resistance in the late 1960s, City Hall in Cincinnati moved rapidly during the 1970s from experimenting with community involvement to eventually establishing a coordinated set of mechanisms to involve communities in municipal decision making. Change came so rapidly that by the early 1980s, the city and its communities had graduated to a new set of concerns, moving from the earlier emphasis on opening the governmental process to an emphasis on using municipal resources to strengthen the councils.

Change of this magnitude occurring with such rapidity would be surprising anywhere, but it is especially surprising in a reform-based, public-interest-oriented government that seemed more likely to resist than to embrace the neighborhood movement. That resistance materialized, as most obviously with two city managers who balked at proposals for community planning, but the changes nonetheless came. Why? The explanation lies, in part, in pressure applied from above by the federal government. The federal War on Poverty raised City Hall awareness of the community issue, then left a legacy of poverty "warriors" in City Hall and in many community organizations. And it was in response to federal CDBG funding that Cincinnati established one of its most important community involvement mechanisms.

On the whole, however, the evidence suggests that the federal role has not been determining. Most of the major changes in the city's community involvement mechanisms came *after*, not during, the War on Poverty, by which time federal pressures had greatly diminished. The CDAC innovation, for example, came when federal pressures were minimal. Federal programs may have been a necessary cause of the Cincinnati evolution, but too much happened away from the weight of federal pressures for them to have been a sufficient cause.

A more important source of the Cincinnati changes has been the community councils themselves. Their presence in increasing numbers by the early 1970s undoubtedly figured in City Hall's decision to experiment with community involvement. In subsequent years the community councils took an even more active role, successfully lobbying City Council and municipal administrators on a variety of neighborhood issues. The greatest asset of the councils in this lobbying may have been their diversity. City Hall might have been much less responsive had the councils represented only low-income communities or only a few middle- to upper-income communities (as was the case as late as 1964). With both those and other types of communities involved, the community movement became difficult for City Hall to ignore.

But the role of the councils, even if combined with the role of the federal government, still misses much of the Cincinnati story. Overlooked is the fact that the new community involvement mechanisms came mostly at the instigation of City Hall figures, rather than over their resistance. Municipal officials *believed* in the changes they were undertaking; they were not acting merely to placate insistent federal or neighborhood constituencies.

The contributions came first from administrative guerrillas, municipal administrators who felt as much allegiance to the communities as to City Hall. The most important of these guerrillas was Planning Director Herb Stevens, who was willing to fight to involve communities in the planning process. Other guerrillas included some of Stevens's community planners, community organizer Chuck Hirt, and a few other figures around City Hall. These mavericks were eventually joined by many other administrators, including City Managers Turner and Donaldson, as the contagion of the community idea spread through City Hall and the guerrillas became the establishment.

What has happened in City Hall in Cincinnati is nothing less than the reform of reform. The reform movement in its many Cincinnati manifestations has reassessed the primacy traditionally accorded both the public interest and decision making by professionals and has concluded that the interests of the city's geographic parts were being slighted, in part because decision making had become too insulated. The reassessment that began with a few administrative guerrillas in the 1960s spread quickly to political leaders and from there to such other traditional supporters of reform principles as the city manager and the League of Women Voters.

This reform of reform may be the concept most useful in explaining the evolution of community involvement mechanisms in Cincinnati. This is not to say that other factors played no role, but those factors might have produced nothing more than symbolic posturing by City Hall had not this rethinking led many City Hall actors to view more community involvement as desirable.

7

Decision Making:
From Politics to Administration,
from Petition to Negotiation

Opening a decision-making process to new actors does not guarantee their participation when decisions are actually made.[1] All too often, providing the mechanisms for more citizen participation has failed to increase actual participation (e.g., Cole and Caputo, 1984). In Cincinnati, however, the new mechanisms for community involvement have increased the neighborhood role in the making of municipal decisions, at the same time helping to transform the very process of municipal governance.

These changes were revealed through in-depth, open-ended interviews with a variety of Cincinnati municipal and community leaders, including five City Council members, representatives from fifteen municipal departments, and fourteen community council leaders.[2] Each was asked about his or her involvement in neighborhood–City Hall interactions. Their answers, as summarized below, suggest how and why community involvement and the process of municipal governance have changed in tandem in recent years.

NEIGHBORHOODS AND THE CHANGING PROCESS
OF MUNICIPAL GOVERNANCE

The community councils in Cincinnati initially favored the City Council in their dealings with City Hall. According to veteran City Council members, the years immediately after the 1971 Charter-Democrat coalition's victory found neighborhood groups coming in increasing numbers to the council. The visibility of the coalition's proneighborhood platform, combined with coalition support for the many fledgling community involvement experiments of these years, presumably encouraged more community attention to elective officials.

89

From politics to administration. Around 1975, however, the trend began to change. The communities for their part probably began to recognize that important municipal decisions are often made by administrators, especially in a reformed city such as Cincinnati. Perhaps more important, most of the new experiments pushed the communities more toward appointive administrators than toward the elective council. Community planning linked the neighborhoods with planners, CDBG decision making pushed them toward the departments targeted for the primary CDBG funding, and more budget involvement sent them to whatever department received particular neighborhood budget requests. The inevitable result was that the community councils gradually turned their attention more toward the city's administrators.

The turn was noted, for example, by two long-time members of City Council. According to Democrat Dave Mann, "One of the things I've observed is an evolution over the years I've been on Council. A lot of the councils have leaderships that have been involved enough that they rely on some of the bureaucratic structures that have been developed to deal with problems." Republican Guy Guckenberger reported similarly that community contacts with his office, over budget issues in particular, "have declined substantially." In the past, he said, "we would find a lot of community councils making a direct [budget] appeal to the City Council. Then we began to see community councils become more educated . . . with the system, and they will make the requests directly to the City administration, the idea being that we [the community leaders] want our request in very early because we want the administration to review it. If we make it after the budget is submitted, it's not possible to get funded because it's out in left field somewhere."

Department officials corroborated those reports, with officials in eight of the fifteen departments reporting increased interaction with community groups in recent years and *no* official reporting a decline in that interaction. Most of the other officials either were in departments with consistently low rates of community contacts or had been with City Hall for too brief a time to comment on historical trends.

The community council leaders also concurred. When asked whom they contacted most often—City Council, the departments, or the city manager— eleven of the fourteen said they usually start at the departmental level. As one leader put it, "We'll initially go to the departments and work through the chain of command," an approach another community leader termed "the kosher way to do it."

The breadth of community involvement with the departments was revealed even more clearly when the council leaders were asked separately about each department. Every leader could recall involvement with a majority of the municipal departments over the previous year, and several cited involvement with *all* of the departments. And in every case involvement meant that the council leader described a specific case of neighborhood-department interaction.

From petition to negotiation. The changing approaches to these interactions are at least as significant as their increasing volume. As the two sides have come into more frequent contact, they have moved from less to more cooperation in their interactions or, stated differently, from petition to negotiation.

Petitioning and public hearings represent the two traditional approaches to community involvement. With petitioning, involvement is initiated by a community when it brings a demand—or "petition"—to government. Most of the community involvement of the 1950s and 1960s, for example, found councils petitioning City Hall to halt changes that threatened the residential status quo. With public hearings, City Hall at least invites the involvement, but the sincerity of the invitation can be questioned because citizens are often allowed to react only to proposals already formulated by government. The approach nonetheless remains important in Cincinnati and perhaps as more than a formality. In Planning, for example, according to former Assistant Director Steve Bloomfield, "it's very difficult to get anything through the Planning Commission unless the community has been notified and has been invited to submit comments."

The trend in Cincinnati, however, has been toward a third approach of "negotiation." Here the departments contact community groups to seek their involvement in program planning and execution, and the contacts come *before* the department has formulated plans. Officials in a number of municipal departments reported this type of involvement, and community leaders corroborated those reports. As Clifton Heights council president Jack Otto said of his dealings with municipal departments, "It's not a win-lose situation anymore. It's 'Let's get it done.'" Josh Weiser of the College Hill Forum commented similarly: "We tend to work with the departments more than we find ourselves in conflict with them."

It has not always been this way. One veteran community leader, after mentioning that city housing officials had recently invited him to City Hall to discuss housing in the neighborhood, noted how much things had changed: "Ten years ago you'd get an invitation like that, you'd fall over dead in surprise. Now they're inviting you to come in, sit down, and go over it." Several department heads also admitted that the negotiation approach differs considerably from the way they once operated. As a veteran of the city's highway construction efforts said, "Back in the forties we'd take our plan and go out to the communities and say, 'This is what we're going to do.' Nowadays we start from scratch with the communities."

Some administrators and community councils have moved yet one step further to an approach best termed "interdependence." In this approach departmental administrators converse with community council leaders on a regular basis, often independent of particular programs, to exchange information that might be of help either to the department or to the community. The most obvious efforts along these lines in 1980 were by the Police and Fire divisions. Although neither division is known for involving communities in high-level policy-making, both were practicing interdependence at the street level by sending a departmental representative, a police officer or a firefighter, to every community council meeting. The goal of maintaining two-way communication was evident, for example, when Fire Chief Norman Wells described why he initiated firefighter attendance at neighborhood meetings: "to answer their questions and, as they [the firefighters] get better recognized at the council, then to present them with things in their communities that are causing us problems—false alarms, careless fire incidence, and so on."

Neither all of the departments nor all of the community councils are involved in negotiation and interdependence, but many are, and in 1980 the numbers appeared to be growing. A third to a half of the departments and a similar proportion of the councils were significantly involved in negotiation or interdependence by that time. The other departments and councils were pursuing community involvement through some mix of the public hearing and petitioning approaches.

The changing role of City Council. Increasing involvement with administrators has not taken the community councils out of the City Council chambers. Some City Council members even dispute the notion that community contacting of them has declined at all. As one said, "It's been a pretty steady decibel level." All City Council members concurred, however, that the *nature,* if not the frequency, of these contacts has changed.

Several of these officials recalled that historically most community contacts were managed by referrals to departments for responses. Here City Council members played either a "switchboard" role, handling requests because community leaders did not know where else to take them, or an "ombudsman" role, intervening when a community group had a complaint with some part of the municipal bureaucracy. Both roles have changed recently. The switchboard role has declined. Community leaders, by both their own accounts and the accounts of City Council members and departmental officials, now usually contact the departments directly or through the CATs. Only one community leader expressed a preference for beginning with the City Council on most issues. The ombudsman role may also have declined as the communities more often worked out their problems with the departments, rather than bringing in City Council as a third party. Many of the community leaders said that they used the City Council less for this role, and most council members concurred. Some departmental officials disputed this judgment, arguing that City Council is still frequently asked to resolve neighborhood-department conflicts. These officials argued, however, that even in such cases council is not serving the same role it once served. Where historically the neighborhoods often gave City Council original jurisdiction on complaints about departments, they now more often use council as an appellate body. Neighborhood complaints come to council only if they cannot be resolved in the department.

The appeals take one of two forms. In the traditional form, a community council wants City Council to do something to force a department to shape up. These appeals often come from low-income areas that tend to perceive City Council as more responsive than the bureaucracy. As the leader of a community council in a small, low-income Appalachian neighborhood said, "The thing is that a neighborhood such as _____ doesn't have as much concern among administrators as other neighborhoods do. But . . . the City Council is usually pretty good about it. Although a _____ vote is never going to put a politician in office, they still have been very good when we've got a complaint." Community leaders who deal only irregularly with the municipal bureaucracy also seem more likely to use council for this type of appeal.

The common denominator for the two types of communities could be inadequate understanding of the complexity of the municipal bureaucracy. When that understanding is limited either by lack of education or lack of experience with the bureaucracy, community leaders may turn more quickly to an available third party, such as City Council. By contrast, leaders having that understanding may be more inclined to resolve conflicts within the bureaucracy.

Having that understanding does not prevent occasional appeals to City Council, but those appeals usually take a different and newer form. Rather than following a conflict between a community and a department, these appeals find the community and the department in alliance, albeit usually a tacit rather than explicit alliance. According to city and neighborhood leaders, a department lacking the money necessary to satisfy a community's request often encourages the community to appeal to the City Council for an increased departmental budget authorization. The department then does its part by appearing at a City Council meeting to announce that, indeed, it cannot do what the community wants unless more money is provided. The department does not actively lobby for the money, however, for fear of appearing to challenge the city's budget priorities.

A number of community council leaders admitted having made such budget appeals, and several department heads acknowledged complicity in those efforts. One department head said that he sometimes invites these appeals by telling neighborhood leaders, "If you want me to respond, what you got to do is expand my budget." A community leader recalled similarly, "I get calls from department heads who say, 'Help me lobby for this.'"

One other type of City Council involvement with the neighborhoods also appears to have grown in recent years. A council member reported an increase in neighborhood–City Council interaction on "the more difficult issues, ones that can't be resolved by the department and have to be resolved by policy action." Interestingly, this could mean that as a consequence of the new community involvement, City Council now deals more with the issues that, according to the theory of council-manager government, city councils *should* be dealing with: broader policy questions, rather than narrow questions of bureaucratic procedure.

The role of the city manager. Much of what the City Council does with the neighborhoods, the city manager also must do. That is obviously true with broader policy questions in which the manager almost always has a say. It is also true with appeals from the neighborhoods on departmental issues, some of those appeals going to the manager rather than to the council.

Communities choose the manager over the City Council for two reasons. First, some problems appear to be more in the manager's sphere of authority. Paul Freshwater, a long-time leader of the Kennedy Heights Community Council, made this distinction: "If it looks like something where the department can do it but needs to be pushed a little bit, then the Manager is probably the right place to go. If it looks, on the other hand, like something where the department is going to have to do something a little extraordinary, like putting money into a project they don't have in their budget, we may have to go to City Council." Second, it sometimes depends on where the community council thinks it can find an interested audience. Several community leaders said that they were more inclined to go to the manager after Sy Murray replaced Bill Donaldson, the latter perceived by some community leaders as unsympathetic to neighborhood groups. On the other hand, one community leader reported more interaction with Donaldson, noting that Murray "doesn't have the same open door policy that Donaldson had."

ADMINISTRATIVE ADVANTAGES
IN COMMUNITY INVOLVEMENT

Most of these changes could have been anticipated from the nature of the community involvement mechanisms adopted by Cincinnati. The growing community involvement with municipal administrators, for example, was clearly inherent in those mechanisms. What might not have been anticipated is how readily municipal administrators have taken to this involvement. Rather than balking, most administrators seem to have embraced the new community involvement. Although the administrators as a group are only modestly more positive than negative in their evaluations, officials in those departments with the most community involvement are almost unanimous in their favorable evaluations. The critical or mixed reviews came only from those departments with the least involvement.

The evaluations are positive because these administrators have not found citizen participation to be, as often described, more of a hindrance than a help in the administrative process (e.g., Cupps, 1977; Barber, 1981). To the contrary, the Cincinnati officials have found that community involvement can have definite administrative advantages, as specified below.

1. *Better channels of communication.* Many administrators reported that councils serve as useful departmental contacts in the communities, giving departments a place to begin when they have questions about community opinions. As Waste Collection Director Don Van Winkle commented, "I think it [community involvement] is for the better. At least we've got somebody as a contact in each of the communities." As well, the councils help the departments to satisfy formal requirements for community input on many programs. As another administrator said, "Community councils eliminate the need for a public hearing because they hold it for you." In the process, of course, the councils may also provide useful information on community preferences.

2. *Improved program implementation.* Several administrators argued that involving neighborhoods in departmental decisions facilitates implementation of those decisions. As Housing Division Director Hugh Guest put it, "They've made it easier for programs to function in neighborhoods because they participated in the decisions."

Another report of this advantage came from the seemingly unlikely source of the city's Engineering Division. Engineering divisions are notorious for opposing community involvement, preferring to run highways through neighborhoods without regard for how residents feel. City Engineer Jim Krusling acknowledged some historical truth to this reputation in Cincinnati but contended that his division had changed its ways, partially in the hope of improving implementation: "As we have learned from our past mistakes—or, let's say, the way we operated in the past—it would be an exercise in futility to make plans for a new street or highway without involving the community. So, where we are planning a new street, we try to bring them on board as soon as possible."

The discovery of this advantage is hardly surprising. Theories of decision making have long postulated that people who are involved in making decisions are more likely to cooperate in putting those decisions into operation (e.g., Vroom and Yetton, 1973). The Cincinnati findings suggest only that what is true of small groups can also apply to decisions made with larger publics.

3. *More services for the dollar.* Participative decision making may also improve organizational productivity. Community involvement can bring an analogous benefit, judging from what many Cincinnati administrators said, by enlisting neighborhoods as active participants in program execution and service delivery, a step beyond passive acceptance of implementation. The result can be more services for the same or lower cost.

This idea has been popularized recently as coproduction, defined as the joint efforts of community groups and local governments to deliver municipal services (e.g., Whitaker, 1980; Albrandt and Sumka, 1983). Most Cincinnati administrators did not use that term, but they did cite numerous examples of community groups' assisting in the delivery of services. Some examples were relatively modest, as with the Highway Maintenance use of community groups to help in neighborhood street inspection, but others were quite substantial, as with the cooperative efforts of the Recreation Department and a community council on a community center. The department built the center but lacked money for its operation, so the community council contracted with the city to handle that operation. This advantage does have its limitations, as discussed in Chapter 10, but most departments with substantial community involvement did perceive dollar benefits from coproduction.

4. *Protection from criticism.* Participation in decision making can also reduce the likelihood of criticism once the decision has been made, because those involved in making the decision take credit for the decision. The more actors who are involved in making the decision, the fewer who may be left to criticize the decision later.

This advantage for administrators was suggested as often by community council leaders as by municipal administrators. Those community leaders who were most involved with the departments expressed reluctance to take conflicts beyond the department. As one leader said, "No one wants to go to City Council with anything unless they have to." They seemed to feel that their relationships with departments could be damaged by appeals to higher authorities (except, of course, when the department supported the appeal). Thus an experienced community council leader spoke disparagingly of those community councils which act as "squeaky wheels" by going to City Council. She argued that they "haven't done their homework," even if they are successful. This attitude can even lead to disdain for City Council, as when another community leader commented: "City Council makes a policy decision, that's big news."

This attitude may spare departmental administrators from some City Council and city manager interventions. As such, working closely with the communities may be a means by which departments can avoid the preoccupation with "brushfires" sometimes said to accompany increased community involvement in municipal affairs (Yates, 1977).

5. *Clout in the budget process.* Just as community involvement can keep some community complaints *against* departments from going to higher authorities, so it can increase the amount of community support *for* departments that gets to those authorities. In particular, many Cincinnati administrators argued that the community councils can be useful allies in the budget process. According to one department head, "If these people can convince City Council that they really need something, it's a good possibility that council will give it to them."

Illustrative of this advantage, two municipal departments in Cincinnati are widely perceived as having avoided most of the budget cutbacks in the late 1970s by virtue of their support from neighborhood groups. When budget cuts were threatened, officials from these departments appeared before City Council with their neighborhood supporters or with the tacit threat that those supporters would appear en masse if the cuts became a reality. An official from one of these departments was candid about the tactic: "We tell council, 'We'll save you from the political dogs if you'll save us from the budgetary dogs.'" What this may reflect is that the organization that presents a united front to its funding base can be more successful in getting funds.

THE LONG LEARNING PROCESS

These advantages have not developed either quickly or easily. They came about as the culmination of a lengthy, often difficult learning process. For departmental administrators, that process probably began with the kind of dogged resistance to community demands that Lipsky (1968) and Kirlin (1973) have described. Only over time did many departmental officials come to hear and eventually adapt to the interests of the new community actors in municipal politics.

The representativeness issue. The officials first had to confront what one city official describes as "that awful question of who does this group of people really speak for." Although much rhetoric argues for community involvement as a means to represent the citizenry, the evidence presented here and elsewhere indicates that community groups are usually far from representative of their communities (e.g., Cole, 1974).

This fact poses major problems for city officials. To begin with, as Councilman Guy Guckenberger noted, "the usual problem is how many people do they represent. You have some neighborhood groups that are very vocal, and you're surprised to find out later that there's a total of ten members in that group. That's a problem because you really don't have a good fix on how many people are actively involved." Alternatively, city officials have to decide whom to believe when more than one group claims to represent an area. Either the boundaries of different groups partially or completely overlap, or dissenting voices in a community claim that the recognized community organization does not speak for the community. One Cincinnati administrator recalled, "One of the community councils had a leader who was a bar owner. I used to get people coming up and whispering to me all the time [at public meetings], 'Don't pay any attention to that guy.'" Even when an administrator has determined whom a particular group represents, that knowledge can quickly become obsolete. The volatile nature of neighborhood groups means that a group may not represent tomorrow the same people it represents today. As Housing Director Guest reported, "You get a group which started and was very active. You still find yourself talking to them, but there's really nothing there anymore."

Most of Cincinnati's administrators were aware of these problems and unwilling to cast them aside quickly. They usually preferred to take a stance such as that taken by Assistant Planning Director Bloomfield: "We assume they [the community groups] represent a number of people. We also assume they don't represent everybody." From there, as a City Council member said, "You just have to guess and ask questions."

A first question asks about the size of a group's membership. According to one administrator, "You get groups when you say, 'Write down the list of your members,' when they get past the fifth line, they start running out of names." Or, in again somewhat tongue-in-cheek terms from the same administrator, "I just have a sense if I can't find a board of directors." The question of size may also be answered by observing the group's turnout at public meetings, perhaps even a series of meetings. As another administrator said, "Often you'll go through a couple of hearings before the true picture can be understood." This approach puts a somewhat different cast on Lipsky's complaint (1968) that public administrators often unnecessarily delay responding to complaints from community groups. Those delays can now be seen as sometimes useful for testing the legitimacy of a group.

A somewhat different approach involves looking at the group's procedures. As one official said, "One way to deal with it [the representativeness problem] is to say, 'Well, you set up a structure, there's an open process.' If there's an open process I don't ask the second question." Community Development director Bud Haupt concurred: "The issue always comes up of, How can you take the word of this group that meets on Thursday nights and assume that they speak for the community? I do think that we have to insist that they have some kind of democratically open procedures. If you can maintain the awareness of people that this group exists, it is going [to] meet and make recommendations to City Hall . . . , then I have no problem whether there's a dozen people or two hundred."

Finally, many administrators test the representativeness of community groups by seeking information from others in the communities. According to one administrator, "On any important issue we'll try to contact as many people as possible in addition to the community councils." Others echoed that opinion.

With the aid of these various techniques, most of Cincinnati's administrators claim that they eventually get a good reading on the representativeness of most groups. According to one, "After a while we know who they represent. They may not represent who they say they represent, but we know who they do represent."

Learning to proceed differently. Cincinnati's administrators also had to learn to proceed differently in making decisions because the entry of the communities adds at least three new elements to decision making. The first and most obvious element is the increased number of decision makers and opinions. As Housing Director Guest says, "There are many more agendas on the table that you have to deal with." Second, the new agendas often differ greatly from the traditional agendas. Communities presumably wanted a role in municipal decision making because they did not like the direction many decisions had taken. Third, many communities initially bring distrustful attitudes to this decision making. As late as 1980, Parks Director Brent Owens reported, "There's a certain amount of mistrust in some of the communities because of how they've been dealt with" in the past.

To cope with these new elements, Cincinnati's administrators have had to learn to do more listening. One administrator said with a smile that he had learned "to have bigger ears than a mouth" in order to understand the new community groups and their priorities. To enhance this listening, many administrators reported that they try to stay in close touch with the community councils. Many have also learned to be patient in the face of communities' initial hostility and distrust. Working with a particular community regularly over a period of time can reduce distrust, with the community gradually becoming more cooperative. As an administrator said of the progress he had made in working with some militant low-income communities: "They come in less with the intent to just beat you up." Lack of patience with that hostility, on the other hand, may create problems with community involvement. It could be more than coincidence that the Cincinnati administrator who complained the loudest about community involvement was also the administrator who said, "If a community group starts giving you too much difficulty . . . , we can just say, 'We'll go some place else.' "

Finally, these administrators had to learn, if it was not already their style, how to bargain and build consensus. One administrator, a relative newcomer from a large and reputedly very political northeastern city, described Cincinnati as different in that "you have to build a consensus, have to build a constituency for any decision." That becomes possible only if the administrator is willing to bend, though perhaps not to the extent suggested by the division head who said, "If it's legal, we're probably going to do it." The more realistic view may be that of another administrator, who said, "There has to be a little trade-off on both sides."

This bargaining may not come easily to administrators who still feel, in the tradition of reformed public interest professionalism, that they alone are best qualified to determine what is good for the community. Illustrative of this point, one administrator complained, "They [the communities] can stop through the political process actions which we might feel are actually in their own best interest." In this case, what to the administrator looked like the optimal choice may have looked to the communities like unacceptable paternalism.

Learning in the communities. A learning process has also been occurring in the communities. As the first step, community leaders had to learn how to establish the legitimacy of their groups and themselves as leaders. For new community groups, that means initially showing the staying power of the group. Community leader Mark Kiley, for example, recalled the City Hall attitude after he formed the Columbia-Tusculum Community Council: "I think for the first three to six months they held their breaths, questioning whether we were going to survive." Establishing legitimacy also means showing knowledge of the community and its needs. As Paul Rudemiller of the Camp Washington Community Council said, "The more data, the more facts you have, the more you get the city to buy in."

The second step is to learn where to go and what to ask for in City Hall. According to Northside community leader Sharon Belmonte, "There is a game. If you're going to be successful, you learn where the pressure points are, who to talk to, how to get things done." According to Belmonte and other community leaders, increasing proportions of their number had learned this game by 1980. Community leader Pat Crum describes the change this way: "Ten years ago neighborhoods were saying we need help in housing, and now neighborhoods will say I need a neighborhood housing service program, and I've got to have access to a three percent loan fund."

The catalysts for taking this second step appear to have been the new mechanisms for community involvement. Belmonte describes the budget involvement, for example, as "a valuable experience in learning how things really work." As for the CDBG involvement, Crum says, "A lot of that [learning] has come because CD existed to reward the communities if they did it right, and to teach them to do it right." A community support worker from an Appalachian neighborhood underscored Crum's point in reflecting on his involvement with the CDBG process: "The other thing we learned is that our neighborhoods are . . . requesting not the best things. We looked at what each of the _____ neighborhoods asked for and found that there were very few housing requests, hardly any economic development requests, but more of them were recreation and public works, which showed you where these neighborhoods' heads were at. It changed my head around. The key issues, and where the bulk of the money is, are in housing and economic development."

The final step is to learn how to lobby and negotiate. As College Hill leader Weiser says, "One of the pieces of the process is to actually go lobby with the departments." The communities then need some ability to advocate, as Crum has pointed out, along with an ability to negotiate and a sense of when to give ground. As long-time Westwood community leader Bob Brodbeck said, "If you're constantly on the offensive, they [department officials] back up and keep backing away from you."

All of this takes time. With the community leaders, Belmonte argued, "this doesn't happen overnight. It takes five or six years to learn." Among the city's administrators, too, the talk was in terms of years. However, for those who are willing, the results may prove worth the time spent. City Engineer Krusling says of his involvement with the communities, "Going back fifteen years ago, they did make the job more difficult. I think they have adjusted and we have adjusted, and the end result is now they are making it easier for us to do our job."

ADMINISTRATIVE DISADVANTAGES
IN COMMUNITY INVOLVEMENT

The difficulties of the learning process are not the only disadvantages that accompany community involvement. However, many of the disadvantages often attributed to community involvement have proved illusory or exaggerated in the context of the extensive Cincinnati community involvement, even as some new, but lesser, disadvantages have emerged. Consider, first, the anticipated disadvantages that did not materialize:

1. *Unpleasant antagonism.* Observers sometimes argue that citizen participation is characterized by unpleasant antagonism. As Cupps (1977: 482) notes, "A frequently voiced complaint is the overdramatization, hyperbole, and shrillness with which citizen groups sometimes present their case." Memories of the 1960s suggest how unpleasant and unproductive this can be and why administrators might wish to avoid it entirely.

Those memories also suggest, however, that the disadvantage could be overstated. The unpleasant confrontation politics of the 1970s has greatly moderated, in part because its high emotional level was difficult to maintain. In addition, the Cincinnati experience indicates that unpleasantness often dissipates when citizen participation evolves into government-community negotiation. Few Cincinnati administrators spoke of much unpleasantness in their dealings with the communities, except to recall it from an earlier era. As for the communities, some are now more protective than critical of favorite departments.

2. *Interference with professional judgments.* Administrators sometimes argue that they have been trained to do their work, and community involvement interferes with their professional judgments (Barber, 1981: ix). That interference, assuming the professonal judgments have validity, may distort policies and programs away from the public interest. This is a difficult problem, but it goes beyond the arguments just presented. If the professional prefers one course of action and a neighborhood prefers another, it may not be readily evident whose judgment should prevail. The judgment derived from technical expertise is not necessarily superior to the less educated, but perhaps more representative, judgment of the community.

Cincinnati's administrators have had to face this problem. A Traffic Engineering spokesperson, for example, said that the division makes decisions "from a traffic control standpoint" (i.e., professional criteria), with the result that on citizen requests for new traffic signals, "we probably recommend against a traffic signal nine times for every one we recommend." Some community leaders argue that those decisions are wrong. Who is right?

As that example indicates, these conflicts have not disappeared in Cincinnati, but the evidence does suggest that they have diminished, largely because of changing professional values. Many municipal professions—in areas ranging from housing and development to police protection to highway engineering—now favor incorporation of community opinions into what had previously been exclusively professional decisions. In Cincinnati these changing values are most obvious among the community planners (see also Needleman and Needleman, 1974), but the change can also be seen in an area such as police, where one official describes community involvement as a "necessary adjunct to the patrol effort. The patrol effort can't go anywhere without it." Several other departments, including some with histories of domination by technicians, also appeared to be routinely incorporating community preferences into departmental decisions. As a result, complaints about interference with professional judgments may be less common than they once were.

3. *Increased dollar costs.* Community involvement is also sometimes faulted for increasing dollar costs as a result of program revisions necessary to satisfy the communities. In the words of a Cincinnati administrator, "A problem we usually find is that their involvement costs the city quite a bit of money because they want embellishments that are far beyond the reasonable utility" of the municipal effort.

The only example of embellishments, however, did not appear to support the contention. City Hall proposed to build a firehouse that, as protection against possible attack, would have concealed, barred windows and no foliage surrounding the building. The neighborhood countered by asking for the more aesthetically pleasing exposed windows and surrounding foliage, "embellishments" that did not appear to be expensive. If in fact they were expensive, it may have been because the city's failure to involve the community in the initial planning of the building meant that the community suggestions could be incorporated only as embellishments, rather than as parts of the initial building plan. Equally important is the question of whose design preferences made more sense: those of siege-oriented administrators, fearing attacks from the community, or those of a seemingly hospitable community seeking a structure not greatly at odds with the existing architecture.

4. *Costly delays.* There have also been frequent suggestions that community involvement produces costly delays in both decision making and implementation. Cupps (1977: 482), for one, argues that "citizen groups are using their growing political influence and administrative and legal leverage to create excessive delays—in some cases near paralysis—of the administrative and judicial processes." That complaint may be valid for some forms of citizen participation, but it does not appear to be valid for Cincinnati's community involvement. When asked, only two of the city's administrators—neither one from a department with extensive community involvement—reported any problems with community-induced delays. The reasons for that finding are not hard to guess. With truly participative decision making, the making of decisions may be slowed because more parties are involved, but the implementation

process can be expedited, as already documented, because those parties are more likely to accept whatever decision is reached. The end result may be no more delays than in a traditional decision-making process.

Many of the supposed problems with community involvement, in other words, are greatest when decision making occurs *outside* a participative mode. Problems of antagonism, interference with professional judgments, dollar costs, and delays are likely to diminish when administrators accommodate community involvement within a participative decision-making style. Unfortunately, some new, if lesser, problems then emerge.

1. *Time costs.* Community involvement takes a great deal of time, just as participative decision making always takes more time. Time is obviously necessary for the learning process; few municipal administrators were so well schooled that they could escape much of that time-consuming process. Additional time continues to be necessary after that because there are, as one Cincinnati administrator said, "more bases to touch" and more negotiations to conduct. Even an administrator sympathetic to community involvement could rue this cost: "When you're up here in City Hall at seven o'clock at night trying to work something out, you may wish you didn't have it [community involvement]."

2. *Personnel costs.* The time costs sometimes translate into significant personnel costs. A number of administrators reported that they had been forced either to reassign existing personnel or to hire new personnel in order to accommodate the volume of interaction with neighborhood groups. (It is probably impossible to determine whether these costs exceed the dollar savings that the departments get through community involvement.)

3. *Unreliability.* Neighborhood organizations can be unreliable, given their tendency to fluctuate between feast and famine. That can become a disadvantage for the public administrator if it means that the neighborhood organization that was so helpful last year is nowhere to be found this year. That possibility is especially troubling as neighborhood organizations assume larger roles in service delivery. Cincinnati has seen at least one recreation center's existence threatened because a community council was unable to fulfill its promise to fund and staff the center's day-to-day operation. This problem is not insuperable, but it does demand that cities be cautious about sharing responsibilities with neighborhood groups. (It may, at the same time, help to explain why cities are sometimes willing to finance the maintenance of these groups.)

COMMENT: THE LIMITED ADMINISTRATIVE ADVANTAGE IN COMMUNITY INVOLVEMENT

The new community involvement mechanisms have transformed the process of municipal governance for neighborhood-related issues in Cincinnati. Community councils have been drawn into the governmental process, and, once there, they have joined in the municipal administrative process, frequently becoming an integral part of negotiations on departmental priorities.

It would be too much, however, to credit the mechanisms alone with accomplishing these wide-ranging changes. The changes have depended, in addition, on the presence of the many neighborhood organizations active in Cincinnati and on the continued backing from a City Council political leadership sympathetic to community involvement. Perhaps most important, the moves from politics to administration and from petition to negotiation have hinged on municipal administrators' finding that community involvement could be advantageous for them as well as for the communities. These administrative advantages go a long way toward explaining how community involvement, and the broader reform of reform, have been able to sustain their momentum in Cincinnati.

The advantages should not be exaggerated. They come, after all, only as the outcome of a long learning process and even then not without some accompanying disadvantages. In addition, there may be conditions that affect whether the municipal administrator can enjoy the advantages. In the first place, advantages are likely to predominate over disadvantages only when citizen participation is real; that is, only when the administrator surrenders some decision-making power to community groups. Community involvement without that actually invites many of the disadvantages commonly attributed to citizen participation. Many citizens have distrusted too long to be safely asked now for their opinions unless those opinions will matter.

Second, not every administrator may be suited to this degree of community involvement. Vroom and Yetton (1973: 198) argue that administrators should be flexible, changing their decision-making styles depending on the problem, but Fiedler (1967) may be closer to the truth when he contends that the individual's leadership style is usually not that malleable. Community involvement may require that the individual be more "relationship motivated" than "task motivated" in order to cope with the many relationships required. It may also require skills at negotiation if both neighborhood and city interests are to be accommodated within a single decision. Not every administrator will have these skills or be interested in developing them. In particular, many municipal professionals, trained decades ago to make the best technical decisions, may find it impossible to adjust to a new standard of group-negotiated decisions. Such may be the case with some Cincinnati administrators who expressed distaste for the new community involvement.

Third, not every department will find community involvement more advantageous than disadvantageous. The advantages will ordinarily be greatest for those service areas, described in more detail in Chapter 8, that hold a regular interest for neighborhood groups. Seeing the groups frequently, these departments can justify special efforts to learn whom the groups represent and how to deal with them. On the other hand, where interactions are infrequent, administrators may not find a net advantage in making those efforts. These administrators may be further deterred if, as in Cincinnati, they are the same administrators who favor the traditional technical, public interest approach to decision making.

In the end, however, there remains the compelling finding that Cincinnati's municipal administrators more often found community involvement advantageous than disadvantageous. That involvement would consequently seem to warrant a considerably better reputation than it has traditionally enjoyed among public administrators.

8

Issues:
The Pursuit of Neighborhood
Goals in Government

Cincinnati's community councils are a diverse lot, varying greatly in origins, types of members, and levels of resources. Nowhere is the diversity more pronounced than in the issues that drive the councils. Consider the responses of three council leaders when asked about the current primary concerns of their organizations:

> For a predominantly black, lower-class area: "Accessibility to services—being able to go shopping without having to drive two miles."

> For an upper-middle-class white area: "The critical issue—zoning. While that has been successfully fought for decades, there is still a tremendous amount of pressure from commercial and business interests to expand the business district in _____."

> For an older neighborhood, demographically similar to the city as a whole: "The most serious issue is still the Colerain expressway issue. That really was an issue which organized this community almost overnight. It is still not resolved."

The diversity does not end there, either. Other leaders mentioned such concerns as preventing a school closing, improving rat control, getting better recreational facilities, slowing displacement of traditional residents, getting a deepwater swimming pool, and changing police handgun policies.

Amid this diversity there is one striking commonality: Almost all of the concerns find the community councils looking to government for assistance—in developing a neighborhood business district (to improve "accessibility to services"), in maintaining residential zoning status (for protection from "commercial and business interests"), and in changing highway construction plans (to resolve the "expressway issue"). In fact, of all the concerns

106

mentioned by fourteen council leaders, only a few did not directly involve government.[1]

This chapter examines this pursuit of neighborhood goals in government. Drawing on newspaper accounts and interviews with community council leaders and municipal officials, the chapter describes the principal substantive issues that concern the community councils, explores how those issues are pursued relative to the forms of governmental involvement described in Chapter 7, and considers which councils are most involved with which issues and why.

PROTECTING THE RESIDENTIAL STATUS QUO

The issues with the longest history among Cincinnati's community councils are those based on perceived threats to the residential status quo. Periodically over the history of the councils, one or another of them has voiced a concern that the neighborhood's current residential nature is threatened, as by some planned physical development. Often City Hall is then asked to intervene to block the development.

The issues. These issues reflect some of the best and the worst aspects of the neighborhood movement. With issues of possible racial change, for example, the best may be evident in the neighborhood efforts to stop "blockbusting" by unethical realtors, whereas the worst can be seen in those neighborhoods that resist integration by saying, as Delmos Jones (1979) paraphrased in his critique of the movement, "Not in my community!" Both aspects are evident in Cincinnati. The best-known versions of these issues came out of the extensive racial migration and urban renewal the city experienced during the 1950s and 1960s, but these issues have contemporary relevance, too. The concern noted earlier about a proposed expressway development, for example, is no different from the concerns that prompted complaints from such neighborhoods as Clifton and the East End in the 1960s.

However, with the slowing of racial change and traditional urban renewal in Cincinnati, the changes that are now perceived as threats to the residential status quo often differ in substance from their predecessors of the 1950s and 1960s. Proposals for public housing, for example, have become a much more common basis for perceiving threats. As early as 1971, residents of the blue-collar neighborhoods of South Fairmount and Price Hill "came en masse, carrying homemade posters," to a City Council hearing to protest the proposed construction of fifty-one units of public housing in their neighborhoods (*Cincinnati Enquirer,* 1971b). A decade later, the prosperous neighborhood of Mt. Washington went on record as opposing a similar plan to construct fifty units of low-income housing inside its boundaries (*Cincinnati Enquirer,* 1981a), with neighborhood leaders voicing fears of "an increasingly transient population.'' Proposals for other types of special residential facilities are also commonly perceived as threats (see Wolch, 1982). Residents of the Hartwell neighborhood objected in 1980 to a plan to place minimum-security prisoners in a section of an area hospital. Around the same time, residents of Hyde Park questioned a plan to place a home for the mentally retarded in their area.

Issues of this kind also frequently grow out of the conflict of residential and commercial interests, as commercial development proposals often arouse opposition from neighborhood residents. Some Hartwell residents, for example, organized in the summer of 1980 to fight a Kroger Company proposal to build a ''mammoth superstore'' in the neighborhood (*Cincinnati Enquirer,* 1980f).

Governmental involvement. Community councils usually approach these issues through petitioning: Neighborhood residents come as a group to a public forum to request a governmental veto of the threatened development. The neighborhood's involvement with government is likely then to be brief, lasting only until the issue has been resolved by a public decision.

Petitioning remains a popular tactic, despite the alternative approaches now available to the community councils, for several reasons. First, it is the only tactic available to challenge the many development projects, especially those planned by most private developers, that continue to be designed without any solicitation of community opinions. Second, even when community opinions are solicited, a community council may prefer petitioning as requiring less time and less sophistication than negotiation. Third, petitioning can be very effective when, as often with concerns for protecting the residential status quo, success requires only a one-time governmental veto. Local officials will only reluctantly ignore the intense public opposition represented by the petitioning of a vocal and unified neighborhood group; and it may take only one ''no'' along the way to stop the proposed development.

Petitions in Cincinnati have many different targets. The most frequent initial target may be the Planning Commission, as it is the body that reviews requests for zoning changes, but many other departments are also targeted. In some cases the petitions go first to licensing bodies, as on questions about liquor licenses. In the summer of 1980, for example, the Oakley Resident's Association considered ''the liquor license route'' in an effort to close a bar after a shooting (*Eastern Hills Journal,* 1980a); in neighboring Madisonville the Coordinating Committee objected to the granting of a new liquor license to a restaurant (*Eastern Hills Journal,* 1980b).

Whatever the initial target of petitions, the most common eventual target may be the City Council. The council must make the final decisions on zoning questions; it is where unsuccessful petitions to municipal departments can be appealed; and it has the original jurisdiction on liquor license issues, with the Human Resources Committee recommending to the state board. Indeed, petitioning probably has become a larger component of City Council involvement with the neighborhoods now that minor service complaints from the communities are most often communicated directly to the relevant departments.

Which neighborhoods? A sense of which neighborhoods are most involved in the petitioning issues can thus be gained by examining community involvement with City Council. Evidence on this involvement came from two council members, a Democrat and a Republican. Working from a list of all the community councils, each indicated which councils had contacted it over the previous twelve months, and one of the two also indicated which councils had been the most active during that period. Combining their responses produced this distribution of activity level for the 47 councils: no activity, 8.5 percent (4 community councils); low activity, 23.4 percent (11); moderate activity, 59.6 percent (28); and high activity, 8.5 percent (4).

Judging from its correlates, this involvement has its principal roots in the communities and the councils. In part, the neighborhoods most involved with City Council are those with the most to protect; that is, those in areas with higher median incomes ($r = .197$), higher home values ($r = .146$), and higher proportions of professionals ($r = .176$). Larger populations are also linked to this involvement ($r = .311$). The factors that can best explain the involvement, however, are the resources of the council themselves. Councils with higher memberships ($r = .428$) and, even more so, greater organizational complexity are the most involved with City Council. As shown in Table 8.1, this involvement rises steadily as organizational complexity increases (gamma = .563).

Still, as the six cases in the lower left-hand corner of Table 8.1 indicate, this involvement does not always require a stable base of organizational resources. These six councils were able to generate relatively high involvement despite low organizational complexity. The reason in each case was an issue sufficiently "hot" to mobilize neighborhood residents, at least temporarily, around this time. Sayler Park mobilized to fight—successfully—a grain-processing plant proposed for the neighborhood. Fay Apartments mobilized around its conversion into a cooperative, a conversion that became a reality that year. The remaining four neighborhoods—Lower Price Hill, Riverside, South Fairmount, and Columbia-Tusculum—had been tentatively designated for "triage" in a controversial classification drafted in City Hall two years earlier.[2] That ranking, as it could have limited community development funding for these areas as a result of the "severe poverty and blight with questionable viability" (*Cincinnati Enquirer*, 1978a, 1978b), gave the neighborhoods a basis for mobilization and involvement with City Council. The clear lesson here is that the right issue can catalyze neighborhood political involvement despite previous lack of organizational resources.

TABLE 8.1
ORGANIZATIONAL COMPLEXITY AND
COMMUNITY COUNCIL POLITICAL ACTIVITY

Political Activity Rating	Level of Organizational Complexity		
	0–.50	.75–1.25	1.50–2.25
0	23% (3)	0% (0)	6% (1)
1	31 (4)	40 (6)	6 (1)
2	46 (6)	53 (8)	69 (11)
3	0 (0)	7 (1)	19 (3)
Totals	100 (13)	100 (15)	100 (16)
		gamma = .563[a]	

[a] Significant at .01 level.

These six cases also reveal that involvement with City Council is not always designed to maintain the residential status quo. Of the six, only Sayler Park acted from such a motivation. The other five were seeking *changes,* such as increased CDBG funding. When the lowest of the low-income communities become involved with City Council, in other words, they may understandably be interested in something other than preserving the status quo.

CORRECTING SERVICE DELIVERY PROBLEMS

While never abandoning their concerns for preventing negative changes, Cincinnati's community councils have gradually developed new interests in creating *positive* change. In many cases, that has meant giving priority to service delivery problems, as councils perform service casework much as congressional representatives do for their constituents.

The channeling of service interests to community councils. This is not a role that all community councils have adopted equally. In most neighborhoods residents may prefer to communicate directly with the relevant public agency on service problems (e.g., Thomas, 1982). Community councils are drawn into the intermediary role on these problems only in certain neighborhoods, particularly those with large black populations and a history of involvement in the federal Community Action Program. As earlier chapters have suggested, blacks may prefer not to approach government directly on service issues, and Community Action may have encouraged directing those issues to neighborhood organizations.

These tendencies can be seen in Cincinnati in the responses of forty-four community council leaders to questions about their organizations' interest in various municipal services. Summing and averaging the responses across the ten services provided an average interest level for each council, an indicator of the extent to which service interests are communicated to the councils. The neighborhood's black proportion is the strongest predictor of this channeling of service interests (see Table 8.2), both in all the communities (r = .523) and in the low-income communities only (r = .753). The OEO involvement is also an important factor as the second strongest predictor of service interests (r = .412) in the sixteen low-income communities. The other intriguing finding involves several community characteristics that do *not* affect service interests. The objective needs of a community are not much of a factor, for one thing. Persons per household is a factor in the overall regression, suggesting that having dependent children—the primary basis for more persons in a household—increases the need for or interest in municipal services. Otherwise, however, percentage vacant is uncorrelated and percentage poor only modestly correlated (r = .288) with these interests. Moreover, the latter correlation essentially disappears in the regression for all communities and actually achieves an *inverse* significance—service interests increasing as objective needs decrease—in the regression on low-income communities only. In other words, greater objective needs lead to more communication of needs to community councils only when combined with the special inclination of blacks or the encouragement of Community Action.

Finally, neither the membership nor the organizational complexity of a community council helps to explain the level of service interests. This underscores the significance of Community Action by demonstrating that of all the organizational resources, only the Community Action resources stimulate the channeling of service interests to community councils.

Governmental involvement. Given that correcting service problems requires positive action by City Hall, petitioning is not the best approach for solving the problems. Petitioning can be more effective when the goal is *no* action. On the other hand, considering the desired changes are usually focused and limited, negotiating is seldom either necessary or desirable on these problems. What is desirable instead is a middle course more conciliatory than petitioning suggests but less involved than negotiating suggests.

The targets of these service concerns tend to be functional city administrators, especially now that the councils mostly communicate directly with departments. Not all municipal departments are involved equally, however, because some services are less subject to the kinds of problems that might be pursued through community councils. With water problems, for example, as Water Works official Denny Davis explained, "If there's a water taste or odor problem, it's something you deal with directly. You don't take it to your community council at its next monthly meeting."

TABLE 8.2
SOURCES OF INTEREST IN MUNICIPAL SERVICES

Community	Relationship to Interests[a]		
and Council	Zero-Order	Standardized Regression Coefficients	
Characteristics	Correlation	All Communities	Low-Income
Percentage black	.523[b]	.523[b]	.753[b]
Persons/household	.261[c]	.276[c]	
Population	.029		
Percentage poor	.228		− .353[c]
Percentage vacant	.013		
Council membership	.009		
Organizational complexity	− .174		
OEO involvement	.458[b]		.412[c]
R^2		.350	.767
Adjusted R^2		.316	.709
N		42	16

[a] One leader from each council was asked in 1979 to rate council interest levels (high, moderate, or low) in each of ten municipal service areas. Responses were averaged for each leader across the ten areas (or however many areas the leader responded to) to create this measure.
[b] Significant at .01 level.
[c] Significant at .05 level.

The departments that are often targeted in this service casework deliver services with a neighborhood-level focus and with a greater potential for problems. In Cincinnati, according to department officials, those departments and the corresponding problems include the following:

1. Health: "environmental problems," including rats, lack of property maintenance
2. Engineering: street rehabilitation, storm drainage, landslides
3. Waste: "refuse problems, dead animal pickups," etc.
4. Highway Maintenance: "routine maintenance," such as pothole repair and snow removal
5. Traffic Engineering: problems with traffic control or street lighting
6. Buildings and Inspections: building code violations

These casework issues were also the most prominent of the casework issues mentioned by community council leaders in their listings of the principal current concerns of the councils.

Which neighborhoods? Evidence on which community councils are most active in seeking service assistance comes from officials in four of these areas, all four being areas in which service casework was reported to be the primary basis for community contacts: the Department of Health and the Public Works divisions of Engineering, Waste Collection, and Highway Maintenance. Reports from these officials on which councils had contacted them during the past year were combined to create a single measure of contacts for service assistance, producing this distribution: 2 percent (1 council) had contacted no division; 32 percent (15 councils) had contacted one division; 28 percent (13), two divisions; 30 percent (14), three divisions; and 9 percent (4), four divisions.

Community council involvement in service assistance, unlike the earlier involvement with City Council, has its roots more in government than in the communities. The primary factor in this involvement, as shown in Table 8.3, is a community's experience with the War on Poverty ($r = .493$). The Community Action and Model Cities experiences apparently induced neighborhood organizations to take on service casework, just as they also encouraged residents to channel their service interests to neighborhood organizations.

TABLE 8.3
SOURCES OF CONTACTS FOR SERVICE ASSISTANCE[a]

Community and Council Characteristics	Relationship to Department Contacts	
	Zero-Order Correlation	Standardized Regression Coefficient
Percentage black	.203	
Persons/household	.205	
Population	− .136	
Percentage poor	.431[b]	
Percentage vacant	.453[b]	.317[c]
Council membership	− .146	
Organizational complexity	.009	
OEO involvement	.493[b]	.493[b]
R^2		.331
Adjusted R^2		.299
N	45	45

[a] Service assistance is defined as councils' contacts with the Department of Health and the divisions of Engineering, Waste Collection, and Highway Maintenance, as reported by municipal officials in those areas.

[b] Significant at .01 level.

[c] Significant at .05 level.

Percentage vacant, the secondary factor in this service assistance involvement, probably also reflects a governmental influence. This factor might suggest that greater community need results in more council involvement in service assistance. That explanation seems unlikely, however, given that greater need did not appear earlier to prompt more channeling of service interests to the councils. It seems more likely that greater need, as evidenced by higher vacancy rates, has prompted more contacting of communities *by* the departments. These departments have initiated some service assistance in the communities, principally through the public-works-oriented Neighborhood Improvement Program, and that assistance has usually focused on neighborhoods with greater needs.[3] In short, community council involvement in service assistance appears to be principally a governmental creation.

From advocacy to service assistance? These findings suggest a variant on Marilyn Gittell's (1980) contention that neighborhood organizations in low-income areas have become too concerned with delivering social services to the neglect of broader advocacy. As such, that does not appear to be a problem in Cincinnati, as council leaders mentioned the delivery of social services (e.g., day care, services for senior citizens, recreational programs) as no more than a secondary function for their organizations. What could be a problem, however, is this emphasis in low-income areas on getting assistance for minor service problems. That emphasis could result in these councils' neglecting the broader programmatic concerns that have a greater potential for improving the neighborhood quality of life. These councils could be ineffective, in other words, because of *what* they choose to advocate for, rather than because of any general failure to advocate. The problem may well extend beyond Cincinnati (see White, 1981).

On the other hand, the inclination toward service casework may not be as counterproductive as that argument suggests. For one thing, as will be seen shortly, service casework has not kept low-income areas in Cincinnati from also pursuing broader municipal and federal spending programs. Nor do these areas appear to be squandering organizational resources on service casework. The councils that take on more casework usually have no better than average organizational resources to begin with, and some of those resources are attributable to federal OEO assistance.

Finally, what resources these councils do expend on service casework may be justified by the desires of neighborhood residents. Black residents, at least, appear in these neighborhoods to bring more of their service needs to community councils. The councils, in performing this casework, may thus be achieving the goal of many recent reforms—to provide channels of communication between alienated citizens and their insulated, professionalized governments.

REDEVELOPING THE NEIGHBORHOOD

It is, however, the broader programmatic concerns that have moved to the forefront of community council concerns in recent years. The councils have become particularly interested in programs that can help in redeveloping neighborhoods. The reasons for this new interest are many. To begin with, the inevitable decline of many urban neighborhoods, accompanied by the escalating costs of moving to suburbs, has increased residents' interest in developing the home neighborhood. The outcome of the Kroger superstore conflict in Hartwell is illustrative. Even as some residents were objecting to Kroger's proposal, the Hartwell Improvement Association, the area's community council, voted 409 to 75 in an open meeting to endorse the plan (*Cincinnati Enquirer*, 1980g). The vast majority of residents of this blue-collar community apparently supported commercial development, where history might have predicted unified residential opposition instead.

Redeveloping the neighborhood has also gained salience from the actions of government. The issue probably got its biggest boost in 1974 when the federal government passed the CDBG program, making substantial funds available for neighborhood development. With City Hall still feeling favorably inclined toward the neighborhoods in the aftermath of the Charter-Democratic electoral success of 1971, Cincinnati's share of those funds was soon available to the community councils, giving them a strong incentive to think more seriously about redeveloping their home areas (e.g., Woods, Andersen, and Grober, 1979). Other federal legislation—making the preservation of designated historical districts eligible for favorable tax treatment, for example—only added to these incentives.

Varieties of neighborhood development. The contemporary interest in neighborhood development goes well beyond a traditional limited concern for commercial development to encompass recreational facilities and housing and housing rehabilitation as well. Recreational facilities may actually have been the first of these areas to interest the neighborhoods in recent times. Recreation officials date the interest to the 1960s, when poverty programs elicited requests from low-income neighborhoods for recreation centers and deep-water pools, items that eventually became principal uses for CDBG spending.

Housing and housing rehabilitation soon interested the neighborhoods, too. Many community councils or related nonprofit development corporations now use CDBG grants or low-interest loans to rehabilitate homes for resale. Other councils pursue housing rehabilitation by seeking historic district designation, the tax advantages of which encourage the desired improvements without any direct CDBG funding. The historic Columbia-Tusculum neighborhood on Cincinnati's East Side, for example, achieved historic district designation through community council lobbying in the late 1970s and had become a home for the new gentry by the early 1980s.

Finally, commercial development remains an important component of neighborhood development in the city. Hartwell is only one of numerous Cincinnati neighborhoods to show a contemporary interest in local commercial revitalization. Other interested communities include low- to moderate-income areas such as Avondale and Madisonville, areas eligible for substantial CDBG funding, and relatively prosperous areas such as College Hill and Kennedy Heights, which may receive other kinds of municipal assistance.

Governmental involvement. On these issues more than any of the others, success is likely to require that neighborhoods work cooperatively with government. Where a confrontational approach may be effective in preventing change, cooperation is usually more effective in promoting development. A cooperative approach becomes all the more desirable when, as frequently on these issues, any of several actors could veto a proposed change. A CDBG-funded neighborhood program, for example, could conceivably be vetoed by the target neighborhood, the relevant municipal department, the Community Development Advisory Council, the City Council, or perhaps even the federal government.

As a consequence, neighborhood involvement with government on issues of redevelopment often means negotiations between the community councils and City Hall, with the key City Hall actors usually being administrators in the Departments of Housing, Development, and Recreation. Negotiations may be able to produce a package upon which all actors can agree, the community councils then gaining substantial outside dollars to use in improving neighborhoods, while City Hall gains neighborhood assistance for such diverse tasks as the required public hearing, reviews by the CDAC, and project implementation.

Which neighborhoods? An indication of which community councils are most involved with these issues was sought by asking the key administrators which neighborhood groups they had worked with over the previous twelve months. Officials from the Housing and Development divisions provided this information. (Recreation officials said they had worked with all forty-seven, and declined to say which they had dealt with most actively.) Combining their responses produced this distribution: worked with neither division, 11 percent (5 councils); worked with one division, 47 percent (22); and worked with both divisions, 43 percent (20). These responses do not, of course, indicate which neighborhoods have *benefited* most from these divisions, but they do suggest which councils are more active.

Given the complex origins of the neighborhood development issues, involvement with these departments might be expected to reflect both community and governmental influences. This is, in fact, the case. The strongest influence comes from the communities, particularly from the councils themselves. Council organizational complexity ($r = .422$) and membership ($r = .322$) are more strongly related to interactions with these administrators than are any other factors, including such community demographics as percentage poor ($r = .143$), percentage commercial ($r = .288$), percentage professional ($r = .013$), and population ($r = .154$).

The governmental influence comes from the federal level and operates through the CDBG eligibility requirements. City Hall in Cincinnati, following the Carter administration regulations in effect in 1980, limited eligibility for primary CDBG spending to neighborhoods with low- and moderate-income populations (i.e., neighborhoods with average incomes of less than 80 percent of the metropolitan average). As indicated in Table 8.4, that eligibility figures prominently in whether community councils were willing to devote their organizational resources to working with Housing and Development officials. Interactions with these officials increase much more rapidly with organizational complexity in areas *eligible* for primary CDBG spending (gamma = .843) than in areas *not* eligible for that spending (gamma = .390). In other words, where federal standards dictate the greatest potential return, community councils are more willing to devote their resources to working with city officials.

TABLE 8.4
COMMUNITY COUNCIL INVOLVEMENT WITH
HOUSING AND DEVELOPMENT

Divisions Worked With	Level of Organizational Complexity		
	0–.50	.75–1.25	1.50–2.25
	Eligible Areas[a]		
0	33%(3)	0%(0)	0%(0)
1	56 (5)	17 (1)	20 (1)
2	11 (1)	83 (5)	80 (4)
Totals	100 (9)	100 (6)	100 (5)
		gamma = .843	
	Ineligible Areas		
0	0%(0)	22%(2)	0% (0)
1	100 (4)	33 (3)	55 (6)
2	0 (0)	44 (4)	45 (5)
Totals	100 (4)	99 (9)	100 (11)
		gamma = .390	

[a] "Eligible" areas are those that have 50 percent or more of two or more person households with income at less than 80 percent of the SMSA average. Neighborhood designations were obtained from the City of Cincinnati (Planning Commission, 1981).

Municipal preferences do not appear to have affected these interactions. Cities supposedly favor economically productive areas because of the potential gains for the municipal treasury (Peterson, 1981: 41). There is no evidence, however, that prosperous or commercial neighborhoods are significantly more involved in these interactions. Nor is there any evidence that the interactions favor "deteriorated but viable" areas, as could have occurred if municipal developmental preferences were compromised with federal redistributive preferences.[4]

Other actors. As neighborhood development issues have grown in salience, they have interested increasing numbers of actors. The private sector has become interested, perhaps recognizing that private development plans are no longer easily imposed on neighborhoods. In the Hartwell case, for example, rather than attempting to force a store on the community, Kroger offered "hundreds of thousands of dollars in new and expanded recreation equipment to the neighborhood in exchange for the community's support of the store" (*Cincinnati Enquirer*, 1980g).

City Council, too, has become an important actor in neighborhood development issues, serving particularly as an appeals body when neighborhoods or departments are dissatisfied with their CDBG standing. Use of the council in this manner was evident, for example, by the communities that protested their possible triage designation (that designation having been suggested as a basis for allocating CDBG funds). There is also the evidence that interactions with City Council members, like interactions with neighborhood development officials, increase somewhat more rapidly with organizational complexity in areas eligible for primary CDBG spending (gamma = .639) than in areas not eligible for that spending (gamma = .489). CDBG eligibility presumably makes community councils more willing to devote their organizational resources to appealing CDAC recommendations to City Council because the potential gains from a successful appeal are so great. What all this may mean, in the end, is that redeveloping the neighborhood is now the most important concern of Cincinnati's community councils.

DEFINING THE COMMUNITY
AND MAINTAINING THE ORGANIZATION

The community councils also face some concerns that traditionally have impinged little on the public sector. At least occasionally councils must be concerned with defining the community's sense of identity. One council leader said that his group's primary concern in 1980 was "a sense of unity insofar as we're a different community because there's a lot of rental property." The councils must also be concerned, given their historically high mortality rates, with maintaining the organizations themselves. The slow times in the life of a neighborhood organization carry too much risk, as this comment from the leader of a recently gentrified Cincinnati neighborhood suggests: "The job has basically been done. Success is here. In the success you lose some of that need for struggle. With the success comes fewer problems, fewer problems to tackle and to solve. I would say that's our biggest problem. We've been too successful."

These concerns for the community and the organization result in a variety of social, communication, and organizational maintenance efforts. The social activities include neigborhood festivals, block parties, neighborhood dinners, and sponsorship of special groups (e.g., youth groups); communication efforts are exemplified by the monthly newsletters published by many councils; organizational maintenance efforts range from membership drives to fund-raising efforts to staff development programs. Each activity does not necessarily correspond to a specific purpose, however. The monthly membership meetings held by most of the councils, for example, commonly serve several purposes at once (e.g., communication, organizational maintenance).

These activities may get more attention from some councils than from others. There is evidence of some councils' adopting a more pronounced social orientation, or at least a lower governmental profile. Cincinnati's traditional civic associations of pre-1956 vintage were often described as predominantly social in orientation and also scored low on most forms of governmental involvement examined in this chapter. That should not be surprising considering that these groups represent relatively prosperous and stable areas less likely to need a neighborhood organization except for social purposes.

The councils vary, too, in the time they give to organizational mainte-nance. That time was estimated using information the councils reported to City Hall in 1980 on activities in areas designated "neighborhood," "school and community," and "community council related," the last corresponding roughly to organizational maintenance activities. Taking the number of those activities as a proportion of the total number of activities provides a crude measure of the proportion of organizational time given to organizational maintenance. Judging from that measure, the councils averaged 41.5 percent of their time on organizational maintenance in 1980, but with a range from 15 to 70 percent.[5]

The principal reason for those variations appears to be the level of council resources, fewer resources resulting in more attention to organizational maintenance (see also Rich, 1980a). Lower membership levels in particular appear to prompt more efforts of this kind, presumably because council legitimacy rests ultimately on membership. This pattern is evident to only a limited extent across the full set of community councils in which organizational maintenance efforts are only a weak inverse function of council membership $(r = -.277)$. Among the dues-based councils for which the meaning of organizational resources is clearer, however, the time given to maintenance is a strong inverse function of membership levels ($r = -.502$, significant at the .01 level for twenty-six cases). No other council or community characteristic is as strongly linked to these maintenance efforts.[6]

The final notable aspect of these organizational and community activities is their relatively recent public side. By the early 1980s, the community councils had tapped into CDBG funding for the Neighborhood Support Program funding of basic organizational tasks and were still receiving Mott Foundation funding through City Hall for similar tasks. This private side of the councils, as with all their other concerns, had become intertwined with the public sector.

COMMENT: THE QUASI-GOVERNMENTAL NEIGHBORHOOD ORGANIZATION

Any notion of the neighborhood organization as private and parochial, concerned only with the home neighborhood, by now should be dispelled. Problems and opportunities facing the home neighborhood are mostly what concern Cincinnati's community councils, but those problems and opportunities in almost all cases find the councils going outside neighborhood boundaries in search of governmental assistance.

This may not always have been so. The issues that bring community councils to government have arisen mostly in recent decades, rather than being traditional concerns of the councils. The new issues began with Cincinnati's racial and physical transformation of the 1950s and 1960s, which prompted many neighborhoods to petition government for help in preserving the residential status quo.

Concerns for the residential status quo have remained salient into the 1980s, but they have declined in relative importance as neighborhoods have become more interested in other government-related issues. Low-income neighborhoods, for example, became concerned with municipal service delivery problems. The growth of services has increased the potential for problems, and the coming of the service-oriented Community Action Program encouraged the channeling of those problems to neighborhood organizations, particularly by blacks who distrusted other channels for communicating with government. Most recently, Cincinnati's community councils have become concerned with issues of neighborhood redevelopment, the current primary interest of the councils. These issues arose both because residents became more concerned about upgrading their home communities and because federal funds became available for that upgrading.

It is these latter issues that have most conspicuously involved neighborhoods in a new kind of relationship with City Hall, where negotiating has often supplanted the once dominant petitioning approach. The negotiations sometimes even involve businesses as many contemporary community councils have become allies of commercial development in neighborhoods. What has changed, according to one long-time neighborhood leader, is that neighborhood groups are now saying, "What's good for the neigbhorhood is good for business," where a quarter-century ago, civic associations were saying, "What's good for business is good for the neighborhoods." In practice, that means a broader definition of neighborhood development to include housing and recreational improvements, as well as economic development.

The community councils have not entirely forsaken the parochial neighborhood issues once thought to be their primary concerns. Many council leaders still express traditional concerns for a sense of community, for sociability, and for maintaining their organizations. Even in these instances, however, government is never far from the minds of the community leaders now that public funding is available for addressing these concerns.

The reasons behind the new government-related neighborhood issues are complex. The neighborhoods have often raised the new issues themselves, perhaps reflecting perceptions of greater needs in the neighborhoods. The city's community involvement mechanisms have also been important by encouraging communities to raise issues in government.

At least equal to these in importance, however, is the federal role. The federal government, like City Hall, has provided mechanisms for channeling neighborhood issues to government, as especially through Community Action. Probably more important, the federal government, through its CDBG funding, has underwritten the new neighborhood redevelopment concerns. Without the gains potentially available from those funds, the neighborhoods might still be keeping most of their issues at home, perhaps letting them go unattended. The federal role also helps to explain why involvement with City Hall on these issues is not much biased by community socioeconomic status. Early federal aid through the War on Poverty increased the resources of many councils in low-income areas, thereby permitting more involvement with City Hall than indigenous community resources could have supported. More recent CDBG assistance has offered additional incentives to those same councils, encouraging their continued involvement with government. As a consequence, the usual bias of involvement with City Hall by *council* resources does not translate to much bias by *community* resources.

With the new City Hall involvements and the new government-focused issues, community councils now resemble quasi-governmental organizations more than traditional voluntary social groups. They lack the authority to be fully governmental, but they could be quasi-governmental in that they exist primarily to influence or work with government. As one community council leader said, "We provide a conduit to City Hall for things to happen." These councils may consequentiy be closer to what Kettl (1981b) has termed "the fourth face of federalism" than to Reagan's hoped-for "voluntarism."

9

Private Interests: Can Neighborhoods Compete in Municipal Politics?

Involvement need not mean influence. In the case of Cincinnati's community councils, the expanded involvement in municipal affairs could conceivably disguise continued political impotence. The resources of the councils, although greater than in times past, might still be too limited for the groups to compete effectively against other powerful urban political actors (see Jones, 1981; Crenson, 1983: 294). The increased neighborhood involvement might even be only ritual participation created by government in an effort to placate neighborhood groups without really responding to their substantive concerns (e.g., Hunter, 1979).

Most of the important actors in Cincinnati do not believe this is the case. In the judgment of most City Council members and municipal administrators, the community councils now exert significant influence over many municipal decisions. Perhaps more important, the community leaders also think they are influential. Almost all fourteen council leaders interviewed in 1980 argued that City Hall had become more responsive to their communities as the result of the increased neighborhood involvement in municipal affairs. Resolving the issue of influence requires a much more rigorous test than this simple show of hands, however. This chapter attempts to provide that test using data on the recent allocations of a number of grants-related programs in Cincinnati. For a number of reasons, these programs promise an excellent test of possible neighborhood clout.

GRANTSMANSHIP AND COMMUNITY CLOUT

Cincinnati's community councils have been interested in grantsmanship since federal and foundation grant programs began to proliferate in the 1960s. The inherent resource problems of neighborhood organizations have forced them always to be on the lookout for additional funding. The wisdom of seeking that funding from grants became increasingly obvious as the grants themselves became more available. The councils have many other interests, as Chapter 8 demonstrated, but it is success in getting grants, rather than in any other endeavors, that the councils value most highly. When asked to list their groups' most significant accomplishments, only a minority of the fourteen council leaders mentioned anything other than grants or grants-funded programs.

This interest is what initially suggests grants as a possible area for testing neighborhood influence; that is, influence can be most fairly tested when an interest in being influential exists. Grants also satisfy the second essential condition for a good test of this influence. As Bachelor and Jones (1981) argue, a show of significant neighborhood influence requires significant stakes to begin with because any influence over trivial stakes could itself be characterized as trivial. The stakes in the grants competition in Cincinnati clearly are not trivial.

Significant stakes are most obvious in the CDBG competition, which is also the grants competition of greatest interest to the community councils. Cincinnati's CDBG allotment averaged over $16 million per year during the 1975–81 period, constituting more than 10 percent of annual total municipal revenues during the period and an even larger proportion of discretionary municipal revenues. The relatively short history of CDBG allocations left them minimally constrained by the past; as a result, a large discretionary component was "up for grabs" each year. The discretionary component of most other municipal spending, by contrast, is limited because earlier decisions—on where to locate fire stations and parks, for example—dictate where so much of the contemporary spending must be directed (see Mladenka, 1980).

Significant allocations. Neighborhood influence in this grants competition requires, first, that the outcomes include substantial allocations for the neighborhoods. The neighborhood share of the significant stakes must itself be significant, in other words. The fourteen council leaders provided the initial evidence on this score when they reported that every one of their councils or neighborhoods had received at least one grant during the 1979–80 period. Fifteen different grant sources were mentioned, some of which were tapped by most or all of the neighborhoods.

The largest funding for the neighborhoods has come through functional grants, which pay the neighborhood or neighborhood organization—usually with CDBG funding—to perform some task (e.g., community development, provision of a social service). Community council success in this phase of grantsmanship is suggested, for one thing, by the fact that almost three-fifths of the city's 1974–78 CDBG funding, or $26.7 million, went to the residential neighborhoods. Only $18.7 million went elsewhere—to projects not allocable by neighborhood or to industrial-commercial projects (City of Cincinnati, Department of Community Development, 1978).[1]

The neighborhoods have received other functional grants, including these that one or more of the council leaders reported for the period around 1980:

1. Urban Mass Transit Administration (for community transportation studies)
2. Law Enforcement Assistance Administration (various programs)
3. Health, Education and Welfare (for community health clinics)
4. Older Americans Act (for senior citizens services centers)

The list might also include the designation of some neighborhoods as Historic Preservation Districts, as that designation amounts to a "tax subsidy," a grant-like tax benefit (Rodgers, 1978).

The community councils have also received organizational grants, under which funds are directed to forming or maintaining a neighborhood organization, rather than paying the organization to pursue some other end. Cincinnati's neighborhood leaders claim as their principal successes in this area of grantsmanship *(a)* the awarding of the Mott Foundation five-year SNAP grant and *(b)* the municipal funding through CDBG of the Neighborhood Support Program. Lesser successes may be evident in these other organizational grants reported by the fourteen council leaders:

1. CDBG (pre-NSP funding for community support workers in a few neighborhoods)
2. Community Action Commission/Community Services Administration (funding for staff for councils in some low-income areas)
3. Comprehensive Employment and Training Act (funding to hire the unemployed as council staff)
4. Urban Appalachian Council (partial funding for a community support worker)
5. Jergens Foundation (partial funding for a community support worker)
6. Community Chest (partial funding for a community support worker)

A role for neighborhood preferences. However impressive, this chronicle of grants still does not establish that the community councils have influenced the grants allocations. The councils might simply be taking credit for grants that came to neighborhoods on the basis of the preferences of other actors, such as the federal government or City Hall. Indeed, the grants could reflect more how government influences neighborhoods than how neighborhoods influence government. As Albert Hunter (1979: 278-79) argues, "Agencies, for the most part, do not deal with *the* neighborhood; rather, they create and maintain specialized neighborhood interest groups. This creation of a neighborhood clientele provides agencies with local support and legitimacy, at the same time providing potential co-optation of local leaders." This possibility can be ruled out only if, as the final piece of evidence necessary to establish neighborhood influence, community council preferences can be shown to have influenced how the grants were allocated. Those preferences need not be controlling, but they must be a significant factor in an allocational process in which several different preferences may be in competition.

1. Developmental (municipal): As Peterson (1981) has explained, the interests of cities lead them ordinarily to favor developmental policies, policies that promote the interests of economically well-off city residents and businesses. If this preference prevails, allocations might favor areas with *(a)* more commercial units and/or *(b)* more residents of higher socioeconomic status.

2. Redistributive (federal): By contrast, redistribution means that those in greater need are targeted either for humanitarian reasons or to co-opt them as a constituency (e.g., Mollenkopf, 1983). This was the federal preference through much of the 1960s and 1970s, the relevant years for the grants at issue here. If this preference is influential, more funding should go to areas with such characteristics as *(a)* lower incomes, *(b)* larger black populations, *(c)* lower home values, and/or *(d)* higher vacancy rates.

3. Triage (federal/municipal): When local developmental preferences conflict with a federal redistributive preference, cities sometimes seek the middle ground of a triage strategy; money is redistributed only to those needy areas that seem to have the greatest potential to improve (see, for example, Downs, 1981: 156–58). This strategy gets its name from the fact that the worst communities are designated for triage (i.e., minimal or no assistance) as too far deteriorated to be helped much by the available funding. Although Cincinnati has never had an official triage policy, one city administrator did draft a classification of the communities along these lines (*Cincinnati Enquirer,* 1978b). As this administrator was close to municipal development planning, his classification could reflect municipal thinking about the communities, such that greater funding would go to communities that are *(a)* both needy and viable (i.e., rehab and conserve) rather than *(b)* only needy (triage) or *(c)* only viable (sound and stable).[2]

4. Distributive (neighborhood): Allocating grants by one or more of those criteria would not necessarily mean that the community councils are being manipulated by government, but it would suggest that funding for neighborhoods reflects federal or municipal priorities only. Influence by neighborhoods requires that their priorities, too, affect the allocations. There should be some kind of distributive pattern indicating that neighborhoods are funded *as claimants,* rather than only as vehicles for achieving other federal or municipal ends (Lowi, 1964: 691; Thomas, 1980).

Neighborhood influence of this kind might result, for one thing, in the distribution of funding equally to all neighborhoods. Such a strategy would suggest the abandonment of other federal and municipal priorities in favor of the strategy least likely to offend particular neighborhoods; that is, if all neighborhoods benefit equally, no one neighborhood is likely to feel slighted relative to its peers. Or neighborhood influence might result in the allocation of funds in proportion to the strength of the community councils. Indeed, this would constitute the clearest evidence of council clout. The influence that could be only cautiously inferred from an equal shares criterion would be strongly implied by any linkage of allocations to the power of the councils themselves.

The roots of council clout. The source of any council clout could lie either in membership or in organizational complexity, judging from the contrasting views of two prominent authorities on American politics: "The Tocqueville model implies that high rates of member participation are essential for goal attainment. The Moynihan model implies that member participation rates are not relevant to goal attainment, since professional activity is the crucial determinant" (Knoke and Wood, 1981: 189).

Both views may have some validity in Cincinnati. Professional activity, as evidenced by organizational complexity, may ordinarily be more influential in a grants competition, such as Cincinnati's, that favors carefully prepared applications and sensitive personal negotiations. Membership numbers are a crude basis for exerting that kind of subtle influence. Those numbers could be important, however, for the low-income communities where council organizational complexity is largely a creation of the War on Poverty. If the critics are correct (Gittell, 1980; Mollenkopf, 1983), the OEO-induced organizational complexity may reflect too much dependency *on* government to be a good basis for advocacy *in* government. Where that is the case, community clout may depend primarily on the force of membership numbers.

These various allocational possibilities are examined in this chapter relative to several types of grants and grants-related programs. Most have in common a primary reliance on CDBG funding, the funding usually cited as of most interest to the councils, but two programs that lack that CDBG reliance are also used to strengthen the test of council influence.

THE INFLUENTIAL COMMUNITY:
SNAP AND NSP ALLOCATIONS

SNAP and NSP, with their availability of funds for a variety of community council uses, offer the most obvious targets for the exercise of council influence. That influence does, in fact, affect the allocations from both programs, but differently with each and as not the only allocational criterion with either.

Equal shares. The first allocational criterion for both programs was the simple rule of "equal shares," each community council being declared eligible for the same amount of program funds. This criterion was established by City Hall for the SNAP allocations, then continued in modified form with NSP. It was also used in dividing funds within any community with more than one neighborhood organization; that is, every eligible organization was to receive an equal part of the community's allocation. Consistent with the idea of neighborhood influence, City Hall appears to have preferred this criterion in part as a means of avoiding the antagonism of the communities. Had City Hall chosen instead to allocate by need, by population, or by some municipal preference, the result could easily have been feelings of inequity and a backlash.[3]

Choice of the equal shares criterion may also have been influenced by two other factors. First, the criterion is easy to administer, where such alternative criteria as need or council representativeness could prove difficult to operationalize. Second, the criterion probably directs more assistance to the councils with greater needs. Although on the surface it may appear inequitable to give the California neighborhood of 636 people the same funding as the Westwood community of 33,580, the smaller community usually has fewer organizational resources to begin with and so may need proportionately greater assistance.

The impact of the equal shares criterion can be seen in Table 9.1. More than half of the councils received all or nearly all of the maximum $14,000 available in the first three years of SNAP, and almost half of the councils received the full amount available in the first year of NSP. Still, not every council was taking advantage of what was available, as the significant variations in the data indicate.

TABLE 9.1
SNAP AND NSP ALLOCATIONS TO THE COMMUNITIES

SNAP funding, 1978–80		NSP funding, 1980–81	
Amounts	Councils	Amounts	Councils
Up to $6,500	17% (8)	None	34%(16)
$6,500–12,500	30 (14)	Up to $6,500	19 (9)
$12,501–14,000	53 (25)	$8,000	47 (22)
Totals	100 (47)	Totals	100 (47)

Sources: NSP and SNAP program records.

Community influence over SNAP allocations. These variations were influenced primarily by the strength of the community councils; stronger councils usually received more of the funding. This is most clearly the case with the SNAP allocations but in a manner that varies depending on the income of the home community.

In the higher-income communities (using City Hall's dichotomy for CDBG purposes) the councils with the greater organizational complexity received the most funding (gamma = .678), as shown in Table 9.2.[4] Fully 82 percent of the high-complexity councils received the largest SNAP shares, compared to only 33 percent of the low-complexity councils. The relationship is not nearly as strong for council memberships, consistent with the notion that an application process of this kind ordinarily favors organizational sophistication over the force of raw numbers.

TABLE 9.2
SNAP ALLOCATIONS BY
COUNCIL ORGANIZATIONAL COMPLEXITY

SNAP	Level of Council Organizational Complexity (1978)[a]		
Allocation	0–.33	.67–1.00	1.33–2.00
	Higher-Income Areas		
Up to $6,000	17%(1)	29%(2)	0% (0)
$8–12,500	50 (3)	14 (1)	18 (2)
$13–14,000	33 (2)	57 (4)	82 (9)
Totals	100 (6)	100 (7)	100 (11)
	gamma = .678		
	Low-Income Areas		
Up to $6,000	22%(2)	22%(2)	0%(0)
$8–12,500	33 (3)	44 (4)	50 (1)
$13–14,000	44 (4)	33 (3)	50 (1)
Totals	99 (9)	99 (9)	100 (2)
	gamma = .013		

[a] In order to serve as a predictor of the SNAP allocations, council organizational complexity must precede those allocations in time. For that reason this measure of organizational complexity uses only 1978 data—on council budgets, paid staff, and block clubs—to explain the 1978–80 allocations.

That organizational sophistication is not effective for the city's low-income communities, however, where organizational complexity is unrelated to the size of the SNAP allocation (gamma = .013). The Community Action influence in these communities apparently has produced an organizational complexity that is not helpful in advocacy. Effective advocacy by these councils rests consequently on the force of membership numbers, which are strongly linked to the size of the SNAP allocation (gamma = .465). Four of the six councils with 150 or more members received the maximum SNAP allocation, compared to only three of the nine councils with 60 or fewer members.

The complicated NSP allocations. NSP, unlike SNAP, draws from CDBG funds, thereby introducing the federal government as another party interested in how the funds are spent. The result is a complicated system of allocations reflecting the joint influence of community clout and the federal redistributive preference. With the higher-income communities (see Table 9.3), community clout based on organizational complexity is the dominant influence on the size of the NSP allocation (gamma = .767), just as it was on the size of the SNAP allocation. The parallel is hardly surprising given that NSP employs an application process modeled after that developed for SNAP. The pattern is exactly the opposite, however, in the lower-income communities. There the councils with the *least* organizational complexity received the *largest* NSP allocations (gamma = − .547). Council membership is also inversely related to the size of the NSP allocation (r = − .511), in contrast to its direct linkage to the size of the SNAP allocation. Community clout appears to exert no influence over these allocations.

TABLE 9.3
NSP ALLOCATIONS BY CDBG ELIGIBILITY
AND ORGANIZATIONAL COMPLEXITY

NSP	Level of Organizational Complexity		
Allocation	0–.50	.75–1.25	1.50–2.25
	Higher-Income Areas		
None	75%(3)	33%(3)	9% (1)
$1,000–6,000	0 (0)	56 (5)	27 (3)
$8,000	25 (1)	11 (1)	64 (7)
Totals	100 (4)	100 (9)	100 (11)
		gamma = .767	
	Low-Income Areas		
None	22%(2)	33%(2)	80%(4)
$1,000–6,000	11 (1)	0 (0)	0 (0)
$8,000	67 (6)	67 (4)	20 (1)
Totals	100 (9)	100 (6)	100 (5)
		gamma = − .547	

The allocations were primarily determined instead by a strong re-distributive criterion that directed more resources to the weaker councils. According to NSP personnel, that criterion took the form of a less restrictive application process for councils in low-income areas. Where funds to councils in higher-income areas were contingent on applications consistent with certain standards (e.g., a potential for increasing citizen involvement), funds were available to low-income areas essentially on request.[5]

The redistributive intent is evident in some other patterns in the NSP allocations. As can be seen in Table 9.4, the low-income neighborhoods were only slightly more likely than the other neighborhoods to receive NSP funds, they were much more likely, if they received funds, to receive the maximum amount. That could hardly be based on any greater promise to their proposals, considering that, as the lower half of the table shows, these councils had much less success with their NSP projects than did the other councils, according to NSP administrators. The only remaining explanation is a redistributive prefer-ence to help the worst of the worst, the weak councils in low-income areas.

TABLE 9.4
NSP CHARACTERISTICS BY CDBG ELIGIBILITY

	Type of Community	
NSP Status	Low Income (CD-eligible)	Higher Income
Project	40% (8)	30% (8)
No project	60 (12)	70 (19)
Totals	100 (20)	100 (27)
	gamma = .226	
$1,000–6,000	8% (1)	42% (8)
$8,000	92 (11)	58 (11)
Totals	100 (12)	100 (19)
	gamma = − .778	
Behind schedule or withdrawn	42% (5)	6% (1)
Some progress	8 (1)	6 (1)
On target	42 (5)	56 (9)
Successful	8 (1)	31 (5)
Totals	100 (12)	99 (16)
	gamma = .676	

Source: NSP program records.

This redistributive preference almost certainly reflects the federal influence. To be sure, the redistributive process—with NSP and with other programs—was assisted by City Hall actors who were sympathetic to redistribution. Had those actors been able to dictate redistribution on their own, however, the NSP pattern in low-income communities might have been duplicated with the SNAP allocations and with the NSP allocations to higher-income areas. Instead, redistribution occurs only when the funds are federal and the communities are low income, indicating that the critical factor is the federal preference.[6]

THE INEFFECTIVE COMMUNITY: ECONOMIC PLANS AND NEIGHBORHOOD IMPROVEMENT PROGRAMS

In contrast to their considerable influence over SNAP and NSP allocations, the communities appear virtually powerless in decisions on who gets some of the city's other grants-related neighborhood programs. Municipal decisions on where to do neighborhood economic plans and neighborhood improvement programs, for two examples, are governed almost exclusively by other allocational criteria.

Neighborhood economic plans. Neighborhood economic plans, an innovation of the city's newly formed Department of Development in the late 1970s, are intended to project how particular neighorhood business districts (NBDs) should be developed, as well as what role City Hall should play in that development. Once completed, the plans have the force of law by being embodied in municipal ordinances. They may then serve as a basis for attracting CDBG or other municipal funding.

Plans are not developed for all NBDs, however. City Hall had been on record for some time as believing that not all NBDs can survive: "Some NBDs should be allowed to die, according to some City administrators. . . . They say a few perhaps should be directly managed out of business and the balance, those which can flourish, should receive concentrated help from both the City and the business community" (*Cincinnati Enquirer,* 1978c). Perhaps as a consequence of this view, plans had been completed for only approximately a third of the city's communities by the summer of 1980, according to Development officials. That raised a question—which those officials refrained from answering—of why plans had been done for some areas but not for others.

As obvious examples of developmental policies, the plans are likely to be targeted primarily to the higher-income areas perceived by City Hall to be most important to its long-term economic health. The only obstacle to such a strategy might be CDBG financing of the plans, which could bring federal pressures for redistribution. As it happens, the plans are only partially CDBG financed, drawing also on the General Fund, the Capital Improvements Budget, revolving loan funds, and private sources; and Development officials say they do not let the CDBG financing dictate where they do plans. The officials are thus free to follow mostly municipal developmental preferences in the targeting of the plans.

This is exactly what has happened. As indicated in the top half of Table 9.5, the first NBD plans were done mostly for higher-income areas, almost half of which had NBD plans by late 1980 as compared to only one-fifth of the lower-income areas. Moreover, that one-fifth was composed of four CDBG "focus" areas where NBD plans were necessary concomitants of federally inspired redistributive efforts. The developmental bias to these plans is not a response to socioeconomic status alone, however. Within the economically better-off areas, the plans have favored communities with larger populations, as the lower half of the table shows. Development officials have probably concluded that if not all NBDs can succeed, the chances for success may be greatest where the potential customers are most numerous.

TABLE 9.5
LOCATION OF ECONOMIC PLANS

Economic Plan?	CDBG Status	
	Low Income	Higher Income
No	80%(16)	52%(14)
Yes	20　(4)	48　(13)
Totals	100　(20)	100　(27)
		gamma = .576

In Higher-Income Areas Only

Economic Plan?	Population	
	Up to 11,500	Over 11,500
No	72%(13)	11%(1)
Yes	28　(5)	89　(8)
Totals	100　(18)	100　(9)
		gamma = .908

As this discussion implies, the clout of the councils played no visible role in the location of the economic plans. That may reflect nothing more than a lack of council interest, perhaps tracing to the fact that many councils were formed to oppose commercial interests, not to promote them. Development officials for their part appear to have been content with this state of affairs, as they admit to having done little to arouse council interest. Instead, as one official commented, "The groups we deal with today are spinoffs from merchants' groups, sometimes subcommittees, which function with an awful lot of autonomy from the community councils." What remains to be seen, however, is whether the lack of council influence has persisted into the 1980s as more and more councils have become interested in neighborhood economic development.

Neighborhood Improvement Programs. In contrast to the sometimes glamorous image of economic development planning, Cincinnati's Neighborhood Improvement Programs (NIPs) concentrate on the more drab problems of basic physical maintenance. Each NIP is intended to make a qualitative improvement in a neighborhood's physical facilities by means of a year-long concentrated dose of Public Works services, including building inspections, highway resurfacing, cleanup of dead trees, repair of traffic signs, and the like. NIPs were initiated in 1974 with municipal funding but have since been funded through CDBG at an average rate of about one million dollars a year. Four to eight communities have received NIPs each year through that period, such that by 1980 NIPs had been undertaken in more than half of the city's communities.

Given the federal funding of NIPs, the choice of communities might be expected to reflect a redistributive criterion. That criterion could make sense from the perspective of need, given that the low-income areas favored in redistribution are more likely to have deteriorated public facilities. A city NIP official suggested the possibility of a different strategy, however, when he described the program as designed "to take a well-targeted area showing the first signs of blight, then provide an infusion of public services in the hope of turning things around." Focusing on areas with the "first signs of blight" implies that areas with severe blight might be of *less* interest, the essence of a triage strategy.

In practice, the NIP targeting appears to have followed both that strategy and a redistributive strategy, but with the latter more influential. The data in the first section of Table 9.6 indicate that the NIPs have been directed primarily to the city's low-income communities, much as a redistributive strategy would dictate. Redistribution is also suggested by the tendency within low-income areas to target NIPs primarily to areas that had not benefited from other programs. As revealed in the second section of the table, the low-income areas most likely to receive NIPs were those that had not previously received War on Poverty funding (funding that, in most cases, subsequently translated to a substantial CDBG entitlement). In the process, any possible triage strategy was ignored by sending NIPs into six of the seven low-income areas suggested for triage in the earlier classification.

TABLE 9.6
LOCATION OF NEIGHBORHOOD
IMPROVEMENT PROGRAMS

NIP?	Community CDBG Status	
	Low Income	Higher Income
No	30% (6)	56%(15)
Yes	70 (14)	44 (12)
Totals	100 (20)	100 (27)

gamma = .489

	Low-Income Areas		
	War on Poverty Status		
NIP?	None	CAP[a]	CAP & MC[a]
No	0%(0)	36% (4)	67%(2)
Yes	100 (6)	64 (7)	33 (1)
Totals	100 (6)	100 (11)	100 (3)

gamma = − .852

	Higher-Income Areas		
	Neighborhood Classification[b]		
NIP?	Triage	Rehab/Conserve	Sound
No	75%(3)	39% (7)	100%(5)
Yes	25 (1)	61 (11)	0 (0)
Totals	100 (4)	100 (18)	100 (5)

[a] CAP = Community Action Program; MC = Model Cities.
[b] Ordinal statistics are not appropriate for curvilinear relationships, but a gamma statistic can be calculated if the "triage" and "sound" communities are combined into a single "not needy or not viable" category. The gamma for their contrast to the "rehab/ conserve" communities is a strong .853.

The triage strategy emerges as important only in the city's other communities, those not eligible for primary CDBG spending. Here, perhaps feeling less constrained by federal redistributive preferences, City Hall followed a triage strategy almost to the letter. As the third section of Table 9.6

shows, all but one of the NIPs in these communities went to areas designated for rehabilitation and/or conservation, with the areas designated either as "sound" or for "triage" almost shut out.

Once again, as with the economic plans, community council clout does not seem to have figured in locational decisions. The absence of that clout is more conspicuous here because NIP officials say that they invite community participation in the nomination of target communities. It could be, however, that the communities for the most part have been no more interested in NIPs than they were in economic plans. Only in the late 1970s, by most accounts, did the communities evince much interest in Public Works services, and then only because several harsh winters had created severe public works problems in the neighborhoods. By that time most of the NIPs examined here had already been completed.

THE JACKPOT:
COMMUNITY CLOUT AND CDBG ALLOCATIONS

It is striking, nonetheless, that decisions on such different programs as NBD plans and NIPs show no signs of community council influence. That fact increases the importance of how the city's CDBG funds have been allocated. Funds that already represented a potential jackpot for the community councils as a basis for neighborhood development now become a jackpot of another kind as the critical test of the clout of the councils. If they can influence the CDBG allocations, the councils would appear to represent a significant force in municipal politics; if not, they would appear to be minor actors, able to influence only the relatively small stakes of SNAP and NSP.

The significance of CDBG. It cannot be said of CDBG funding, as was suggested of the NIPs and economic plans, that it excites no interest among the community councils. The funding is probably *the* primary interest of the councils. When the fourteen leaders were asked in 1980 about their groups' accomplishments, nine mentioned CDBG-assisted programs first—the building of deepwater pools, the renovation of neighborhood parks, and the rehabilitation of existing structures for use as recreation centers, senior citizen centers, or health centers, or for resale as private homes. The only major CDBG programs not mentioned were NIPs and NBD plans, reinforcing the impression of limited council interest in those programs. In addition, among the few leaders who did not mention a specific CDBG program, two spoke of turning City Hall attention to their areas in a manner that promised more CDBG funding.

Nor could the CDBG funding be characterized as only small change, as might be said of the SNAP and NSP funding. The city's CDBG allotment across the 1975–81 period ranged from a low of $13.4 million in 1976 to a high of $22.4

million in 1980, totaling almost $116 million for the full seven-year period. Those are figures of considerable magnitude in a city that, in the middle of that period, reported General Fund revenues of only $113 million.[7] Not all of the CDBG funding went to the neighborhoods, of course, but the bulk of it did.

In order to get the best sense of how the councils have fared in the CDBG competition, this analysis examines spending for the entire seven-year period. That should eliminate any year-to-year fluctuations that might not accurately reflect the long-run results of the competition. Within the seven-year period, however, the analysis is limited to those funds designated for *specific* neighborhoods, omitting any spending designated for groups of neighborhoods or for neighborhoods in general. That limitation reflects a judgment, confirmed by municipal officials, that funds spent in a neighborhood without being specifically allocated to the neighborhood—a rehabilitation loan to a particular homeowner, for example—are not a fair test of council influence. The exclusion does not greatly limit the significance of the analysis because $33 million in CDBG allocations to neighborhoods remain to be explained, out of a total of $91 million spent or encumbered by Cincinnati by 1982 (City of Cincinnati, Department of Finance, 1982).

Redistribution by neighborhood type. Allocation of the $33 million was influenced first by the federal redistributive preference. Federal pressures were limited at the outset of CDBG (see Dommel et al., 1982: 41–43), but City Hall felt obligated to honor earlier War on Poverty commitments. By the time any sense of obligation could have waned, the Carter administration had promulgated new, stricter guidelines requiring targeting consistent with a redistributive standard. According to municipal officials, those guidelines have actually become more strict under the Reagan administration. As a consequence, the 1975–81 per capita CDBG allocations to the city's low-income neighborhoods eligible for primary CDBG spending were more than three times as large as the allocations to the other neighborhoods—$131 per capita on the average (median rather than mean) for the low-income neighborhoods; $38 per capita for the others.

Within each type of neighborhood, however, the variations are considerable. The range in per capita allocations to the higher-income neighborhoods, for example, is from 0 to $155—a maximum higher than the *median* for the *low*-income communities—with a standard deviation of $45. There is obviously room for the community councils to have exerted influence, but only within each type of community where the redistributive criterion may no longer be controlling.

Allocations to higher-income areas. Eligibility for only the smaller part of the CDBG pie has not kept some of the city's higher-income communities from gaining substantial allocations. College Hill supposedly "made off like a bandit," according to a city official, with CDBG funding that included $934,650 for an NBD revitalization (*Cincinnati Enquirer,* 1980e). And the small riverside community of Sedamsville, with a 1980 population of only 3,007, received over $350,000 in CDBG funds in 1980 alone for neighborhood development (*Cincinnati Enquirer,* 1980a).

Judging from the results shown in Table 9.7, these varying allocations to the higher-income communities trace primarily to the clout of their community councils.[8] Council organizational complexity emerges in the regression analysis as the best predictor, explaining 30 percent of the variation in the CDBG allocation. Here, as with the SNAP and NSP allocations, the advantage apparently goes to the council with the staff and other resources necessary to prepare good proposals and then to lobby for them.

TABLE 9.7
EXPLAINING CDBG SPENDING
IN HIGHER-INCOME AREAS

Community Characteristics	Relationship to CDBG Allocations[a]		
	Zero-Order Correlation	Regression Coefficients	Variance Explained
Organizational complexity[a]	.550[b]	.550[b]	.303
Membership	.287		
Households	.549[b]	.440[b]	.182
Percentage black	.223		
Percentage poor	.335		
Percentage vacant	− .236		
Percentage occupancy change	− .112		
Percentage commercial	− .111		
Triage ranking	.193	− .411[c]	.100
R[2]			.585
Adjusted R[2]			.523
N of cases			24

[a] Both CDBG allocations and council memberships are expressed as square roots to reduce the impact of extreme cases. Both membership and organizational complexity figures are for the year 1978.
[b] Significant at .01 level.
[c] Significant at .05 level.

Once the effects of organizational complexity are controlled, population emerges as the second most important factor in the CDBG variations, more money going to communities with larger populations (i.e., more money in absolute terms, not per capita).[9] Need also affects the allocations, consistent with the federal redistributive preference, as the correlations show more funds going to communities with larger proportions of the poor and the black (though not, interestingly, to areas with higher turnover or higher vacancy rates). In addition, the triage rankings are the third most important predictor of these allocations, meaning that more dollars went where needs were ranked as greatest (i.e., communities ranked at the triage end of the scale).

That means, of course, that the triage rankings were not used in anything like the manner anticipated. Rather than the worst of the higher-income communities getting less of the pot, they actually received *more*—with or without controls for the other predictors. What happened, apparently, is that publication of the draft triage rankings created a controversy that killed the possibility of any future use of the rankings. Faced with the threat of less CDBG funding, the so-called triage communities mobilized as the Inner-City Neighborhood Coalition to oppose the triage plan. Their success—and additional evidence of community council influence—is evident in these CDBG allocations.

Allocations in low-income areas. The primary beneficiaries of CDBG in Cincinnati are the low-income communities. Several, including Avondale, the West End, and Walnut Hills, received $5 million or more each over the program's first seven years, far exceeding what any of the higher-income communities received. That money could conceivably have been used to manipulate or co-opt the neighborhoods, as Hunter (1979) has suggested. These communities are certainly the most likely targets for such a strategy. Their neighborhood organizations were often created *by* government through Community Action or Model Cities, raising the suspicion that from the start they may have been tools of government. With populations that are less educated and less professional, these communities could also lack the intelligent leaders able to see through manipulative strategies. Finally, any leaders who might emerge could, given their probable low-income backgrounds, be susceptible to efforts by City Hall to buy them off without really aiding their communities (see, for example, Peterson, 1970).

But a successful manipulative strategy should mean that funds go where *government* wants them to go, not where the communities want them to go. The analysis of allocations to these communities, as shown in Table 9.8, strongly implies that this has not happened in Cincinnati. Instead, community influence exerted through the force of raw numbers has largely determined which communities got more funds: The larger the membership of the community council, the larger the neighborhood's CDBG allocation.

This does not necessarily mean that manipulation of these neighborhoods has not been attempted. At least the hint of a manipulative strategy can be found in the ineffectual nature of the federally induced organizational complexity of councils in these neighborhoods. To the extent that the War on Poverty

TABLE 9.8
Explaining CDBG Spending
in Low-Income Areas

| Community Characteristic | Zero-Order Correlations | Most Clout[b] | | Least Clout |
		Regression Coefficients	Variance Explained	Variance Explained
		Relationship to CDBG Allocations[a]		
Organizational complexity	.259			
Membership	.789[c]	.789[c]	.622	.205
Households	.658[c]	.252[d]	.044	.433
Percentage black	.311			
Percentage vacant	.588[c]	.278[d]	.061	.109
Percentage commercial	.209			
Percentage occupancy change	.175			
OEO history	.479[c]	.373[c]	.136	.117
Total R^2			.863	.863
Adjusted R^2			.827	.827
N of cases			20	20

[a] CDBG allocations and council memberships are again expressed as square roots.
[b] The two equations provide the maximum and minimum estimates of the role of council resources in explaining CDBG allocations.
[c] Significant at .01 level.
[d] Significant at .05 level.

has been relied upon for organizational strength, in other words, the community councils are not very effective at advocacy, just as manipulation would imply. Only membership numbers—numbers not much affected by the War on Poverty—help these councils to advocate.

Those numbers can explain 62 percent of the variation in the allocations if membership, as the strongest bivariate predictor, is treated as the first cause of the allocations in the initial, "most clout" regression equation. An argument could be made, however, that some other predictors should be controlled before examining the influence of membership. The pressures of membership might conceivably become relevant only after allocating according to population, earlier War on Poverty commitments, and perhaps even percentage of housing units vacant. The impressive fact about the influence of council membership is that even when the potential influence of these other factors is considered first, membership still explains more than 20 percent of the variations in CDBG allocations to these communities, as shown in the second, "least clout" regression equation.

Those other factors should not be overlooked, however, for they, too, say something about how the CDBG allocations have been handled. To begin with, the factor of population means, once again, that larger communities get larger allocations. In addition, earlier governmental decisions on where to target War on Poverty programs affect where CDBG funding goes, indicating that even this relatively recent funding is not immune to influence by historical decisions. Community need also figures in which low-income communities get more funding, as higher proportions of vacant residential units lead to higher CDBG allocations. The importance of physical need, rather than strictly human need (as would be reflected in percentage poor or percentage black), undoubtedly reflects the CDBG focus on physical structures, rather than on poverty per se. As that finding hints, the triage rankings were no more influential with these low-income communities than with the other communities. Per capita figures show that the worst of the low-income communities did at least as well as the other low-income communities in the CDBG competition.

Finally, the results for both types of communities strongly suggest that the residential community councils prevailed over neighborhood commercial interests in the first CDBG years. None of the indicators of community commerce (e.g., number of commercial units, commercial units as a ratio to residential units vacant) was much correlated with CDBG allocations in either type of community, and none was important in any of the regression analyses.

COMMENT: THE COMPETITIVE NEIGHBORHOODS

Much of the competition in urban politics moved during the 1960s and 1970s to the area of grants. Grants have the attraction of a sizable discretionary component, a consequence of lacking the historical constraints that dictate where so much traditional municipal spending goes. Neighborhood organizations are among the claimants that have joined in this competition, and judging from the Cincinnati evidence, they have competed effectively. Wherever community councils have been active in grants-related programs, they have influenced the allocation of substantial program benefits. They have persuaded City Hall in Cincinnati to provide equal shares or shares proportionate to council strength.

In the city's higher-income communities, that strength has been wielded principally through organizational complexity, a composite measure of staff, committee, budget, and block club resources. The role of this complexity may reflect how a professionally dominated city government such as Cincinnati's values a similar professionalism in its neighborhood organizations. Municipal professionals in City Hall may respond favorably to the attractive grant proposals and articulate lobbying that the professional community council can produce. Higher-income communities may also prefer working in this manner to the alternative of cruder political pressures. Cruder pressures may prove useful, however, when an effective organizational complexity is lacking, as in Cincinnati's low-income communities. Handicapped apparently by an externally induced council complexity, these communities have still been able to translate their membership numbers into influence over which areas got the larger SNAP and CDBG allocations.

The communities have not, by any means, been the only players influencing the results of the grants competition. The most influential of the other players appears to have been the federal government, with the traditional federal preference for redistribution affecting how benefits were allocated from all but one of these programs, the foundation-funded SNAP effort. Although redistribution may not be in the municipal interest (Peterson, 1981: 43), City Hall in Cincinnati has generally followed the redistributive criterion when required by federal policy.

By following that federal preference on some allocations and the dictates of community clout on others, City Hall became perhaps the weakest of the three principal actors in this competition. Far from manipulating the community councils, City Hall has often subordinated its preferences to those of the communities or of the federal government. Only in the area of neighborhood economic plans is the municipal preference clearly controlling, and that control may have been possible only because the communities were uninterested.

Cincinnati's grants competition thus strongly resembles the usual intergovernmental grants process (e.g., Pressman, 1975; Ingram, 1977) in that, as the term "competition" implies, one actor seldom dominates. Instead, the process is usually characterized by bargaining: Each party gives some and gains some in order to reach a resolution. That perspective helps to explain why these neighborhood organizations have mostly not been manipulated by government. True, federal Community Action efforts created some organizations that do not seem to function as effective neighborhood advocates, a finding suggestive of manipulation. For the most part, however, drawing these groups into the grantsmanship competition, as government did when it created or sustained various of the groups with earlier grants, did not necessarily buy off the groups. To the contrary, it apparently served to interest the groups in successive rounds of the competition, at which time the groups could push harder for their preferences than for government's preferences. That tendency, described elsewhere at the national level (Walker, 1983), can now be seen at the local level as well.

Eventually the groups can gain a foothold to ensure that their influence will persist even if the grants themselves diminish. In Cincinnati in the 1980s, for example, although a dwindling CDBG allotment has probably meant less funding for neighborhoods, the clout of the community councils has not disappeared. The locus of neighborhood influence has only changed, according to many local observers, as the councils have responded to declining control over federal funding by asserting a growing influence over local funding—in the general budget process and in the capital improvements budget process.

10

The Public Interest:
Can the Whole Survive
the Sum of the Parts?

Few gains come without costs. In Cincinnati the political gains achieved by the neighborhoods could come at a cost to the city as a whole. What is good for the private interests of the many neighborhoods could prove inimical to the citywide public interest. The new power of neighborhoods raises the specter of "hyperpluralism" (see Lineberry, 1983: 54-60), a brand of politics in which many—supposedly too many—private interest groups dominate public decisions. According to some observers, neighborhood groups and other new urban interest groups have made so many demands of municipal governments that harried public authorities have sometimes lost sight of the broader public interest (e.g., Bell and Held, 1969; Yates, 1977), resulting in problems ranging from financial crises (Haider, 1979) to paralysis of the very process of municipal decision making (Yates, 1977). No one has suggested such dire prospects for Cincinnati as a consequence of the rise of the community councils, but some observers have warned that the new neighborhood power could undermine pursuit of the citywide interest. The city's primary daily newspaper, for example, has coupled praise of "citywide approaches to community issues" with a warning that "it would be wrong to abandon that vision in behalf of neighborhood organizations" (*Cincinnati Enquirer,* 1980d).

This chapter considers whether that vision has, in fact, been sacrificed. It attempts to determine, specifically, how and why the citywide interest has been affected, either positively or negatively, by the new power of neighborhoods in Cincinnati.

NEIGHBORHOOD SUBVERSION
OF THE CITYWIDE INTEREST?

Determining whether the public interest has been neglected hinges on being able to define the public interest in the first place. That is no easy chore given the common practice of using "the public interest" as a rhetorical disguise for particular private interests. Conceptually, the public or citywide interest should refer to any ends that are of demonstrable value to at least a majority of the city's residents. The problem, of course, is determining what that means operationally.

That problem was solved here by using several different approaches to define the public interest and its possible neglect in Cincinnati. First, the literature on hyperpluralism was reviewed for ways in which the citywide public interest might be neglected. Second, local newspaper accounts were followed for suggestions of whether and how the public interest might be suffering in Cincinnati. As traditional voices for citywide interests, newspapers represent an excellent source. Third, those city officials whose positions encourage a citywide perspective (e.g., City Council members elected at large) were asked to recall any recent conflicts between neighborhoods and City Hall. To aid their recall, follow-up questions were asked about specific public interest concerns related to hyperpluralism. This combination of approaches produced several possible or actual areas of neighborhood-induced neglect of the citywide interest.

A more difficult governing process? First, with the many new neighborhood groups involved, governing itself could be much more difficult. Government may have become, as Lineberry (1983: 54) suggests, "so decentralized and pluralistic that it has trouble getting anything done." The chaos the new groups bring to municipal decision making could even make the city "ungovernable" (Yates, 1977).

This does not appear to have happened in Cincinnati. City Council members were unanimous in reporting that their jobs had not become more difficult with the rise of neighborhood groups, and most department heads concurred. Nor did the City Council members feel that dealing with neighborhood issues was taking time away from public interest issues and broader policy questions. As one council member said of the neighborhoods, "Generally, their issues are so specific that it's not a problem. You can deal with that issue and be done with it, and go on to other issues. You really don't have the parochialism that exists under a ward system." A few council members even contended that the city's citizen participation mechanisms, by channeling particularized demands to the departments, were helping the City Council to spend more time than in the past on broader policy questions.

City hall reactions to the neighborhoods may not always have been so positive; the current accommodation represents the outcome of a long learning process (see Chapter 7). Early in that process, in the late 1960s and early 1970s, city officials may have been much less sanguine about the effects of the neighborhoods on municipal governance.

Distortions in public spending? Although problems with the governmental process can be important, hyperpluralism has more commonly been associated with problems in governmental policies, primarily distortions in public spending. The many new urban groups have been accused, for one thing, of pushing the level of municipal spending beyond the fiscal capacity of City Hall (e.g., Haider, 1979).

Whatever the validity of this argument in other cities, it does not hold for Cincinnati. Rather than seeing its budget expand beyond municipal means, Cincinnati actually cut spending between 1975 and 1978, when community involvement in municipal decision making was accelerating (see Thomas, 1981; Levine, Rubin, and Wolohojian, 1981).

But the neighborhoods probably could not be expected to affect overall municipal spending levels greatly, as state law requires the city to keep its budget in balance. Any neighborhood-induced distortions in municipal spending must consequently occur *within* the budget cap. Neighborhoods may not be able to affect the size of the pie, but they could affect how the pie is divided.

Such distortions are probably most likely in Cincinnati in the area of CDBG spending. This is where the neighborhoods have focused their primary attention, and it is also where observers in other cities have suggested that the public interest may suffer as a consequence of "the demand for widespread distribution of benefits" to many neighborhoods (Kettl, 1979: 451). That concern has been raised in Cincinnati, too, as by Community Development Director Bud Haupt in 1980: "You can't take eighteen to twenty million dollars a year and address the needs of half the city. If we want to make a difference, so you can see it . . . , you're going to do it by saying to forty-odd communities, 'Sorry, fellas, we're going to make a difference.' "

Still, this did not appear to be much of a problem in Cincinnati during the 1970s. Although the neighborhood influence was strong enough for the CDBG allocational process to be described as a "grabbag" (Woods, Andersen, and Grober, 1979), through 1978 the city had still been able to concentrate two-thirds of the CDBG spending in only six neighborhoods, with the remaining forty-one neighborhoods splitting the other one-third (City of Cincinnati, Department of Community Development, 1978).

A question did arise in 1980, however. The new city manager, Sylvester Murray, wanted to target primary CDBG spending to Avondale to compensate for what urban renewal and urban riots had done to the community. Could his view of the citywide interest prevail over neighborhood preferences for dispersed spending? Or, in Haupt's words again, "The 64 dollar question, or the 64 *million* dollar question, is in the next year or so how are we going to dampen this notion of pork barrel, equity, every community gets it fair share, and take half the bucks into Avondale. We're caught up in that dilemma."

Within three years the question had been answered in the city's and Avondale's favor. The citywide interest, as the manager had defined it, prevailed as considerable CDBG and other municipal money was infused into Avondale, resulting in the opening of a new neighborhood shopping center in an area that a short time before had been "vacant and barren" (*Cincinnati Enquirer*, 1983). Moreover, the Avondale funding apparently did not result from the manager's overpowering the neighborhoods. According to another Community Development official, the neighborhood representatives on the CDAC became "supportive" of increased focusing of CDBG spending after the concept of focusing was explained. Despite the apparent incentives, the neighborhoods had not attempted to stop the manager's pursuit of his sense of the citywide interest.

Interference with economic development? Neighborhoods have also been accused of endangering the public interest by interfering with local economic development. This accusation came most pointedly in 1980 from two City Council members who cited an issue involving a grain-processing company that proposed to build a new plant in Cincinnati, a plant promising employment and a boost for the city's declining tax base. Unfortunately for the company, and perhaps for the city, the company wanted to build in the primarily residential riverside community of Sayler Park. Neighborhood residents objected and eventually persuaded a City Council majority to deny the zoning change requested by the company. In the minds of the two council members, that outcome was not in the city's best interest. One described the issue as "probably the classic case of a conflict between the overall good and the local position." The other concurred: "If Sayler Park had been a community of itself, it would have found a way to get the plant in there."

Even here, however, the case for neighborhood-induced neglect of the citywide interest is far from clear. Several other municipal officials argued that the fault lay more with the company than with the community. Sayler Park, they pointed out, is a relatively high-income, predominantly homeowner community unlikely to need or want a new industrial facility. The company had erred, these officials contended, by not selecting a different neighborhood, one more likely to be receptive to a new plant. The growing interest of some neighborhoods in economic development suggests that such areas could be found in the city.

There are also grounds to argue that despite the results in the Sayler Park case, the neighborhood movement on the whole may help more than hinder municipal economic development. Companies are now known to value quality of life considerations in making locational decisions. The community councils share that concern for neighborhood quality of life and so could improve the urban environment in ways attractive to commercial interests. Cincinnati's neighborhoods took a dramatic step in this direction in 1980 when they supported a property tax levy for the city's school system, an important component of the services and amenities that constitute an area's quality of life. The *Cincinnati Enquirer* (1980j) speculated that the neighborhood support may even have been the crucial element in the levy's passage: "Many recognize that, for whatever reasons, a neighborhood-backed levy passed after eleven previous levies were defeated. That success lends a new credibility to neighborhood influence."

Barrier to low-income housing? The community councils have not been as kind to the interests of low-income, publicly assisted housing. Development of this housing had progressed so slowly up to 1980 that a lawsuit was filed against City Hall, charging that "to date the city hasn't moved to facilitate construction of even one rent-subsidized, low-income apartment complex" (*Cincinnati Enquirer,* 1980b). Much of the blame has to fall on the neighborhoods, particularly those middle-to-upper-income neighborhoods that had steadfastly resisted all proposals for low-income housing in their areas. Even federal officials tacitly recognized this fact: " 'The need is obviously there,' said Cincinnati area HUD planning and development official Bill Rogers, 'but it's doggone hard to find sites for new housing, especially if it's assisted' " (*Cincinnati Enquirer,* 1980b).

On the other hand, preventing the construction of this housing does not necessarily represent subversion of the public interest. Low-income housing may reflect the *private* interest of the low income or of those who believe in residential integration of social classes (i.e., through placement of low-income housing in higher-income neighborhoods), rather than the public interest in the sense of a goal shared by a city majority. Viewed in that light, the real lesson from Cincinnati's problems with low-income housing is that the neighborhood movement is an unlikely force for radical change favoring the disadvantaged. Neighborhood groups include some of the disadvantaged and will on occasion support redistribution to the disadvantaged, as with Avondale in the early 1980s. But aiding the disadvantaged is not what the movement is mostly about. As much might have been surmised from the well-documented importance of protection of turf to so many neighborhood activists.

NEIGHBORHOODS ON THE SIDE
OF THE PUBLIC INTEREST?

This analysis of the city's housing problems keeps intact the almost spotless record of the community councils on citywide public interest issues. The interests of Cincinnati as a whole appear to have suffered only minimally at the hands of the neighborhoods during the late 1970s and early 1980s. This probably cannot be attributed to any inability of the neighborhoods to prevail when matched against proponents of the citywide interest. Actually, neighborhood power was directly opposed to the apparent citywide interest only in the Sayler Park case, and then neighborhood preferences prevailed.

A consensus on the citywide interest. Explaining the survival of the citywide interest must begin, instead, with the fact that the neighborhoods have seldom been opposed to that interest. The community councils have usually agreed with others in the city on the major public interest issues. During retrenchment, for example, these groups mostly concurred with City Hall on what had to be done. As CATs coordinator Ken Bordwell commented, "There's a pretty widespread realization now that the city can't do everything, and that other resources are going to have to be tapped. That doesn't seem to be a sticking point. Communities seem to understand that. Nobody wants more taxes." Similarly on such other issues as CDBG targeting to Avondale and the need for a school tax levy, neighborhoods either accepted or actively supported what appeared to be in the citywide interest.

This support has developed, it appears, because of how the neighborhoods have been involved in determining the citywide interest in Cincinnati. Rather than simply being told by city officials what is in the city's interest, the neighborhoods have usually participated through the city's community involvement mechanisms in defining that interest. That participation has then helped to persuade the neighborhoods of the wisdom of the resulting definition.

At least three examples can be cited in support of this argument. First, by being involved in the budget process as retrenchment was occurring, the community councils became more aware and more accepting of the city's need to cut back. More than one community council leader indicated a willingness to go along with retrenchment, so long as they were involved in deciding how the cuts would be made. City officials for their part often mentioned the cooperation of the communities in the retrenchment process. A City Council member, for example, praised the community councils for their "realism" on the budget, noting that community budget requests "have declined sharply . . . in the last five or six years."

Second, through their involvement in the Community Development Advisory Council, neighborhood representatives were persuaded of the citywide interest in concentrating large chunks of CDBG funding in a few neighborhoods, such as Avondale. They were persuaded, however, only because *(a)* city officials took the time to explain why this targeting was in the citywide interest and *(b)* the neighborhood representatives then had the opportunity to approve or even modify how that interest was put into operation.

Finally, the neighborhoods united behind the 1980 school tax levy after they were involved, as they had not been with previous unsuccessful levies, in deciding on the nature of the levy. The need for a levy was explained to the councils in a series of neighborhood meetings held before the size of the levy had been specified, such that the eventual size could reflect neighborhood input. The neighborhoods then played a primary role in the campaign as School Board officials let the "neighborhoods run whatever kind of levy campaign they wanted" (*Cincinnati Enquirer,* 1980h). It was an unusual campaign, too, according to community council and levy campaign leader Pat Crum: "As the thing was originally organized, it was a pretty ordinary kind of campaign—you know, speakers going out here and there—but very quickly neighborhood people began coming in with wild ideas, and we just started saying, 'Why not?' " The outcome was victory by a 55 percent majority, a sharp contrast to a two-to-one ratio of defeat for a similar levy scarcely a year earlier, and on a budget of less than half that of the earlier campaign (*Cincinnati Enquirer,* 1980d).

The lesson of these examples is clear. Increasing power to the parts of the city need not produce neglect of the citywide interest *if* those parts are given a role in defining that interest. That role can persuade them to accept and sometimes promote whatever interest emerges as the citywide interest, even if that interest is, as often in Cincinnati, more someone else's conception than their own.

THE NEIGHBORHOOD ROLE
IN SERVICE DELIVERY

Neighborhood organizations may even be capable of promoting the public interest on more than the occasional basis implied by the retrenchment, CDBG, and school levy examples. More neighborhood groups could conceivably mean more partners available to aid cities on an everyday basis in the delivery of urban services. With many services, some observers argue, that production should be reconceptualized as "coproduction," in which services are produced or delivered jointly by government and neighborhood or other citizen groups (e.g., Rutter, 1980; Percy, 1983).

With its many neighborhood organizations, Cincinnati offers a natural environment for coproduction. Community interest in the role has, in fact, grown as the councils have watched dwindling revenues reduce City Hall's capabilities. According to former community organizer Chuck Hirt, "The key thing I saw happen out of that [the city's retrenchment] was that the neighborhoods realized they had to take much more seriously the whole concept of self-help and doing for yourself. I think that was absolutely essential, and it probably was a very healthy kind of thing." By 1980, in any event, the neighborhoods had assumed a significant role in service delivery. Interviews with departmental and community council leaders revealed council involvement in at least four forms of coproduction, all either new or recently expanded.

1. *Joint decision making.* To begin with, as earlier chapters have documented, the community councils are now extensively involved in municipal decision making. The councils frequently provide information on neighborhood preferences and have a say in the eventual shape of municipal programs to

meet those preferences. This involvement has obvious significance for the neighborhoods and for City Hall. Still, it represents a limited form of coproduction in that neighborhoods only participate in decision making, rather than assisting in the actual delivery of services.

2. *Program and service monitoring.* Another kind of information provision does take neighborhoods into actual service delivery. In this form of coproduction neighborhood residents monitor municipal programs and service problems, then report their observations to municipal officials, who may modify the services.

Departmental officials offered numerous examples of this form of coproduction. City CDBG officials reported that many neighborhood groups provide information on how CDBG-funded programs are progressing in the field. A Highway Maintenance official claimed that the community councils "serve as our inspection force, or supplement our inspection force," a claim heard in varying forms from officials in other departments as well. In an example common to many cities, police-sponsored neighborhood "block-watch" programs ask citizens to observe and report crimes and other suspicious activities. By the summer of 1980, the Fire Division was encouraging neighborhood organizations to adopt a similar role on fire-related problems (e.g., arson, fire hazards).

3. *Unskilled labor.* The neighborhood role in service delivery becomes even more active when the community councils supplement the municipal supply of unskilled labor for occasional cleanup and maintenance work. Three departments—Parks, Highway Maintenance, and Waste Collection—report extensive use of neighborhood groups for this kind of work. One official said, "We've been encouraging more and more of the self-help on cleanup." This involvement most often comes through short-term cleanup campaigns, as when a community council asks residents to assist in picking up the neighborhood on a given weekend.

4. *Program operation.* There is, finally, a significant neighborhood role in program operation, as some community councils now administer particular services with financial assistance from City Hall. This coproduction has two principal forms in Cincinnati. In the first, a number of councils run neighborhood service centers. A few have assumed day-to-day responsibilities for running recreation centers, in at least one case after the Recreation Department indicated that it could pay to build a center but not to staff it. A few others are involved in administering neighborhood health clinics on contracts with the city's Health Department.

In the second form, neighborhood groups rehabilitate buildings, usually residential homes, helped by grants or low-income loans from City Hall. A growing number of neighborhood development corporations, formed as non-profit arms of the community councils, have contracted with City Hall on such projects. According to Housing official Hugh Guest, "We use the development corporations as an extension of our staff," then "keeping a smaller staff at City Hall," much as proponents of coproduction have envisioned. For the development corporations the rehabilitated homes can eventually be sold in the private market, with profits recycled into more housing rehabilitation. In late 1980, for example, the western riverside community of Sedamsville was asking $50,000 for a home it had bought for $500 and renovated with a $27,500 low-interest loan from the city (*Cincinnati Enquirer*, 1980a).

DEFINING THE LIMITS I:
WHERE COPRODUCTION FALTERS

These examples demonstrate that coproduction with neighborhoods has assumed significant proportions in Cincinnati. The city's experience also suggests, however, that the magnitude of this neighborhood role should not be exaggerated. There are clear limits to neighborhood coproduction and thus, as well, to the potential magnitude of the neighborhood contribution to the citywide interest.

Neighborhood coproduction is limited, first, by usually being confined to areas where minimal expertise is required. This occurs both because municipal professionals resist citizen intrusions on their professional prerogatives and, perhaps more important, because citizens seldom have the professional expertise they are both willing *and* able to contribute to the provision of services. This limitation is implied by the first three forms of coproduction in which community councils provide only information or unskilled labor. Although the limitation has not prevented more advanced coproduction, it could help to explain the varying service quality often accompanying that coproduction. A Health Department official noted this variability in describing the community-run health clinics as including "the best and the worst" of the city's clinics.

Coproduction is limited, second, by usually being confined to areas where municipal departments need not depend on it, as with maintenance City Hall might otherwise postpone or cleanups it could otherwise manage unassisted. On the latter, for example, one division head argued that "what we get in the cleanup campaigns could be collected all year round" by regular department personnel. Information provision might also qualify as nonessential assistance. Even the program operation by neighborhood groups is restricted, as in other cities, to "peripheral or supplementary services, as opposed to . . . core public good services" (Ahlbrandt and Sumka, 1983). This limitation could be City Hall's creation, with departments acting from two motivations. For selfish reasons officials may resist the farming out of essential services to volunteer help because that threatens the jobs of regular municipal employees. Or, concerned for service continuity, officials may balk at surrendering essential municipal responsibilities to volunteer help who could volunteer "out" as easily as they volunteered "in."

The validity of this concern is borne out by what happened when City Hall contracted to have several community councils run recreation centers. The first such effort worked well, with City Hall paying to renovate a building as a recreation center for the Madisonville neighborhood and the community council arranging to run the center through a YMCA. Problems developed only when two other neighborhood groups, observing the Madisonville success, proposed to do the same thing. The municipal Office of Research, Evaluation, and Budget (REB) opposed the proposals, arguing that the groups lacked the capacity to run the centers. The proposals were nonetheless recommended by the CDAC, and both centers were developed. Shortly thereafter REB's prediction proved accurate; both neighborhood groups were unable to support the everyday operations of the centers. City Hall had renovated two recreation centers that could not be opened. The volatile nature of volunteer help, abetted by the CDAC's inattention to that volatility, ran two centers aground at considerable expense.

The need for a financial reward. What these problems suggest is that neighborhood involvement in substantial and reliable coproduction—involving, in other words, more than sporadic provision of information and unskilled labor—seldom springs spontaneously from the grass roots of the neighborhood as needs arise. When faced with those needs, neighborhoods will instead, as one council leader said, "usually try to get an agency in the community to provide those services or get the city to do it."

The councils have been both willing and able to assume major service delivery responsibilities only when a substantial subsidy was available. Subsidies were necessary in the successful Madisonville case, in which the municipal construction subsidy leveraged the community's willingness to administer the recreation center, and for the numerous housing rehabilitation projects executed by neighborhood organizations. The lack of sufficient subsidies, on the other hand, helps to explain the two aborted recreation centers, cases in which partial subsidies proved insufficient. More generally, years of public support of the community councils probably figure in *all* of their coproductive involvement.

Herein lies the most serious limitation on coproduction. Simply put, coproduction requires up-front money, but in an era of austerity there is little of that around. City governments lack discretionary money, and any efforts to divert nondiscretionary money from traditional programs are likely to be blocked by municipal employee groups.

None of this is to deny a potential in coproduction for a significant neighborhood contribution to the citywide interest. Realization of some of that potential is already evident in Cincinnati's numerous coproductive efforts with the neighborhoods. That potential is sometimes exaggerated, however, by viewing coproduction as a "free good" bringing only gains without any associated costs. There are definite costs, ranging from the initial subsidies to the possible eventual sacrifice of service quality or continuity, and they limit the net contribution that coproduction can make to the citywide interest. Without a continued municipal ability to pay those initial costs, moreover, even that limited contribution can be only episodic rather than everyday in nature.

DEFINING THE LIMITS II:
THE ACCOUNTABILITY PROBLEM

There is an accountability issue that could also figure in how the community councils affect the citywide interest in Cincinnati. Until the mid-1980s, a number of factors forced the councils to be especially accountable to their home areas. Their relative newness meant, for one thing, that the councils needed to demonstrate their legitimacy as neighborhood representatives in order to be credible with City Hall. In addition, any council that might neglect that legitimacy risked being challenged by a competitor group, as the entry costs for starting a new neighborhood organization were relatively low. Those costs probably were lowest, in fact, in the late 1970s and early 1980s, when SNAP and NSP funds were available to any neighborhood group able to demonstrate some standing in its home community. These factors constrained the community councils to stay in relatively good touch with the wishes of their constituencies. Those wishes may often have corresponded to citywide interests, such that the greater accountability could have contributed to the usual neighborhood support for those interests.

Significantly, these forces for accountability were weakening in the mid-1980s. With most of the councils having been around for some time, City Hall now seemed less concerned for their representativeness and legitimacy than for their organizational complexity. It is that complexity, in any event, which has proved most effective recently in winning assistance from City Hall. Perhaps for that reason the councils themselves, as is common with neighborhood organizations (see Cooper, 1980), appeared to be spending less time improving representativeness and more time building that complexity, as in the campaign for municipal financing of community support workers.

To make matters worse, entry costs for new neighborhood organizations were going up. Since the early 1970s the community councils had sought official City Hall recognition of the existing set of councils, an action that could have excluded or discouraged the formation of new neighborhood groups. City Council consistently resisted those pressures and in so doing kept the entry costs relatively low. In 1982 the councils took a new tack, but with the same potential effect, through their efforts to build the Invest in Neighborhoods endowment. The endowment would provide support only for existing groups that had contributed to the endowment's base, thereby putting any new neighborhood group at a relative financial disadvantage. In effect, the existing community councils would become the incumbents, with some of the financial advantages that incumbents enjoy elsewhere in American politics.

The likely consequence of this arrangement would be the exclusion of some new neighborhood groups in years to come. That would have been the effect, certainly, had the City Council acceded to the earlier requests for official credentialing of particular groups. That recognition would not have extended to a number of community councils that did not then exist but that are now important actors in the neighborhood movement in Cincinnati.

This evolution reflects a tendency common with most organizations; it is not unique to neighborhood groups (e.g., Clark and Wilson, 1961). As organizations mature, they often become more concerned for maintenance than for their original purposes, and so grow more interested in making life difficult for potential competitors. That inclination could lead to a loss of some of the freshness and vitality that the neighborhood movement has brought to urban politics. With that loss could come a decline in the impressive community council support for the citywide interest in Cincinnati.

COMMENT: THE WHOLE SURVIVES

Contrary to what might have been anticipated, the new attention to the parts of the city in Cincinnati has not detracted from the interests of the city as a whole. Indeed, rather than just surviving the sum of the parts, the whole—the citywide interest—for the most part has benefited from the presence of the many new representatives of the city's neighborhoods. The reasons are several. In the first place, by involving neighborhood representatives in defining citywide interests on crucial issues, City Hall has usually won neighborhood support for those interests and at minimal cost in terms of neighborhood redefinition of those interests. More groups need not mean increased antipathy toward common interests, especially if the groups are treated as though they, too, share those interests.

Second, the municipal service concerns of the community councils have made possible even more regular neighborhood contributions to citywide interests. Rather than coming in only amateur and episodic fashion, those contributions now sometimes come on an expert, everyday basis through coproduction. The gains from coproduction are probably not as great as sometimes advertised, nor are they likely to reach the advertised levels, but they do appear to represent net gains rather than a net loss.

Third, the relative youth and vitality of the neighborhood groups has kept them in close touch with the grass roots of the city, possibly making them stronger proponents of citywide interests. The organizational selfishness of which interest group critics sometimes complain may be partially a by-product of organizational maturation and decay, which the relatively young community councils have yet to know. Ironically, an eventual decay may be avoided only if there are *more* groups, or at least lower entry costs for new groups.

That argument and the other findings suggest, again, that more groups and more participation need not be unhealthy for the urban political system, as the hyperpluralism argument implies. Perhaps more groups are worse under some circumstances, but the Cincinnati experience counsels that under the right circumstances, more groups can actually enhance the citywide interests initially thought to be at risk.

11

Conclusions:
The Meaning
of the Neighborhood Movement

Although the neighborhood movement has been significant for Cincinnati, its greatest importance may lie beyond the city's boundaries. What has happened with community councils in Cincinnati exemplifies what has happened in many American cities in recent years, as a new, more vibrant brand of urban politics has emerged. That new politics suggests a surprisingly positive evaluation of the role government has played in urban political development. Indeed, thanks largely to that governmental role, this more lively urban politics seems likely to persist despite a recent shift in governmental priorities. It is in these themes that the meaning of the neighborhood movement will probably be found.

THE NEW URBAN POLITICS

It has been popular in recent years to characterize urban politics as mostly apolitical—lacking in organized groups, lacking in conflictual decision making, and lacking, consequently, in policies with a clear political content (Peterson, 1981). That characterization probably fit Cincinnati and many similar cities a decade or two ago. It no longer does in the 1980s, as Cincinnati and other cities like it have experienced a political revival, producing what can accurately be termed a new urban politics.

This new politics has at least three elements. First, a growth in the incentives for urban political groups has produced a corresponding growth in the number of such groups. In Cincinnati, a renewed salience for the homeowner's traditional stake in urban politics has coincided with the introduction of the new stakes from a variety of governmental program innovations to bring a new breed of community councils into municipal politics. Similar incentives elsewhere may explain why neighborhood groups and Community Action groups, in combination, now represent the most common local interest groups in a representative sample of fifty-one American cities (Schumaker and Getter, 1983). As early as 1972, in fact, fully 65 percent of America's large cities (i.e., a population of 250,000 or more) had formal systems of "neighborhood, area, or district councils representing residents" (Advisory Commission on Intergovernmental Relations, 1972).

The new incentives have not had the same effect everywhere, by any means. Where they have not produced the new neighborhood groups, however, they appear to have produced new groups of other kinds. Groups representing blacks and Hispanics, for example, have become much more common in many cities (e.g., Johnson, Booth, and Harris, 1983; Browning, Marshall, and Tabb, 1984; Jackson, 1978). The political climate has become more hospitable to urban political groups of one kind or another.

Even as the groups were growing, municipal government was gradually becoming more sympathetic toward them, providing the second element in the new urban politics. The attitude of municipal government in Cincinnati has been transformed by changes in political leadership, in administrative personnel, in professional values, in formal decision-making procedures, and in the spending programs available to groups. As a consequence, the way municipal decisions are made has changed in Cincinnati, to the point where the community councils are now routinely involved in a manner almost unimaginable a quarter-century ago.

Other cities have seen these changes, too. "Guerrillas" have been sighted in other municipal bureaucracies (e.g., Needleman and Needleman, 1974); a new generation of political leadership more sympathetic to insurgent groups has ascended to power in many cities (e.g., Clark and Ferguson, 1983: 104–10); many municipalities have altered their decision-making procedures to permit more citizen and community involvement (Advisory Commission on Intergovernmental Relations, 1979; Hallman, 1980); and the relevant federal spending programs have reached most or all large American cities. By the early 1980s systematic neighborhood involvement in CDBG decision making or in the general municipal budget process could be observed in at least these cities: Birmingham, Alabama, and Dayton, Ohio (Hallman, 1984: 245–46); a number of smaller cities in both Connecticut (Kettl, 1979) and Texas (Busson, 1983); and New York City, St. Paul, Atlanta, and Portland, Oregon (Hallman, 1980).

None of the changes, either in the urban groups or in the attitude of municipal government, has gone unnoticed. For the most part, however, the changes have been viewed in isolation, such that their cumulative effect on the character of urban politics could be overlooked or underestimated. That atomistic perspective on these changes could permit, in particular, a consistent underestimation of what the changes mean for the power of the new groups and the nature of urban policies.

In actuality, the new urban groups bear a striking resemblance to many interest groups that have emerged on the national scene in recent years. Like the national groups (see Walker, 1983; Hansen, 1985), the new urban groups have built their organizations from a combination of *(a)* shared interests, *(b)* threats to those interests, *(c)* the socioeconomic status of members or prospective members, and *(d)* government and foundation support. The new urban groups also resemble the national groups in their increasing involvement with government and in the willingness of government to support that involvement (e.g., Beer, 1976; Thomas, 1980). Yet even as the power of the national groups is widely feared (e.g., Bell, 1975; Beer, 1977), the new urban groups are generally described as ineffectual (e.g., Peterson, 1981: 117-19). Even some students of neighborhood groups have asserted, often without any real evidence, that the groups are too weak to affect urban policies (e.g., Crenson, 1983: 294-96).

Here, then, is the third element in the new urban politics. The presence of the new groups has combined with the changing municipal attitudes to produce a new power for the groups and, as a consequence of that power, a new political content in many municipal programs. Where decisions on traditional urban programs have usually been dominated by forgotten history and unseen administrators, decisions on the newer programs reflect the competition of a number of political actors, including the new groups. The influence of the new groups is perhaps most evident in Cincinnati, as on the CDBG spending, but a comparable influence has also been reported elsewhere (e.g., Kettl, 1979; Sekul, 1983; Browning, Marshall, and Tabb, 1984; Abney and Lauth, 1985). Given how local elective officials tend to succumb to pressure rather than risk open conflict (e.g., Pressman, 1975: 65-68; Boulay, 1983), that influence may well be found wherever the groups themselves are found.

Judging from the Cincinnati experience, this new urban politics may represent mostly a positive development. New segments of the population have been mobilized, contributing to broader participation in community life. The municipal decision-making process has become much more permeable than it was twenty or thirty years ago, making for a more democratic system. Equity, too, may have been enhanced as funding has been distributed to more neighborhoods, rather than going primarily to commercial renewal areas. In addition, if observers of other cities can be believed, the quality of life may have been enhanced as neighborhood groups have lowered crime rates (Kohfelt, Salert, and Schoenberg, 1981) and promoted renovation and stabilization of deteriorating areas (e.g., Clay, 1979: 93; Taub, Taylor, and Dunham, 1984: 140). Finally, none of these changes appears to have exacted much cost from the interests of the city as a whole. The new organizational vitality between citizen and city may have given more than it has taken from the cities.

THE GOVERNMENTAL ROLE
IN POLITICAL DEVELOPMENT

The years when this new urban politics was growing include the years when government was trying to promote political development in American cities. That political development, as Pressman (1975: 141) has noted, encompassed both "(1) the ability of a wide range of people to participate in politics and make demands on government, and (2) the ability of government to satisfy those demands." Governmental efforts focused on both dimensions in these years and, judging from the Cincinnati experience, with more success than has generally been recognized.

The achievements. The Cincinnati evidence indicates, first, that government has helped in building neighborhood organizations. Federal Community Action can be credited with creating approximately a third of the contemporary community councils; CDBG spending has proved moderately effective, if in an unintended manner, in increasing council memberships; and the SNAP subsidies have been very helpful in building those memberships. These latter subsidies originated, admittedly, with a private foundation, but their allocation was both planned and administered by local government in Cincinnati; thus their effectiveness seems unlikely to derive principally from their origin outside of government.

These governmental efforts at building neighborhood organizations have not been without their disappointments. In particular, compensatory programs directing assistance to relatively disadvantaged areas have been only partially successful. Federal Community Action, for example, built organizations but could not mobilize neighborhoods as the goal of "maximum feasible participation" implied. Municipal compensatory programs have not fared much better; the municipally run Neighborhood Support Program has proved much less effective when allocated to low-income areas on a compensatory basis than when allocated to other areas on something like a merit basis.

This problem may have less to do with the capabilities of government than with the hazards of a compensatory strategy. That strategy is usually pursued because low-income areas are viewed as lacking the indigenous resources necessary to build viable organizations on their own. Unfortunately, the absence of indigenous resources often signals a neighborhood's inability to make effective use of any outside resources, thereby dooming a compensatory strategy to a rate of success lower than could be anticipated from a different strategy. This is not to argue against compensatory strategies; the desire to compensate may be the strongest argument for governmental assistance to neighborhood organizations in the first place. It may mean, however, that compensatory programs should not be undertaken unless their probably lesser effectiveness is understood at the outset.

Second, governmental action has also helped to increase the involvement in municipal decision making of both the community councils and the neighborhoods they represent. The insistence of the communities themselves certainly figured in this increased involvement, but it seems unlikely that the communities on their own could have created the changes observed in Cincinnati.

The extent and rapidity of those changes actually belie the magnitude of the governmental effort required for their production. Had the city merely offered the opportunity for more involvement, as by holding more public hearings, the new involvement might never have developed (see also Cole and Caputo, 1984). But governmental efforts in Cincinnati went well beyond that minimum:

1. City Hall has usually scheduled community involvement for the earliest stages in the decision-making process, when municipal preferences were more fluid and so more susceptible to influence.
2. City Hall assisted the communities, as most dramatically through the Community Assistance Teams, in learning how to work with city government.
3. The city and federal governments jointly made available substantial discretionary CDBG funding, thereby providing a strong incentive for the communities to join in municipal decision making.

Of all these factors, the last could be the most important. Although more timely opportunities and assistance in using those opportunities can facilitate community involvement, that involvement might not have been viewed as worth the effort had a substantial payoff not been possible.

Finally, government has proved moderately effective at redistributing public spending to low-income areas. Although the evidence does not say whether benefits actually reach low-income populations, the findings in Cincinnati do indicate that government has succeeded at least in directing benefits disproportionately to the *areas* with the largest low-income populations. This redistribution has occurred principally because of federal influence, but a generation of that influence has left a legacy of important local actors also sympathetic to redistribution.

The critique from the left. This record of achievement contrasts sharply with how the governmental efforts at political development have usually been evaluated elsewhere. Even as the neighborhood movement as a whole has drawn praise, the role of government in the movement has more often drawn criticism—and from both ends of the political spectrum. That criticism loses some of its force when seen in light of the Cincinnati findings.

Consider, first, the critique from the left. Government, many on the left have argued, has created organizational structures in low-income neighborhoods but has not really organized the neighborhoods. The structures exist only as organizational overlays without real roots in neighborhoods (O'Brien, 1975: 144–48). Compounding the problem, these organizations supposedly limit themselves to concerns with services, thereby depriving neighborhoods of any effective advocacy (Gittell, 1980, 1983; Mollenkopf, 1981). As the end product, these neighborhoods are effectively co-opted by government, as government achieves support from the organizations without giving any significant programmatic concessions to the neighborhoods (Hunter, 1979). Any potential for a unified, change-oriented neighborhood movement is consequently lost (Mollenkopf, 1981: 31; Katznelson, 1981: 179–90).

The Cincinnati experience with the War on Poverty gives some support to these criticisms. OEO assistance did create complex organizations without mobilizing neighborhoods and also appears to be a principal reason for the greater concern of these organizations with service problems. And that assistance has proved relatively ineffective in prompting advocacy of broad programmatic change for the neighborhoods. But the criticism ignores what could be said on behalf of the poverty program. In the first place, the case of Cincinnati suggests that OEO support has created stronger neighborhood organizations than would otherwise exist in low-income areas. The alternative to weak federally induced organizations appears to be weaker or nonexistent organizations, rather than the militant and autonomous organizations the left might prefer. In the second place, the emphasis of the OEO-based organizations on service delivery issues may in part reflect what local residents prefer, rather than indicating a disdain for their preferences. Evidence from Cincinnati and elsewhere suggests that minority residents of low-income areas often want neighborhood organizations to be available as intermediaries on service delivery problems (see also Sharp, 1980; White, 1981). In short, the War on Poverty was not quite the unqualified failure that the critique from the left suggests.

Moreover, more recent governmental efforts have sometimes succeeded where the War on Poverty failed. Both the CDBG funding and the SNAP subsidies have increased community council memberships, rather than merely complicating organizational structures. These larger memberships can stand on their own as evidence of governmental success or can be seen as valuable as a source of greater lobbying effectiveness—for example, in the case of the SNAP and CDBG allocations.

The influence of those memberships suggests that the left has erred, too, in depicting governmental programs as only co-opting neighborhood organizations in low-income areas. Organizations can hardly be viewed as co-opted when, as in Cincinnati, the force of their CDBG membership numbers largely dictates how the substantial funds are spent. The lesson here is that organizations, even if created by government, need not always remain under the control of government. Many will instead develop their own powers and priorities.

The left might be accurate, however, in arguing that governmental funding has helped to keep the neighborhood movement from becoming a unified force for change in the city. Neighborhoods in Cincinnati have seldom presented a united front to City Hall, perhaps in part because of the opportunity to bring large chunks of CDBG funding back to the home neighborhoods. Still, it is difficult to imagine Cincinnati's community councils' uniting on many issues, whatever the level of governmental support. The neighborhoods are themselves too diverse to find many common interests under any circumstances. In addition, without governmental assistance, these organizations would be weaker and therefore even less able to organize in support of the radical change the left has in mind.

The critique from the right. The view from the right is somewhat different but no less critical of the governmental efforts at political development. This critique complains, first, that government has created too many artificial groups, such as neighborhood organizations, which exist only because of governmental inducements (see Bell and Held, 1969). Second, these groups are accused of converting their governmental funding to organizational uses rather than directing it to the public purposes for which the funding was intended (e.g., Stockman, 1975). Third, with the aid of the funding, the groups supposedly become so effective at lobbying that the public interest is eventually sacrificed in order to satisfy the many private special interests (e.g., Bell, 1975).

This criticism is only partially corroborated by the Cincinnati findings. For one thing, although government has financially supported many of Cincinnati's neighborhood organizations, government is not solely responsible for them. All or most of the community councils either began for other reasons or eventually found other reasons to exist: protecting the residential status quo, redeveloping the neighborhood, or obtaining assistance on municipal service problems. In other words, government support could be a necessary cause for these community councils, but it is not a sufficient cause.

In addition, if one were really concerned to eliminate governmental support for neighborhood organizations, attention should also be given to the more subtle forms of support seldom mentioned in the critique from the right. These include the tax advantages that have facilitated gentrification and the formation of new community councils in a number of Cincinnati neighborhoods, along with the Federal Housing Administration and Veterans Administration mortgage insurance programs that have underwritten so much of the homeownership that drives many of the councils. A fair attack would need to take on these forms of support, as well as the direct subsidies—something the right has seldom recognized.

The critique may be more on target in portraying these groups as using funds for organizational purposes. The role of the CDBG funding in stimulating council memberships, for example, suggests that public funds targeted for other purposes have sometimes proved useful in maintaining neighborhood organizations. Some diversion of this funding may be desirable, however, in order to build the organizational capacity necessary to achieve the core functional goals of the funding. Any time government uses a third party as an agent in pursuing a goal, some diversion of funds to the third party itself may be both inevitable and desirable.

The right is also partially accurate, judging from the Cincinnati case, in complaining that the original governmental funding has helped these organizations to lobby effectively for continued funding. That complaint can be easily distorted, however, by giving the funding *too* much credit. In Cincinnati the lobbying effectiveness of a community council may actually be *inversely* related to the extent to which the council relies on public funding. In the extreme, when councils were created and sustained by the War on Poverty, lobbying effectiveness appears virtually nonexistent.

Where the critique really falters is in the claim that the public interest is neglected as a consequence of the new groups' entering the governmental process. Perhaps that was once true—when the groups were new, more numerous, more abrasive, and more alien to the experience of municipal officials. Critics on the right err, however, if they assume the persistence of that early difficult phase of the neighborhood movement. In the early 1980s Cincinnati's community councils appeared more likely to promote than impede the pursuit of the citywide interest. Moreover, the effect councils have on that citywide interest probably depends more on how they are involved in its definition than, as the right suggests, on either their numbers or the level of their support from government.

A positive assessment. With the Cincinnati neighborhood movement, in short, government has served as a more positive force for political development than either of the polar critiques suggests. The governmental role has not been as effective for low-income areas as the left might have wanted, and it has sometimes been more costly than the right finds acceptable. Even these frustrations, however, are largely attributable to government's taking on the more difficult low-income areas, areas that private forces have mostly neglected. Attempting to help these areas has inevitably produced problems, but it has also given the neighborhood movement a degree of representativeness perhaps otherwise unattainable.

Government has played this beneficial role, to be sure, usually in alliance with private sector actors. Although the now popular claims for "public-private cooperation" are frequently exaggerated (see Langton, 1983), the Cincinnati evidence suggests that the best forms of political development result from a combination of public and private influences. Governmental support has been most successful when it has coincided with indigenous neighborhood interests, rather than being used to create both the interests *and* the corresponding activities.

This judgment could be colored by the phase of the neighborhood movement examined here. The period of the 1970s and early 1980s could have been the best years of the movement, the period of peak performance likely to follow the difficult early years of growth in the 1960s and early 1970s. What remains to be seen is whether the movement can retain its vitality—and its influence—in the later 1980s and beyond.

THE FUTURE
OF THE NEIGHBORHOOD MOVEMENT

As extensive as the changes have been in recent decades to create the neighborhood movement, one wonders whether the coming years will bring changes of a comparable magnitude, but now perhaps hostile to neighborhoods. A number of changes have, in fact, already occurred—or loom as threats—that could change the character of the movement.

Changing governmental priorities. Most obviously, governmental priorities have changed in several ways potentially detrimental to the interests of neighborhood organizations. Federal spending has been substantially cut and further cuts are likely. The CDBG allotment to Cincinnati, for example, dropped by a third, from more than $22 million in 1980 to less than $15 million in 1985. At the same time, local financial problems continue to force cities, with Cincinnati prominent among them, to find ways to cut local spending. Spending on neighborhoods could be particularly vulnerable because it focuses more on optional than on basic municipal services.

Compounding the problem is the companion turn in municipal priorities toward economic development. On the surface this might not seem to pose a problem for neighborhoods, as they, too, are interested in economic development, but neighborhood developmental preferences often differ from municipal preferences. Neighborhoods usually favor spreading funds to many areas, in contrast to the municipal interest in targeting funds to a few selected areas (e.g., the central business district). Successful assertion of the municipal preference could result in less CDBG funding for most neighborhoods. In Cincinnati in the 1980s, for example, municipal attention has once again turned to the downtown, prompting efforts to direct more CDBG spending there.

These new governmental priorities are likely to retard the further growth of neighborhood organizations in Cincinnati and elsewhere. The absence of new discretionary governmental funding should make neighborhood organizing a less attractive option, with the result that new organizations will be less common in the coming years than in the 1960s or early 1970s. There may also be a winnowing of the organizations already in existence, much as happened in Cincinnati in the 1970s when governmental assistance proved insufficient to support more than one organization per neighborhood. Low-income areas, the primary beneficiaries of this assistance, may be especially hard hit.

Even in those areas, however, the prospects for a wholesale reduction in the number of neighborhood organizations appear remote. For one thing, municipal officials may want the groups to survive because of their utility when difficult spending decisions must be made. Broad community participation can sometimes save municipal officials from the political fallout that unpopular spending decisions can bring. Community involvement in Cincinnati, for example, helped City Hall in persuading the communities of the need for municipal retrenchment in the late 1970s and of the desirability of targeting CDBG spending to Avondale in the early 1980s.

On the other side of the coin, municipal officials may invite disaster if they choose to challenge neighborhood groups in an effort to change local spending priorities. Mollenkopf (1983: 248-51) makes a strong case that the confrontational politics of northeastern and midwestern cities in the 1960s figured prominently in their economic decline, as commercial interests looked elsewhere for more tranquil environments in which to settle. A new round of confrontations with neighborhoods might similarly discourage yet another generation of urban economic development. Perhaps most important, it is no longer clear that municipal officials can expect to win in a confrontation with neighborhood groups. The power of these groups may now be sufficient in many cities to ensure the groups' hold on governmental support even under challenge from municipal officials and changing municipal and federal priorities.

This certainly seems to be the case in Cincinnati, judging from the outcomes of two recent City Hall–neighborhood conflicts. In the first, new City Manager Sylvester Murray attempted in 1980 to change the CDAC's recommendations for CDBG spending, making "mincemeat" of the CDAC plan, according to one observer. An angry chair of the CDAC "lit into Murray like a buzzsaw," causing him to back off on his recommendations and subsequently to ask the municipal CDBG staff to help him in understanding how the process worked. The neighborhoods were even more clearly the winners in a second conflict, the 1983 battle over whether the Neighborhood Support Program would be continued. After initial City Hall talk of ending NSP, the program was eventually continued with *increased* funding, despite the more limited CDBG and municipal general fund revenues.

The clout of neighborhoods has also been demonstrated in other cities in recent years. Consider the case of Minneapolis, where the City Council, faced with budget problems, voted in 1982 to cut funding for neighborhood organizations. Within two years, many council members who had supported those cuts had been voted out of office, and most of the cuts had been restored to the budget (Hult, 1984). The lesson may be that municipal officials sometimes confront neighborhood organizations at more risk to their own jobs than to the survival of the organizations.

This is not to suggest that neighborhoods can hold on to all of their support from government. It is more likely, in hard times when municipal priorities are changing, that some support will be lost. According to both municipal and community leaders, governmental support for Cincinnati's neighborhoods has declined in recent years as the result of reduced CDBG funding and new municipal priorities for that funding. That decline appears to have come, however, as the outcome of the same kind of bargaining process that determined the level and allocation of this support in the first place. In the end, Cincinnati's neighborhoods may still receive the primary CDBG funding—the larger part of a "60-40 split," in the opinion of one City Hall observer—and they also may have been able to make increasing inroads on other parts of the municipal budget.

Changing organizational priorities. The greatest threat to the vitality of neighborhood organizations could come from within rather than from without. As they age, these organizations could prove susceptible to the same atrophy of purpose that has drained the vitality from so many other organizations. With neighborhood organizations, that might take the form of a loss of accountability to the home community.

Cincinnati's community councils could already be sensing encouragement to think less about accountability to the home communities and more about appearances in City Hall. Such encouragement is implicit in the recent municipal tendency, when allocating funds, to pay more heed to the organizational complexity of the councils than to the breadth of their memberships. Only with low-income communities, where the War on Poverty created a mostly ineffectual organizational complexity, were council memberships an important factor in determining municipal allocation.

Municipal officials may have slighted council representativeness out of a sense that they know by now who the different groups represent. That knowledge can rapidly become obsolete, however, as neighborhood organizations wax and wane in their community backing. Municipal officials in Cincinnati are not unaware of this volatility, but they are still responding mostly to organizational complexity, thereby perhaps discouraging the representativeness that has been the core claim to legitimacy for the community councils. The councils, for their part, have been moving in directions that could exacerbate the problem. There is a particular risk in the new Invest in Neighborhoods endowment that the councils are building. That fund could discourage new neighborhood organizations by subsidizing only the existing community councils that have bought into the endowment. If competition among these organizations becomes more difficult, the existing councils will have less incentive to maintain their ties to the home communities, and the ties could consequently become attenuated. At the extreme, the councils might be transformed into only another organizational layer, a far cry from the effective intermediaries they now appear to be.

If that happens, the community councils will have reached that tipping point thought to be characteristic of many organizations in the public realm.

They will have moved from bringing net benefits to the life of the city to incurring net costs. At the moment, fortunately, that outcome is not in sight.

What government can do. The fate of the neighborhood movement depends in large part on the actions of government. The Cincinnati experience, viewed against the backdrop of contemporary constraints on governmental action, suggests some guidelines for those actions. In general, a governmental role in the neighborhood movement remains desirable and unavoidable. It is desirable because the qualities of equity and representativeness associated with the movement derive largely from governmental involvement. It is unavoidable because government is involved in too many different ways—including poverty program financing, CDBG funding, FHA and VA mortgage insurance, and rehabilitation tax incentives—for anyone to anticipate reasonably that the involvement could be entirely terminated. At the same time, government probably cannot contemplate any major new spending initiatives in neighborhoods in the near future. The limited success of programs such as Community Action and the current climate of fiscal austerity both argue against significant new spending in the future.

Within those broad limits, the optimal governmental strategy might have four general components. First, government should continue to strive for accessibility of its decision-making processes to interested citizens' groups, such as neighborhood organizations. Continued emphasis on accessibility seems all the more desirable in light of the considerable evidence of only limited effectiveness whenever government action is undertaken without citizen cooperation (e.g., Whitaker, 1980). On the other hand, steps in this direction are not worth taking if they provide only nominal access. Such access, as through the use of pro forma public hearings, amount at best to a modest waste of time for those who attend the hearings. At worst, the efforts can backfire if aroused citizens' groups choose to fight already formulated governmental plans. In either case no useful purpose is served.

Second, government should continue to fund the activities of neighborhoods and their organizations. The argument for an inherent shortage of resources for most neighborhood organizations remains cogent; many of these organizations could not survive on the basis of indigenous resources alone. In addition, these organizations are increasingly proving helpful to government to an extent that their survival may now be in the best interest of government. Contrary to what the rhetoric of "voluntarism" might suggest (Joyce, 1982), however, that help will be only minimal unless there is at least some public financing.

Third, any such funding should continue to be targeted more to the areas with greater needs. The relative representativeness of the neighborhood movement hinges on government's continuing to show the concern for equity inherent in a compensatory approach. Yet, as the fourth element in this strategy, the pursuit of equity must be conditioned by the need for better productivity from governmental contributions to neighborhoods. Compensatory approaches cannot be expected to be as productive as some of the alternatives. When resources are limited and governmental action is viewed skeptically, however, compensatory efforts must be pursued cautiously in order to avoid outright rejection of governmental involvement. The way out of this quandary may be through a leveraging strategy, in which funding is targeted to those low-income areas that show a potential for using this funding to stimulate other private funding. This is, in essence, the controversial triage strategy (i.e., no money for areas that can raise none of their own funding). Controversy might be avoided, however, if money is awarded only in response to applications, rather than as an entitlement.

As for the federal role specifically, the successes of the neighborhood movement in Cincinnati argue against any radical contraction. Federal involvement has been invaluable for giving the neighborhood movement some virtues that could not have developed had the movement been left only to the resources of cities and neighborhoods. In addition, neighborhoods and cities could use some continuity in federal urban policies, given that the traditional flux of these policies is itself a source of inefficiency (e.g., Haider, 1979).

The federal role should also retain its primary redistributive thrust. On this point Paul Peterson's (1981) arguments are compelling: The competition forced on cities by their open borders precludes many redistributive initiatives by municipal governments, assuming they follow self-interest. Only the federal government faces the more limited competition that permits occasional initiatives on behalf of the relatively disadvantaged. Fortunately, the federal redistributive emphasis in CDBG spending has actually been strengthened under the Reagan administration, according to Cincinnati officials, although the funds themselves have been greatly reduced.

As for local governments, the findings argue for maintaining the existing involvement of neighborhood groups—and other citizen groups—in the municipal decision-making process. New programs of involvement, however, should not be initiated unless municipal resources are sufficient to cover the accompanying costs. Community involvement requires more expenditure of staff time, more time for making decisions, and perhaps more discretionary funding to attract community groups. Municipal governments risk trouble if they begin this involvement without first knowing that these costs are affordable. This probably means that a municipal government would be unwise to initiate a new community involvement program during a budget crunch, such as those faced by many large cities in the 1980s. Community involvement can be helpful in cutting back if the involvement is established *before* retrenchment begins because it then adds no complications not already a part of municipal decision making. It does add to those complications if the involvement is initiated *only as retrenchment is occurring*. A city in that position is essentially taking on two difficult tasks at once.

When cities want to increase the involvement of neighborhoods in municipal affairs, they should seriously consider having discretionary municipal funding available on a competitive basis. The Cincinnati evidence strongly suggests that increased involvement requires the enticement of discretionary funding, as well as the invitation implicit in a more accessible decision-making process. The funds need not be available simply for organizational purposes, as municipal officials often find difficult to justify, because neighborhood organizations are almost as interested in funding for functional purposes.

If funding is made available for organizational purposes, a good balance of equity and productivity may be possible if several principles suggested by the Cincinnati experience are followed. First, equal funding should be available to all neighborhoods. This funding principle creates the politically attractive appearance of evenhandedness, yet it is also likely to have a redistributive impact by sending more funding to the smaller neighborhoods that have more difficulty sustaining organizations. Second, funding probably should not be restricted to a preexisting set of neighborhood organizations. Such a restriction improves the competitive position of these incumbent organizations, thereby potentially reducing their accountability to the home communities.

Assuming the funds are designed to leverage rather than to serve as the primary support for organizations, two additional principles should be followed. First, the funds should be kept relatively modest, perhaps in the $5,000–$10,000 range of SNAP and NSP funding available annually to Cincinnati's community councils in recent years. Organizations are likely to see such limited funds only as assistance, not as basic sustenance, and so should be more likely to leverage with the funds. Second, the funds should be allocated in response to applications, rather than as simple entitlements. The mere act of applying demonstrates some mobilization of indigenous resources, hinting at the desired goal of leveraging neighborhood resources with municipal resources.

Beyond the funding question, local government might also consider trying to organize some neighborhoods that, despite the inroads of the neighborhood movement, remain relatively unorganized. These include a number of relatively disadvantaged public housing communities and Appalachian white neighborhoods in Cincinnati. These neighborhoods might benefit from outside assistance in organizing, such as that offered by Cincinnati Human Relations Commission staffers briefly in the mid-1970s.

Neighborhood organizing has been a troublesome task for government in the past, as the frustrations of federal Community Action and local community planning attest (e.g., Needleman and Needleman, 1974; O'Brien, 1975). New governmental efforts probably could be justified only if they were modest in scope, rather than requiring a major commitment of municipal resources, and targeted according to a leveraging strategy. That strategy could mean making assistance available only to disadvantaged neighborhoods that express both an interest in organizing and some confusion as to how to proceed.

Whatever the specifics, government must continue to play an active role if the neighborhood movement is to remain a positive force in cities. Government may have contributed the least to neighborhoods and cities when it was the most intrusive, as in the combative days of the War on Poverty, but government would do even greater damage by attempting to withdraw. With neighborhoods, as probably with the nation as a whole (see Reich, 1983), success in the future requires that both the public and the private sectors be involved.

Notes

CHAPTER 2
THE ARGUMENT: NEIGHBORHOOD ORGANIZATIONS AND THE NEW URBAN POLITICS

1. Succeeding references to the Peterson book report only page numbers (parenthetically).

2. The logic of this argument can be extended to predict occasional high levels of activism by renters. Renters ordinarily have less stakes and greater ease of exit and are therefore likely to show little or no activism. Why stay and fight if the stakes are low and exit is easy? In cities with rent control, however, holding a favorable rental agreement may raise both the stakes and the exit costs to an extent sufficient to justify some renters' choosing voice over exit whenever serious threats are perceived (e.g., Navarro, 1985).

CHAPTER 3
BEGINNINGS: THE RISE OF THE COMMUNITY COUNCIL IN CINCINNATI

1. "Community" is often used to mean something larger than "neighborhood." The two terms are treated here as synonymous and interchangeable, however, reflecting the way they are used in Cincinnati.

2. The dates and reasons for formation of the various neighborhood organizations are drawn from a variety of sources, between which disagreements are common. The primary sources were (1) a 1970 study of the city's community councils by the reform-oriented Charter Committee (Charter Research Institute of Cincinnati, 1970) and (2) a series of telephone interviews, conducted by a graduate assistant, with community council leaders in the summer of 1979. These have been supplemented by other sources too numerous to mention. Disagreements on dates or causes of origins were resolved in a manner to reflect the preponderance of evidence.

3. For Map 3.3 a neighborhood was considered to have experienced "major black population growth" between 1950 and 1970 if the community's percentage of blacks in 1970 minus its percentage of blacks in 1950 equaled at least 20 percent.

4. Population size was not a factor. Both the communities with new councils and the predominantly black communities where councils did not form are comparable in population to the average Cincinnati community.

5. A few of these communities reportedly had neighborhood organizations prior to Community Action, but the dates and reasons for their formation are so vague or nonexistent that the earlier groups were treated as dormant and the Community Action groups treated as new groups. Where Community Action clearly did build on an existing group—in Avondale and the East End—the earlier dates of formation were used for classifying the groups.

6. The Bond Hill and Paddock Hills groups, which formed in 1965, might have been included in this era as similar exceptions. They are included in the previous era because *(a)* they formed before Community Action was fully under way and thus were unlikely to have been influenced by it, and *(b)* their rise has never been attributed to Community Action.

CHAPTER 4
PEOPLE:
THE SEVERAL FACES OF NEIGHBORHOOD ACTIVISM

1. The survey instrument was constructed on the basis of input from citizens and municipal officials on the important aspects of the service areas. It was administered to a random sample of 2,334 Cincinnati residents (18 years of age or older) by telephone in early 1978. The sampling technique was random-digit dialing. The survey included all Cincinnati exchanges using a computer-generated list of random phone numbers. A matrix was used for random selection of respondents within households, and as many as six calls were made to assure that the appropriate respondent was reached. The survey was conducted by professional interviewers (including twenty-two white females, two black females, and two white males) employed by the Behavioral Sciences Laboratory at the University of Cincinnati. The completion rate was 72 percent, with the remaining 28 percent divided between refusals, partial interviews, those interviews impossible to complete because of language or hearing problems, and respondents the interviewers were unable to contact. The sample appears to be representative of the Cincinnati population on most demographic dimensions. For example, the sample included 29.2 percent blacks, which falls between census figures of 27.6 percent in 1970 and 33.8 percent in 1980. This is consistent with other studies (e.g., Klecka and Tuchfarber, 1978) that have found random-digit dialing to be as representative as face-to-face interviews.

2. In the few cases in which 1980 data were unavailable on council memberships, 1978 data were substituted.

3. With council-reported memberships, proportions were calculated relative to total population or total households, depending on which unit of membership the particular council employed.

4. Socioeconomic status equals the sum of the scores on education, a seven-category variable, and income, an eight-category variable. If one score was missing, a measure was created by multiplying the available score by two. This single measure serves both as a more accurate indicator and as an indicator with fewer cases of missing data.

5. Ratings were provided in the summer of 1980 by Community Assistance Team quadrant leaders, each of whom worked closely with approximately one-fourth of the community councils (see Chapter 6). Their ratings could not have reflected census data because the 1980 census data used here were not then known. Their ratings of the age mix of council members, incidentally, were essentially unrelated to the age mix in the community (gamma = .074), underscoring the significance of the high correspondence on race.

6. Not only do the reported patterns fit the basic theory, they also reflect the statistically strongest patterns after every pattern observed on one group was tested on the three other groups. Undoubtedly, however, relationships would have been stronger had more attitudinal predictors been available in addition to the demographic predictors. Socioeconomic status, for example, is not a good substitute for actual measures of political efficacy and civic duty.

7. Following this logic, white homeowners might also be influenced by the presence of blacks immediately *outside* a community's boundaries. However, a measure of this proximity was unrelated to the neighborhood activism of white homeowners. That may attest to the psychological reality of neighborhood boundaries for the city's residents: Residents react most strongly to changes occurring *within* those boundaries.

8. This is consistent with Sharp's (1980) argument that a lack of personal efficacy in dealing with government agencies leads blacks to pursue public service problems through neighborhood organizations. The findings do not, however, support Sharp's suggestion that service problems are what prompt neighborhood activism among blacks. Service use is a much stronger predictor than service problems for the community council membership of both black renters and black homeowners. Blacks may channel service problems through community councils in Cincinnati, but it is the use of services, rather than problems with the services, that underlies blacks' council membership.

CHAPTER 5
ORGANIZATIONS: THE UNEQUAL RESOURCES
OF COMMUNITY COUNCILS

1. Percentage black could be a measure of threat in the perceptions of white homeowners, but that is not the only possible meaning.

2. These reports came in response to a mail survey conducted by the municipal Office of Neighborhood Housing and Conservation. In the few cases in which councils did not respond to that survey, 1978 membership figures were substituted (Robinson, 1978). In addition, membership estimates had to be developed for two communities— Sayler Park and Kennedy Heights—where the councils counted all community residents as members. These estimates were developed from membership proportions obtained for each neighborhood from the citywide survey discussed in Chapter 4. Those proportions were multipled by each community's population, then discounted to reflect how survey proportions overestimated actual reported council memberships in four similar neighborhoods.

3. Three councils—those in Madisonville, Paddock Hills, and South Fairmount— are omitted because their membership figures refer to delegates selected from the community. Delegate counts are unlikely to have the same meaning as other membership figures.

4. It is also possible that the important relationships are curvilinear rather than linear, as assumed in this regression analysis. On socioeconomic status, for example,

membership levels might initially rise, then begin to decline at some middle to higher socioeconomic level, in the kind of curvilinear fashion described by Rich (1980a). Or on race, memberships might be highest in more volatile, racially mixed areas than in either predominantly black or predominantly white neighborhoods. The data, however, do not support either argument. With or without a control for population, there is no sign of higher membership levels in the middle ranges of any measure of community socioeconomic status or community racial mix.

Nor does it appear to be the case that the wrong membership statistic is being used. Rich (1980a) argues that gross membership figures are less important than membership as a proportion of neighborhood population, which may reflect an organization's success in tapping its membership potential. The problem is that the community councils do not seem to think in these terms. The inverse relationship between this proportion and population (r = − .350) suggests that councils in large neighborhoods readily settle for large but manageable membership levels, rather than worrying because those levels represent a small proportion of the total neighborhood population. Nor does City Hall appear to hold this proportion in high regard. Municipal officials were much more impressed by raw numbers, judging from the much stronger linkages of reputed council organizational strength to membership levels (r = .582), than to membership as a proportion of community population (r = .256).

5. All regression analyses in this and later chapters were examined carefully for possible problems of multicollinearity, and none of the regressions reported here contained any pair of independent variables correlated at more than ± .4. Residuals from the regressions were also examined for any unusual patterns, such as outliers or heteroskedasticity. None of the reported regressions contained such a pattern.

6. Pearson product-moment correlations are used for all of the membership relationships, whereas gammas are used for the relationships between the other resources. Parenthetical figures refer to the number of cases on which the statistic is based.

7. The square root of membership, rather than actual membership, is also used in the analysis of organizational complexity. It is a much stronger predictor of complexity: .636 as opposed to .538 for actual membership.

8. The $16,000 cutoff was chosen instead of the citywide median of $16,872 for two reasons. First, the lower figure still includes all of the Community Action communities plus a number of other low to moderate income communities, including two (South Fairmount and Carthage) with incomes higher than those for any of the Community Action areas. Second, the $16,000 figure excludes several communities that, despite below-average incomes, do not appear to have lower socioeconomic status. Bond Hill and East Walnut Hills, for example, have incomes below the citywide median (at $16,187 and $16,405, respectively) but have home sale values and professional proportions substantially above the median.

CHAPTER 6

CHANNELS: THE DEVELOPMENT
OF MECHANISMS FOR COMMUNITY INVOLVEMENT

1. The single most helpful source in compiling this history was a box of memoranda and other materials accumulated by CATs coordinator Ken Bordwell since his days as one of the city's first community planners. I am indebted to him for allowing me the free use of those materials.

2. Membership data were missing for either 1975 or 1980 for a number of councils, and CDBG spending data were not available for three recently organized neighborhoods. These problems reduced the number of cases available for analysis to thirty-seven.

CHAPTER 7
DECISION MAKING: FROM POLITICS
TO ADMINISTRATION, FROM PETITION TO NEGOTIATION

1. I thank Don Heisel for suggesting the phrase "from petition to negotiation," as well as for providing many other insights. I am also grateful to Mark Weinberg for his helpful comments on an earlier version of this chapter.

2. Though open ended, the interviews proceeded from standard formats, with a different format designed for each of the three groups. Most of the interviews were tape recorded (with the knowledge of the interviewees) and subsequently transcribed by the author. The sample of administrators covered all of the fifteen major service delivery areas of the city: Parks, Recreation, Development, Planning, Police, Fire, Building and Inspections (in particular, the Housing Division), Health, Public Works (including the divisions of Highway Maintenance, Engineering, Traffic Engineering, Waste Collection, and Municipal Facilities), Water Works, and Sewers. At least one official was interviewed in each area, with that official being either the department or division head or, with a few of the largest departments, the official primarily involved with the community councils. Five members of the City Council were interviewed, including two Democrats, two Republicans, and one Charterite, a breakdown representative of the actual partisan makeup of the council in 1980. Finally, fourteen community council leaders were interviewed, including eight white males, four white females, and two black males. The fourteen were chosen as a roughly representative cross-section of the different types of city neighborhoods.

CHAPTER 8
ISSUES: THE PURSUIT
OF NEIGHBORHOOD GOALS IN GOVERNMENT

1. The neighborhood preoccupation with government is also evident on specific municipal services. Asked to rank the level of their councils' interest in each of ten services as "low, moderate, or high," the forty-four council leaders usually responded "high"—the modal rating for six services and the second most common rating for three of the other four.

2. The classification mentioned "Columbia–East End" rather than Columbia-Tusculum alone, reflecting how City Hall then combined the Columbia-Tusculum and East End neighborhoods. Although it is unclear whether the Columbia-Tusculum area was much influenced by the triage designation since the area subsequently was gentrified, its inclusion among these deviant cases is at least a striking coincidence.

3. The NIP presence in a neighborhood was only modestly correlated (r = .193) with contacts with the three Public Works divisions, and that presence did not emerge as significant in the regression analysis of the combined contacts with those divisions and Health. NIPs thus do not appear to be the principal basis for these contacts.

4. Neighborhoods in the "triage" and the "sound and stable" categories are the least likely to be involved with both divisions, with rates of 30 and 20 percent, respectively, consistent with the expectation. However, the neighborhoods *most* likely to be involved are the "triage or rehab" areas, running counter to the prediction; and rates vary unsystematically across the other four categories of neighborhoods.

5. The council reports enumerated activities but did not suggest how much time was devoted to each activity. Consequently, the proportions also refer only to activities, not to actual time spent.

6. Once the influence of membership is controlled, no other council or community characteristic is significantly linked to the time given to organizational maintenance.

CHAPTER 9
PRIVATE INTERESTS: CAN NEIGHBORHOODS COMPETE IN MUNICIPAL POLITICS?

1. The $26.7 million figure probably significantly underestimates the share of the funding that went to the neighborhoods. According to former Community Development Director Bud Haupt, much of the other $18.7 million also went to the neighborhoods, but not in a manner attributable to specific neighborhoods (e.g., projects for all or many neighborhoods).

2. A regression analysis of the triage classification, using a variety of community demographics and council characteristics as predictors, suggests that the best neighborhoods in the eyes of this official were those (standardized regression coefficients in parentheses) with (1) higher home sale value (.750), (2) larger populations (.397), (3) a smaller percentage of residential units vacant ($-.271$), and (4) lower percentages of households with children under 18 ($-.251$). Any influence for the triage rankings, however, probably could not be attributed to official city policy. The rankings themselves were not formulated until 1978, after many of the programs examined here had been completed; and they were formulated by one person who had not shared them with the other departments.

3. The fear of antagonizing particular neighborhoods also helps to explain why City Hall has long resisted pressures for an official credentialing of neighborhood groups. The closest the city has come was in naming the eligible groups in the initial SNAP proposal; and the city later decided to provide additional funds for any omitted groups that showed an interest in SNAP funding.

4. By any objective definition, most of these communities would probably qualify only as working or middle class, not "high income." They are "higher-income communities" only in CDBG terms; that is, in contrast to the city's low-income communities.

5. Redistribution cannot explain the lack of NSP funding for four high-complexity councils in low-income areas (see Table 9.3). Those four apparently spurned NSP because of claims they had on other CDBG funding. Three of the four were in the "focus" areas—the West End, Avondale, and Walnut Hills—targeted to receive the largest CDBG allocations.

6. As an exception to this rule, City Manager Sy Murray was principally responsible after 1980 for sending substantial municipal funding into the former riots community of Avondale, ostensibly to compensate for what he felt the city had taken from the community. His efforts may have been facilitated by federal CDBG funding, but that funding was far from the only basis for the effort.

7. The total revenue figures are exclusive of CDBG funding but do include federal General Revenue Sharing and Anti-Recessionary Fiscal Assistance (City of Cincinnati, Department of Finance, 1978: viii).

8. The use of funds from the full 1975–81 period posed a problem in the selection of some predictors. Although the community characteristics important as predictors are the same as in earlier analyses (i.e., community demographics, community council characteristics, municipal rankings of the communities, and OEO programmatic histories of the communities), it is not obvious from what years some predictors should be drawn. That is, what is the appropriate year for recording a measure to be used to predict funding across a seven-year period? The year 1975 might be too early because the factors could have greatly changed years later when they would still be in use to predict CDBG allocations. On the other hand, the year 1980 or 1981 would probably be too late for the cause-effect sequence to remain intact. The year 1978 was eventually selected as a compromise between the equally undesirable polar options of 1975 and 1980. In addition, most of the CDBG funding came *after* 1978, such that 1978 predictors actually precede most of the CDBG spending they are intended to explain. As it was, the 1978 rule could not be followed with some predictors, but exceptions were made only for demographic data (e.g., percentage poor) where the date of the data seems less important.

All variables entered in the regression analyses were first examined for possible skewness, and transformations were performed to ensure that no score registered at more than three standard deviations removed from the mean. Each regression was also examined for possible multicollinearity, and no reported equation contains any pair of independent variables correlated at more than ± .4.

9. An argument could be made that the role of population in these allocations should be controlled *before* looking at the role of other factors. Doing so makes no material difference, however, in the importance of organizational complexity for explaining the CDBG allocations.

References

Abney, Glenn, and Thomas P. Lauth. 1985. "Interest Group Influence in City Policy-making: The Views of Administrators." *Western Political Quarterly* 38 (March): 148-60.

Advisory Commission on Intergovernmental Relations. 1979. *In Brief: Citizen Participation in the American Federal System*. Washington, D.C.: Government Printing Office.

———. 1972. *The New Grass Roots Government? Decentralization and Citizen Participation in Urban Areas*. Washington, D.C.: Government Printing Office.

Ahlbrandt, Roger S., Jr., and James Cunningham. 1979. *A New Public Policy for Neighborhood Preservation*. New York: Praeger.

Ahlbrandt, Roger S., Jr., and Howard Sumka. 1983. "Neighborhood Organization and the Coproduction of Public Services." *Journal of Urban Affairs* 5 (Summer): 211-20.

Alford, Robert R., and Harry M. Scoble. 1968. "Sources of Local Political Involvement." *American Political Science Review* 62 (December): 1192-1206.

Ambrecht, Biliana C. S. 1976. *Politicizing the Poor: The Legacy of the War on Poverty in a Mexican-American Community*. New York: Praeger.

Axelrod, Robert. 1984. *The Evolution of Cooperation*. New York: Basic Books.

Bachelor, Lynn W., and Bryan D. Jones. 1981. "Managed Participation: Detroit's Neighborhood Opportunity Fund." *Journal of Applied Behavorial Science* 17: 518-36.

Barber, Daniel M. 1981. *Citizen Participation in American Communities*. Dubuque, Iowa: Kendall/Hunt Publishing Co.

Bartelt, David W. 1981. "Neighborhood Reinvestment Strategies: The CRA Experience." *Journal of Community Action* 1 (November/December): 5-12.

Beer, Samuel H. 1977. "Political Overload and Federalism." *Polity* 10 (Fall): 5-17.

———. 1976. "The Adoption of General Revenue Sharing: A Case Study in Public Sector Politics." *Public Policy* 24 (Spring): 127-95.

Bell, Daniel. 1975. "The Revolution of Rising Entitlements." *Fortune* 91 (April): 98-103, 183, 185.

Bell, Daniel, and Virginia Held. 1969. "The Community Revolution." *The Public Interest* No. 16 (Summer): 142-77.

Berger, Peter L., and Richard John Neuhaus. 1977. *To Empower People: The Role of Mediating Structures in Public Policy*. Washington, D.C.: American Enterprise Institute.

Birch, David L. 1981. "Who Creates Jobs?" *The Public Interest* No. 65 (Fall): 3–14.

Boulay, Harvey. 1983. *The Twilight of Cities: Political Conflict, Development and Decay in Five Communities*. Port Washington, N.Y.: Associated Faculty Press.

Boyle, John, and David Jacobs. 1982. "The Intra-City Distribution of Services: A Multivariate Analysis." *American Political Science Review* 76 (June): 371–79.

Boyte, Harry C. 1980. *The Backyard Revolution: Understanding the New Citizen Movement*. Philadelphia: Temple University Press.

Brown, Michael K., and Steven P. Erie. 1981. "Blacks and the Legacy of the Great Society: The Economic and Political Impact of Federal Social Policy." *Public Policy* 29 (Summer): 299–330.

Browning, Rufus P., Dale Rogers Marshall, and David H. Tabb. 1984. *Protest Is Not Enough: The Struggle of Blacks and Hispanics for Equality in Urban Politics*. Berkeley: University of California Press.

Busson, Terry. 1983. "The Impact of Neighborhoods and Neighborhood Organizations on Community Development Block Grants." *Journal of Urban Affairs* 5 (Summer): 193–202.

Cater, Douglass. 1964. *Power in Washington*. New York: Vintage Books.

Charter Research Institute of Cincinnati. 1970. *Community Councils of Cincinnati, Ohio*. Cincinnati.

Chernoff, Michael. 1981. "The Effects of Superhighways in Urban Areas." *Urban Affairs Quarterly* 16 (March): 317–36.

Cincinnati Enquirer. 1984. "Neighborhood Leaders Criticize Citizen Review Memo." July 3.

———. 1983. "Sparkling Avondale Center Off to Spotty Start." October 3.

———. 1982. "Neighborhoods: Self-Help Agency Seeks Funding for New Ventures." June 19.

———. 1981a. "Mt. Washington Still Opposed to City's Public Housing Bid." June 19.

———. 1981b. "Figures Don't Surprise Community Leaders." June 1.

———. 1980a. "Sedamsville Renovation Project Ready for Owners." December 29.

———. 1980b. "Complaint Could End HUD Grants for City." August 9.

———. 1980c. "Communities Want Paid Staff." July 30.

———. 1980d. "School Levy Campaign a Bargain after 1979." July 19.

———. 1980e. "Avenue Mall Caps Plans to Draw New Shoppers." June 30.

———. 1980f. "Neighborhoods: A Larger Voice for Organizations Could Be an Error." June 19.

———. 1980g. "Hartwell Association Supports Development of Kroger 'Superstore.' " June 18.

———. 1980h. "Kroger Superstore Stirs Controversy in Hartwell." June 9.

———. 1980i. "He Rocked Boat, Set It on Course." June 8.

———. 1980j. "Old Foes Find Togetherness Less 'Taxing.' " June 5.

———. 1978a. "Poor Lobbying Blamed in Community 'Neglect.' " August 22.

———. 1978b. "Neighborhood Organizations Rap Limitations on Renovation Fund." August 20.

———. 1978c. "Too Many Pocket Districts? Some Officials Say Kill Few So City Can Save Others." August 6.

———. 1971a. "Neighborhood Renewal High in Coalition's Plans." November 29.

———. 1971b. "Housing Protests Fly in Council." August 5.

City of Cincinnati, Department of Community Development. 1978. Neighborhood Analysis of CDBG Expenditures. Cincinnati, Ohio.

City of Cincinnati, Department of Finance. 1982. Community Development Program Report. Cincinnati, Ohio.
————. 1978. Annual Financial Report for the Year 1978. Cincinnati, Ohio.
City of Cincinnati, Department of Neighborhood Housing and Conservation. 1981. "Neighborhood Support Program, 1981-83." Brochure.
City of Cincinnati, Department of Urban Development. 1972. From Housing Rehabilitation to Neighborhood Development. Cincinnati, Ohio (September).
City of Cincinnati, Office of Research, Evaluation and Budget. 1982. Planning Resource Document, Prepared for Town Meeting IV. Cincinnati, Ohio.
City of Cincinnati, Office of the Manager. 1979. "Project SNAP—Year 3. A Proposal Submitted to the Charles Stewart Mott Foundation." Cincinnati, Ohio (August).
City of Cincinnati, Planning Commission, Planning and Management Support System Division. 1981. Cincinnati Neighborhood Profiles 1980: Interim Report. Cincinnati, Ohio.
Clark, Peter B., and James Q. Wilson. 1961. "Incentive Systems: A Theory of Organizations." *Administrative Science Quarterly* 6: 129-66.
Clark, Terry Nichols, and Lorna Crowley Ferguson. 1983. *City Money: Political Processes, Fiscal Strain, and Retrenchment*. New York: Columbia University Press.
Clay, Phillip L. 1979. *Neighborhood Renewal: Middle-Class Resettlement and Incumbent Upgrading in American Neighborhoods*. Lexington, Mass.: Lexington Books.
Cole, Richard L. 1981. "Participation in Community Service Organizations." *Journal of Community Action* 1 (September/October): 53-60.
————. 1975. "Citizen Participation in Municipal Politics." *American Journal of Political Science* 19 (November): 761-81.
————. 1974. *Citizen Participation and the Urban Policy Process*. Lexington, Mass.: Lexington Books.
Cole, Richard L., and David A. Caputo. 1984. "The Public Hearing as an Effective Citizen Participation Mechanism." *American Political Science Review* 78 (June): 404-16.
Cooper, Terry L. 1980. "Bureaucracy and Community Organization: The Metamorphosis of a Relationship." *Administration & Society* 11 (February): 411-44.
Cox, Kevin R. 1982. "Housing Tenure and Neighborhood Activism." *Urban Affairs Quarterly* 18 (September): 107-29.
Cox, Kevin R., and Jeffery J. McCarthy. 1980. "Neighborhood Activism in the American City: Behavioral Relationships and Evaluation." *Urban Geography* 1: 22-38.
Crenson, Matthew A. 1983. *Neighborhood Politics*. Cambridge, Mass.: Harvard University Press.
Cronin, Thomas E. 1980. *The State of the Presidency* (2nd ed.). Boston: Little, Brown.
Crum, Pat. 1974. "Planning with Communities." Cincinnati (mimeo).
Cunningham, James V. 1981. "Assessing the Urban Partnership: Do Community Forces Fit?" *National Civic Review* 70 (November): 521-26.
Cupps, D. Stephen. 1977. "Emerging Problems of Citizen Participation." *Public Administration Review* 37 (September/October): 478-87.
Dommel, Paul R., John Stuart Hall, Victor E. Bach, Leonard Rubinowitz, Leon L. Haley, and John S. Jackson III. 1982. *Decentralizing Urban Policy: Case Studies in Community Development*. Washington, D.C.: Brookings Institution.
Donovan, John C. 1973. *The Politics of Poverty* (2nd ed.). Indianapolis: Bobbs-Merrill.
Downs, Anthony. 1981. *Neighborhoods and Urban Development*. Washington, D.C.: Brookings Institution.

Eastern Hills Journal (Cincinnati). 1985. "Local Communities Invest in Invest." August 21.

———. 1980a. "ORA Grapples with Oakley Hotel Disturbances." July 9.

———. 1980b. "Madisonville Committee Frowns on Latest Liquor License Nod." June 25.

Fiedler, Fred E. 1967. *A Theory of Leadership Effectiveness.* New York: McGraw-Hill.

Friedland, Roger. 1980. "Corporate Power and Urban Growth: The Case of Urban Renewal." *Politics & Society* 10: 203–24.

Gamson, William. 1975. *The Strategy of Social Protest.* Homewood, Ill.: Dorsey Press.

Geiser, Miriam. 1968. "Planning with People." *Journal of Housing* 23 (July): 298–301.

Gittell, Marilyn. 1983. "The Consequence of Mandating Citizen Participation." *Policy Studies Review* 3 (August): 90–95.

———. 1980. *Limits to Citizen Participation: The Decline of Community Organizations.* Beverly Hills, Calif.: Sage.

Goering, John M. 1979. "The National Neighborhood Movement: A Preliminary Analysis and Critique." *American Planning Association Journal* 45 (October): 506–14.

Greer, Scott. 1965. *Urban Renewal and American Cities.* Indianapolis: Bobbs-Merrill.

Haider, Donald H. 1979. "Sayre and Kaufman Revisited: New York City Government since 1965." *Urban Affairs Quarterly* 15 (December): 123–45.

Hallman, Howard W. 1984. *Neighborhoods: Their Place in Urban Life.* Beverly Hills, Calif.: Sage.

———. 1980. "Citizens and Budgets: Some Local Innovations." *National Civic Review* 69 (April): 191–96.

Hansen, John Mark. 1985. "The Political Economy of Group Membership." *American Political Science Review* 79 (March): 79–96.

Harrigan, John J. 1981. *Political Change in the Metropolis* (2nd ed.). Boston: Little, Brown.

Hartsock, Paul. 1977. "Cincinnati's Response to Its Communities." *Neighborhood Ideas* 2 (September): 1, 3–5.

———. 1975. "Proposed Work Program for the Cincinnati Planning Commission." November 3.

———. 1974. "A Framework for Integrating City Programs to Provide a Comprehensive Response to Community Budgetary Needs." Memorandum prepared for the Cincinnati City Planning Commission, June 21.

Haveman, Robert H. 1977. "Poverty, Income Distribution, and Social Policy: The Last Decade and the Next." *Public Policy* 25 (Winter): 3–24.

Hawkins, Robert B., Jr., ed. 1982. *American Federalism: A New Partnership for the Republic.* San Francisco: Institute for Contemporary Studies.

Henig, Jeffrey R. 1982a. *Neighborhood Mobilization: Redevelopment and Response.* New Brunswick, N.J.: Rutgers University Press.

———. 1982b. "Neighborhood Response to Gentrification: Conditions of Mobilization." *Urban Affairs Quarterly* 17 (March): 343–58.

———. 1981. "Community Organizations in Gentrifying Neighborhoods." *Journal of Community Action* 1 (November/December): 45–55.

Hersey, Paul, and Kenneth N. Blanchard. 1977. *Management of Organizational Behavior: Utilizing Human Resources.* Englewood Cliffs, N.J.: Prentice-Hall.

Hessler, Iola. 1961. *Cincinnati: Then and Now.* Cincinnati: League of Women Voters.

Hirschman, Albert. 1970. *Exit, Voice, and Loyalty.* Cambridge, Mass.: Harvard University Press.

Howe, Elizabeth, and Jerome Kaufman. 1979. "The Ethics of Contemporary American Planners." *Journal of the American Planning Association* 45 (July): 243–55.

Hult, Karen M. 1984. "Institutionalizing Organized Citizen Participation: Challenges and Opportunities." Paper prepared for delivery at the annual meeting of the Urban Affairs Association, Portland, Ore., March.

Hunter, Albert. 1979. "The Urban Neighborhood: Its Analytical and Social Contexts." *Urban Affairs Quarterly* 14 (March): 267–88.

Hunter, Floyd. 1953. *Community Power Structure: A Study of Decision-Makers.* Chapel Hill: University of North Carolina Press.

Hutcheson, John D., Jr. 1983. "Representation in Participatory Planning." Paper prepared for presentation at the annual meeting of the Urban Affairs Association, Flint, Mich., March.

Ingram, Helen. 1977. "Policy Implementation Through Bargaining: The Case of Federal Grants-In-Aid." *Public Policy* 25 (Fall): 499–526.

Isaac, Larry, and William R. Kelly. 1981. "Racial Insurgency, the State, and Welfare Expansion: Local and National Level Evidence from the Postwar United States." *American Journal of Sociology* 86 (May): 1348–86.

Jackson, Pamela Irving. 1978. "Community Control, Community Mobilization, and Community Political Structure in 57 U.S. Cities." *Sociological Quarterly* 19 (Autumn): 577–89.

Johnson, David R., John A. Booth, and Richard J. Harris, eds. 1983. *The Politics of San Antonio: Community, Progress, and Power.* Lincoln: University of Nebraska Press.

Johnson, Jorene K. 1975. "An Evaluation of the Metropolitan Project in the City of Cincinnati, 1973–75." Master's thesis, University of Cincinnati.

Jones, Bryan D. 1983. *Governing Urban America: A Policy Focus.* Boston: Little, Brown.

———. 1981. "Party and Bureaucracy: The Influence of Intermediary Groups on Urban Public Service Delivery." *American Political Science Review* 75 (September): 688–700.

Jones, Bryan D., Saadia Greenberg, Clifford Kaufman, and Joseph Drew. 1978. "Service Delivery Rules and the Distribution of Local Government Services." *Journal of Politics* 40 (May): 332–68.

———. 1977. "Bureaucratic Response to Citizen-Initiated Contacts: Environmental Enforcement in Detroit." *American Political Science Review* 71 (March): 148–65.

Jones, Delmos J. 1979. "Not in My Community: The Neighborhood Movement and Institutionalized Racism." *Social Policy* 10 (September/October): 44–46.

Jones, E. Terrence, Thomas Gosebrink, and Phyllis Evans. 1982. "The Neighborhood Professional and Urban Politics." *Journal of Community Action* 1 (January/February): 43–47.

Joyce, Michael S. 1982. "Voluntarism and Partnership." Pp. 193–208 in Robert B. Hawkins, Jr., ed., *American Federalism: A New Partnership for the Republic.* San Francisco: Institute for Contemporary Studies.

Judd, Dennis R. 1979. *The Politics of American Cities: Private Power and Public Policy.* Boston: Little, Brown.

Kansas City Star. 1984. "Effort for Integration Recalled." February 14.

Kansas City Times. 1984. "Blacks Feel Accepted in White Suburbs." August 6.

Karnig, Albert K. 1975. " 'Private-Regarding' Policy, Civil Rights Groups, and the Mediating Impact of Municipal Reforms." *American Journal of Political Science* 19 (February): 91–106.

Katznelson, Ira. 1981. *City Trenches: Urban Politics and the Patterning of Class in the United States.* New York: Pantheon.

Kennedy Heights Community Council. 1978. "Kennedy Heights Community Council, 1963–1978: 15 Years Together." Cincinnati.

Kettl, Donald F. 1981a. "Blocked Out? The Plight of the Poor in Grant Reform." *Journal of Community Action* 1 (November/December): 13–18.

———. 1981b. "The Fourth Face of Federalism." *Public Administration Review* 41 (May/June): 366–71.

———. 1979. "Can the Cities Be Trusted? The Community Development Experience." *Political Science Quarterly* 94 (Fall): 437–51.

Kerr, Norman D. 1964. "The School Board as an Agency of Legitimation." *Sociology of Education* 38 (Fall): 34–59.

Kirlin, John J. 1973. "The Impact of Increasing Lower-Status Clientele upon City Governmental Structures: A Model from Organization Theory." *Urban Affairs Quarterly* 8: 317–43.

Klecka, William R., and Alfred J. Tuchfarber. 1978. "Random Digit Dialing: A Comparison to Personal Survey." *Public Opinion Quarterly* 42: 105–14.

Knoke, David, and James R. Wood. 1981. *Organized for Action: Commitment in Voluntary Associations.* New Brunswick, N.J.: Rutgers University Press.

Kohfelt, C. W., Barbara Salert, and Sandra Schoenberg. 1981. "Neighborhood Associations and Urban Crime." *Journal of Community Action* 1 (November/December): 37–44.

Kotter, John P., and Paul R. Lawrence. 1974. *Mayors in Action: 5 Approaches to Urban Governance.* New York: John Wiley.

Kovak, Richard M. 1972. "Urban Renewal Controversies." *Public Administration Review* 32 (July/August): 359–72.

Lamb, Curt. 1975. *Political Power in Poor Neighborhoods.* Cambridge, Mass.: Schenkman.

Langton, Stuart. 1983. "Public-Private Partnerships: Hope or Hoax?" *National Civic Review* 72 (May): 256–61.

League of Women Voters of the Cincinnati Area. 1975. "Update: On Systems for Citizen Input into the City Budget, City Planning and Community Development Funding (City and County)." Newsletter, August.

Levine, Charles H., and Paul L. Posner. 1981. "The Centralizing Effects of Austerity on the Intergovernmental System." *Political Science Quarterly* 96 (Spring): 67–86.

Levine, Charles H., Irene S. Rubin, and George C. Wolohojian. 1981. "Resource Scarcity and the Reform Model: The Management of Retrenchment in Cincinnati and Oakland." *Public Administration Review* 41 (November/December): 619–28.

Levy, Frank S., Arnold J. Meltsner, and Aaron Wildavsky. 1974. *Urban Outcomes: Schools, Streets, and Libraries.* Berkeley: University of California Press.

Lineberry, Robert L. 1983. *Government in America: People, Politics, and Policy* (2nd ed.). Boston: Little, Brown.

———. 1977. *Equality and Urban Policy: The Distribution of Urban Services.* Beverly Hills, Calif.: Sage.

Lineberry, Robert L., and Edmund P. Fowler. 1967. "Reformism and Public Policy in American Cities." *American Political Science Review* 61 (September): 701–16.

Lipsky, Michael. 1971. "Street-Level Bureaucracy and the Analysis of Urban Reform." *Urban Affairs Quarterly* 6: 391–409.

———. 1968. "Protest as a Political Resource." *American Political Science Review* 62 (December): 1144–58.

Long, Norton E. 1980. "The City as a Local Political Economy." *Administration & Society* 12 (May): 5–35.

Lowi, Theodore J. 1979. *The End of Liberalism: The Second Republic of the United States* (2nd ed.). New York: W. W. Norton.

———. 1968. "Gosnell's Chicago Revisited via Lindsay's New York." Pp. 7–16 in Harold F. Gosnell, *Machine Politics: Chicago Model*. Chicago: University of Chicago Press.

———. 1964. "American Business, Public Policy, Case Studies, and Political Theory." *World Politics* 16 (July): 676–715.

Marcuse, Peter, Peter Medoff, and Andrea Pereira. 1982. "Triage as Urban Policy." *Social Policy* 12 (Winter): 33–37.

Marini, Frank, ed. 1971. *Toward a New Public Administration: The Minnowbrook Perspective*. Scranton, Pa.: Chandler Publishing.

Martin, George C. 1975. "A Proposal for the Community Assistance Team Program." Memorandum, City of Cincinnati, November 28.

Mladenka, Kenneth R. 1980. "The Urban Bureaucracy and the Chicago Political Machine: Who Gets What and Limits to Political Control." *American Political Science Review* 74 (December): 991–98.

Mollenkopf, John. 1983. *The Contested City*. Princeton, N.J.: Princeton University Press.

———. 1981. "Neighborhood Political Development and the Politics of Urban Growth: Boston and San Francisco 1958–1978." *International Journal of Urban and Regional Research* 5: 15–39.

Montgomery, John D. 1983. "When Local Participation Helps." *Journal of Policy Analysis and Management* 3 (Fall): 90–105.

Moynihan, Daniel P. 1969. *Maximum Feasible Misunderstanding*. New York: Free Press.

Murphy, Patrick V. 1976. "The Development of the Urban Police." *Current History* 70 (June): 245–48, 272–73.

Nathan, Richard P. 1978. "The Outlook for Federal Grants to Cities." Pp. 75–92 in Roy Bahl, ed., *The Fiscal Outlook for Cities: Implications of a National Urban Policy*. Syracuse, N.Y.: Syracuse University Press.

Nathan, Richard P., and Fred C. Doolittle. 1984. "The Untold Story of Reagan's 'New Federalism.'" *The Public Interest* No. 77 (Fall): 96–105.

Navarro, Peter. 1985. "Rent Control in Cambridge, Mass." *The Public Interest* No. 78 (Winter): 83–100.

Needleman, Martin L., and Carolyn Emerson Needleman. 1974. *Guerrillas in the Bureaucracy: The Community Planning Experiment in the United States*. New York: John Wiley.

O'Brien, David J. 1975. *The Logic of Collective Action*. New York: Schocken Books.

Olsen, Marvin E. 1970. "Social and Political Participation of Blacks." *American Sociological Review* 35: 682–97.

Olson, Mancur, Jr. 1971. *The Logic of Collective Action: Public Goods and the Theory of Groups*. New York: Schocken Books.

Orbell, John M., and Toru Uno. 1972. "A Theory of Neighborhood Problem Solving: Political Action vs. Residential Mobility." *American Political Science Review* 66 (June): 471–89.

Peirce, Neal R. 1980. "Neighborhood Movement Faces Choices in the '80s." *Memphis Commercial Appeal*, January 2.

Percy, Stephen L. 1983. "Citizen Coproduction: Prospects for Improving Service Delivery." *Journal of Urban Affairs* 5 (Summer): 203–10.

Peterson, Paul E. 1981. *City Limits*. Chicago: University of Chicago Press.

———. 1970. "Forms of Representation: Participation of the Poor in the Community Action Program." *American Political Science Review* 64 (June): 491–507.

Piven, Frances Fox, and Richard A. Cloward. 1971. *Regulating the Poor: The Functions of Public Welfare*. New York: Pantheon.

Pressman, Jeffrey L. 1975. *Federal Programs and City Politics: The Dynamics of the Aid Process in Oakland*. Berkeley: University of California Press.

———. 1972. "Preconditions of Mayoral Leadership." *American Political Science Review* 66 (June): 511–24.

Reich, Robert B. 1983. *The Next American Frontier: A Provocative Program for Economic Renewal*. New York: Penguin.

Rich, Richard C. 1980a. "A Political-Economy Approach to the Study of Neighborhood Organizations." *American Journal of Political Science* 24 (November): 559–92.

———. 1980b. "The Dynamics of Leadership in Neighborhood Organizations." *Social Science Quarterly* 60 (March): 570–87.

Ripley, Randall B., and Grace A. Franklin. 1976. *The Congress, the Bureaucracy, and Public Policy*. Homewood, Ill.: Dorsey Press.

Robinson, Ben C. 1978. "Memorandum to the City Manager on Community Councils." City of Cincinnati, July 5.

Rodgers, Harrell. 1978. "Welfare Policies for the Rich." *Dissent* 25 (Spring): 140–43.

Rohe, William M., and Lauren B. Gates. 1981. "Neighborhood Planning: Promise and Product." *Urban and Social Change Review* 14 (Winter): 26–32.

Ross, Bernard H., and Louise G. White. 1981. "Managing Urban Decentralization." *The Urban Interest* 3 (Spring): 82–89.

Rossi, Peter H., and Howard E. Freeman. 1985. *Evaluation: A Systematic Approach* (3rd ed.). Beverly Hills, Calif.: Sage.

Rutter, Lawrence, ed. 1980. *The Essential Community: Local Government in the Year 2000*. Washington, D.C.: International City Management Association.

Schattschneider, E. E. 1960. *The Semi-Sovereign People*. New York: Holt, Rinehart & Winston.

Schill, Michael H., and Richard P. Nathan. 1983. *Revitalizing America's Cities: Neighborhood Reinvestment and Displacement*. Albany: State University of New York Press.

Schoenberg, Sandra Perlman, and Patricia L. Rosenbaum. 1980. *Neighborhoods That Work: Sources for Viability in the Inner City*. New Brunswick, N.J.: Rutgers University Press.

Schumaker, Paul, and Russell W. Getter. 1983. "Structural Sources of Unequal Responsiveness to Group Demands in American Cities." *Western Political Quarterly* 36 (March): 7–29.

Seidman, Harold. 1980. *Politics, Position, and Power: The Dynamics of Federal Organization* (3rd ed.). New York: Oxford University Press.

Sekul, Joseph D. 1983. "Communities Organized for Public Service: Citizen Power and Public Policy in San Antonio." Pp. 175–90 in David R. Johnson, John A. Booth, and Richard J. Harris, eds., *The Politics of San Antonio: Community, Progress, and Power*. Lincoln: University of Nebraska Press.

Shapiro, Henry D., and Zane L. Miller. 1976. *Clifton: Neighborhood and Community in an Urban Setting. A Brief History*. Cincinnati: The Laboratory in American Civilization.

Sharp, Elaine B. 1984. "'Exit, Voice, and Loyalty' in the Context of Local Government Problems." *Western Political Quarterly* 37 (March): 67–83.

———. 1980. "Citizen Perception of Channels for Urban Service Advocacy." *Public Opinion Quarterly* 44 (Fall): 362–76.

Shingles, Richard D. 1981. "Black Consciousness and Political Participation: The Missing Link." *American Political Science Review* 75 (March): 76–91.

Sleeper, Jim. 1982. "Neighborhood Gentrification." *Dissent* 29 (Spring): 169–75.

Snow, David A., and Peter J. Leahy. 1980. "The Making of a Black Slum-Ghetto: A Case Study of Neighborhood Transition." *Journal of Applied Behavioral Sciences* 16: 459–81.

Steggart, Frank X. 1975. *Community Action Groups and City Governments: Perspectives from Ten American Cities*. Cambridge, Mass.: Ballinger.

Stenberg, Carl W. 1972. "Citizens and the Administrative State: From Participation to Power." *Public Administration Review* 22 (May/June): 190–98.

Stevens, Herbert W. 1972. "Report to Councilmember Taft on Second Community Planning Team." Memorandum, City of Cincinnati, January 3.

———. 1971. "A Report of the Community Planning Priorities Committee on the Matter of Selection of Communities for the New Planning Program." Memorandum prepared for the Cincinnati City Planning Commission, June 10.

Stockman, David A. 1975. "The Social Pork Barrel." *The Public Interest* No. 39 (Spring): 3–30.

Stone, Clarence N. 1980. "Systemic Power in Community Decision Making: A Restatement of Stratification Theory." *American Political Science Review* 74 (December): 978–90.

Taub, Richard P., D. Garth Taylor, and Jan D. Dunham. 1984. *Paths of Neighborhood Change: Race and Crime in Urban America*. Chicago: University of Chicago Press.

Thomas, John Clayton. 1982. "Citizen-Initiated Contacts with Government Agencies: A Test of Three Theories." *American Journal of Political Science* 26 (August): 504–22.

———. 1981. "The Class Impacts of Budget Cutbacks: The Process and Outcome of Retrenchment in Cincinnati." *The Urban Interest* 3 (Spring): 51–61.

———. 1980. "Governmental Overload in the United States: A Problem of Distributive Policies?" *Administration & Society* 11 (February): 371–91.

Verba, Sidney, and Norman H. Nie. 1972. *Participation in America*. New York: Harper & Row.

Vroom, Victor, and Philip Yetton. 1973. *Leadership and Decision Making*. Pittsburgh: University of Pittsburgh Press.

Walker, Jack L. 1983. "The Origins and Maintenance of Interest Groups in America." *American Political Science Review* 77 (June): 390–406.

Wandersman, Abraham. 1981. "A Framework of Participation in Community Organizations." *Journal of Applied Behavioral Science* 17: 27–58.

Warren, Donald I. 1975. *Black Neighborhoods: An Assessment of Community Power*. Ann Arbor: University of Michigan Press.

Wellman, Barry, and Barry Leighton. 1979. "Networks, Neighborhoods, and Communities." *Urban Affairs Quarterly* 14 (March): 363–90.

Whitaker, Gordon P. 1980. "Coproduction: Citizen Participation in Service Delivery." *Public Administration Review* 40 (May/June): 240–46.

White, Louise G. 1981. "Functions of Neighborhood Advisory Groups." *Journal of Voluntary Action Research* 10 (April/June): 27–39.

Wilson, James Q. 1963. "Planning and Politics: Citizen Participation in Urban Renewal." *American Institute of Planners Journal* (November): 242–49.

Wolch, Jennifer R. 1982. "Spatial Consequences of Social Policy: The Role of Service-Facility Location in Urban Development Patterns." Pp. 19–35 in Richard C. Rich, ed., *The Politics of Urban Public Services*. Lexington, Mass.: Lexington Books.

Woods, William K., William G. Andersen, Jr., and Susan Grober. 1979. *Cincinnati's Community Councils: An Assessment of Capacity Building for Citizen Involvement in the Budget Process*. New York: National Municipal League.

Wurdock, Clarence J. 1981. "Neighborhood Racial Transition: A Study of the Role of White Flight." *Urban Affairs Quarterly* 17 (September): 75–89.

Yankelovich, Daniel. 1967. *Evaluation of the Cincinnati Community Action Program.* Cincinnati: Daniel Yankelovich, Inc.

Yates, Douglas. 1977. *The Ungovernable City: The Politics of Urban Problems and Policy Making.* Cambridge, Mass.: The MIT press.

Zeitz, Eileen. 1979. *Private Urban Renewal: A Different Residential Trend.* Lexington, Mass.: Lexington Books.

Zimmerman, Joseph F. 1972. *The Federated City: Community Control in Large Cities.* New York: St. Martin's Press.

Index

The acronyms CDBG and SNAP are used throughout the index for Community Development Block Grant and for Stimulating Neighborhood Action Programs.

189